This book was donated to the

Independence Public Library's
Aviation shelf

by the Polk County
Oregon Pilot's Association

D0341531

The Boats of Cherbourg

Abraham Rabinovich

THE BOATS OF CHERBOURG

NAVAL INSTITUTE

Seaver Books / Henry Holt and Company — New York

INDEPENDENCE PUBLIC LIBRARY
175 Monmouth Street
Independence, OR 97351   2956-0052

Copyright © 1988 by Abraham Rabinovich
All rights reserved, including the right to reproduce this
book or portions thereof in any form.
Published by Seaver Books/Henry Holt and Company, Inc.,
115 West 18th Street, New York, New York 10011.
Published in Canada by Fitzhenry & Whiteside Limited,
195 Allstate Parkway, Markham, Ontario L3R 4T8.

Library of Congress Cataloging-in-Publication Data
Rabinovich, Abraham.
The boats of Cherbourg / Abraham Rabinovich.
p. cm.
Bibliography: p.
ISBN 0-8050-0680-X
1. Israel-Arab War, 1973—Naval Operations, Israeli. 2. Israeli
Missile Boats Incident, Cherbourg, France, 1969. 3. Fast attack
craft—Israel. 4. Gabriel (Guided missile). I. Title.
DS128.16.N3R33   1988   87-22933
956'.048—dc19   CIP
First Edition

Designed by Jeffrey L. Ward
Printed in the United States of America
1   3   5   7   9   10   8   6   4   2

ISBN 0-8050-0680-X

INDEPENDENCE PUBLIC LIBRARY
175 ()   Street
Independence, OR 97351
2950 - 0052

Contents

Preface

It was two years after the Yom Kippur War when I first heard of the performance of the Israeli missile boats in that conflict. The brief account was given by Admiral Binyamin Telem, commander of the Israeli navy, at an international conference in Jerusalem on the military and political implications of the war. The media, including the Israeli media, had reported virtually nothing about the navy's activities in the conflict. The navy had clearly played a marginal role in the war, when Israel's existence seemed to hang on its air force and its armored corps battling in Sinai and on the Golan Heights. Mildly curious about what had been going on at sea, I sat in on Telem's talk.

It was a revelation. There had indeed been battles at sea, and they had been fought—for the first time in history, Telem said—not with gunfire but with missiles, at ranges of up to forty-five kilometers. The Arab missile boats outnumbered the Israeli missile boats by more than two to one, and the Styx employed by the Arab navies had more than twice the range of the Israeli Gabriel. Yet the Israeli missile boats had survived the battles intact while sinking almost every Arab vessel they encountered. The Israeli naval concept, said Telem, was an original one, and Israel was the first country except the Soviet Union to develop an operational missile-boat system.

This, then, was not some irrelevant skirmishing of gunboats on the margins of a bloody land war but a major turning point in the history of naval warfare. More impressive to me than the revolutionary technological innovations employed, or the fact that the navy had committed its fortunes and the lives of its men to an untested electronic umbrella, was the display of national will that had permitted a country of three million to develop an advanced weapon system that did not exist anywhere in the Western world.

It was only several years later, in an idle moment of rumination triggered by some passing remark, that I thought back to Telem's talk and made the connection between the missile boats and the Cherbourg boats. The realization that they were the same boats gave the tale an irresistible new dimension. The thread that connected the two parts was not just the boats themselves but the aspect of national will surmounting conventional bounds.

I wrote to the Israeli Defense Ministry twice during the coming years to request access to the appropriate military sources in order to write a book on the subject. The request was declined, on the grounds that the matter was still too sensitive, particularly the Cherbourg aspect. I tried again in late 1982. This time I received a reply from naval headquarters in Tel Aviv inviting me for an interview. A naval captain and a junior woman naval officer questioned me politely about my background and about the kind of book I intended to write. A few weeks later I was invited back. The captain, looking solemn, informed me that after due consideration the navy had decided it could not cooperate on the project and could not provide me access to documentation, as I had requested. Crestfallen, I was about to take my leave when he added, "But we won't stand in your way if you want to interview people on your own. We could even provide telephone numbers of specific people you ask for."

"But where do I begin?" I said. "I don't even know whom to ask for."

The captain wrote something on a piece of paper and handed it to me. On it were the names of two persons unknown to me and their telephone numbers.

I left the office uncertain whether to be depressed or elated. It took me a while to come to understand what was happening. The navy did not want to get involved in the project officially, perhaps for fear of damaging its reputation if the book gave a distorted account. The captain had mentioned that, after seeing a recent movie on Israel's naval commandos, the naval command had regretted cooperating with the film company that had made it. On the other hand, the navy would clearly like to see a book recounting its exploits—exploits unknown even to the Israeli public—and would encourage such a project indirectly.

The names on the slip of paper given me by the naval captain were Hadar Kimche and Moshe Tabak. I called Kimche first, and traveled up to his home in Haifa on a winter evening early in 1983, without knowing what edge of the story I was about to touch. It was only after we began talking that I realized that I was not at the edge of the story but at its very center. Kimche had commanded the Cherbourg breakout and had been the first commander of the missile-boat flotilla. When I left his home, after four hours, the piece of string the captain in naval headquarters had handed me had become a web leading in a dozen different directions. From Tabak, who had been Kimche's deputy at Cherbourg, I received an expanded picture and the names of still more people to track down.

There would be more than a hundred interviews in the coming years. I would have lengthy talks with the former commanders of the Israeli navy instrumental in the development of the missile-boat concept, including Yohai Bin-Nun, whom I met at his kibbutz on the Mediterranean coast; Shlomo Erell, inspector general of Israel's defense establishment, in his Tel Aviv office; and "Binny" Telem on his small farm near Netanya. The officer who commanded the flotilla during the war, "Yomi" Barkai, gave a vivid account of the battles as we sat in the cabin of the small boat he lived on for half the year in the Tel Aviv Marina, between sailings as captain of a merchant vessel.

I had two long sessions with Yitzhak Shoshan, the commander of the destroyer *Eilat,* in the office of the paving-stone plant near Netanya where he worked as managing director. He still clearly bore the emotional scars inflicted by the loss of his vessel and a quarter of his crew. Many of the interviews with ex–naval officers were conducted in electronics plants in the Haifa and Tel Aviv areas, where they had found employment upon completion of military service. The navy made serving personnel available for interviews at naval headquarters and at the Haifa naval base. I was permitted to sail aboard one of the missile boats on a training mission, and even to simulate firing a missile at night. Moshe Arens, a former aeronautics professor at the Technion who had been involved in the Gabriel project and gone on to become Israel's defense minister, discussed the Gabriel in the Jerusalem office where he was serving as minister-without-portfolio.

A key figure in the story, Mordecai (Mocca) Limon, who had master-minded the Cherbourg breakout, initially refused to be interviewed, noting that he had received numerous requests from journalists over the years and had always declined because of the political sensitivity of the subject. He relented, however, when informed of the broad nature of the book and of the navy's indirect cooperation. We met twice in his executive offices in Tel Aviv, where he manages Rothschild interests in Israel. While remaining discreet about certain areas, he was generally forthcoming and exceedingly helpful.

To meet another key figure in the story, Ori Even-Tov, the developer of the Gabriel, I traveled to the United States, where he had set up an electronics plant in a Philadelphia suburb. In Washington, D.C., declassified documents on the Sixth Fleet activities during the Yom Kippur War were made available at the Naval Historical Division in the navy yard. Retired admiral Daniel Murphy, who had commanded the Sixth Fleet during the Yom Kippur War, shed light during an interview on the largest confrontation ever between American and Soviet fleets. American naval authority Norman Polmar offered helpful insights on missile development as well as encouragement, noting that there was virtually no literature on the subject of Israel's missile boats. Retired Rear Admiral Julian Lake (USN), a senior member of the American naval team that had debriefed Israeli naval officers following the Yom Kippur War, provided extremely useful background on the development of electronic warfare (EW) as well as observations on the EW capacity displayed by Israel during the 1973 war.

In Cherbourg, which I visited twice for the story, I met with Monsieur Corbinais, who had headed the missile-boat construction project at the Amiot shipyards. On the basis of the Israeli success, his shipyard had won numerous orders for similar boats from other countries, including Arab countries. Local journalists who had covered the story, particularly René Moirand of *La Presse de la Manche*, were generous with their time. A shipping agent in Cherbourg provided me with the Paris telephone number of a shadowy figure, Victor Zipstein, who had been to Cherbourg with Limon the night of the escape and who had been alluded to in various reports as a one-time Mossad agent. From a public telephone booth in a Paris railway station, I contacted Zipstein, who, after initially refusing to speak, went on to offer important confirmation and new revelations about central points in the Cherbourg affair as a long line of impatient Parisians formed behind me and finally dispersed in search of other working phones.

I was able to meet in Paris with General Cazelles, who had been sacked by the Pompidou government for his inadvertent role in the affair, and found the distinguished old officer still dazed at what had happened. From retired French officials who had been connected with the matter, I was able to obtain copies of relevant documents, including reports by the secret police on the flight of the Cherbourg boats. Ex-Premier Jacques Chaban-Delmas described in an interview the government's deliberations when the flight was discovered.

In the end, all these strands emanating from the piece of investigative string offered by the captain in Israeli naval headquarters would weave together into a single tale.

In maritime encounters involving missiles after the Yom Kippur War, the missile would be king. The British, despite electronic defenses, lost two vessels to Exocet missiles fired by Argentine planes in the Falklands Campaign and had another damaged by a land-launched Exocet. In the Persian Gulf, tankers would become slow-moving targets in a shooting gallery for Iranian and Iraqi missiles and even the American destroyer, USS *Stark*, would fall victim. The Israelis had shown in the Yom Kippur War, however, that the missile could be beaten.

The virtual absence of references even in professional literature to the Israeli missile boat performance in the Yom Kippur War—a major naval landmark—is probably due to the secrecy with which the Israeli navy initially shrouded the events out of immediate security considerations, long habit, and lack of publicity consciousness. Even in Israel, the story of the homemade electronic defenses that permitted the Israeli missile boats to overcome the technology of a superpower is hardly known outside the navy itself. The story of the Cherbourg breakout is likewise told here for the first time on the basis of interviews with the principals involved.

Among the numerous persons not mentioned in the text who were extremely generous in providing information, I would like to express my thanks to Zvi Tirosh, Moshe Oren, Hirsh Goodman, Michael

Lazarus, Louis Lipsky, Arye Barak, the late Munya Mardor, Ephraim Talmon, Yitzhak Zoran, Jacques Derogy, and Jacques Bruneau. My special thanks to the number-two man on the Gabriel team—anonymous, at his own request—who was able to introduce my nontechnical mind to the arcane world of electronics.

THE CONCEPT

1

The *Eilat*, 1967

The bridge of the destroyer *Eilat* was crowded, as it always was toward sunset, when the watch is doubled against the surprises lurking in a world half drained of light yet unprotected by darkness.

Through his binoculars, Commander Yitzhak Shoshan, captain of the *Eilat*, could make out the tops of cranes in Port Said silhouetted against the horizon to the west. Around him, commands were being given laconically into intercoms with the exaggerated enunciation used for clarity in shipboard communication.

Shoshan's orders were to skirt the edge of Egyptian territorial waters twelve miles from Port Said; he was 13.5 miles out and intending to get no closer. After asking the watch officer to confirm the distance with a radar check, he ordered the vessel turned south, toward the Sinai coast.

Ever since Israel's spectacular victory in the Six Day War four months before, the navy had been patrolling Sinai's coasts against infiltration and showing the flag up to the limits of Egyptian territorial waters. In its forays along the approaches to Port Said, the northern entranceway to the Suez Canal, the navy was not only showing the flag but ramming it down the Egyptians' throat. It was highly unlikely that the devastated Egyptians would do anything about this, particularly since the Israeli vessels kept to international waters.

Despite Israel's postwar euphoria, Shoshan had been ill at ease about these close brushes with Port Said ever since a night action three months before. Two unidentified vessels had been detected on the *Eilat*'s radar emerging from Port Said and turning eastward. His standing orders were to attack if the Egyptian vessels ventured into territorial waters off Sinai. Shoshan took his destroyer ten miles out to sea and ordered two torpedo boats operating with him to lie close to the shore at Romani, where the land mass behind them would mask them from radar detection. The intruders sailed steadily eastward and were soon abreast of Sinai. When the Egyptians' escape route had been cut off, the torpedo boats sprang from hiding.

The Egyptian vessels turned out to be torpedo boats as well. They split in two directions as soon as they detected their pursuers, one running back along the coast and the other heading out to sea. The two Israeli boats overtook the inshore vessel and raced in an Indian circle around it, the gunners keeping their fire bearing on the Egyptian vessel in the center until it burst into flames. The other Egyptian boat was intercepted by the *Eilat* and blown out of the water.

Instead of reveling in this classic ambush, Shoshan was troubled. The Egyptian navy, he felt, was unlikely to let the humiliation pass without attempting revenge. Shoshan was one of the few people in Israel who had reason to believe that the Egyptians had the means to achieve it.

Since 1962, Egypt had been receiving vessels from the Soviet Union designated as missile boats. No one in Israel knew the nature of those missiles—neither their range nor whether they had the capacity to home in on a target. Neither the Egyptians nor the Syrians had ever attempted to use them, not even in the Six Day War, when they had twenty-four missile boats between them. Skeptical of Egyptian technical abilities, Israeli military circles believed that even if the Soviet-made missiles had some kind of homing capacity—and that was far from certain—the Egyptians were unlikely to maintain them and operate them sufficiently well in combat conditions for the vessels to constitute a serious danger. In any case, Israel's ability to punish the Egyptians severely made it unlikely that they would even attempt to fire the missiles.

Before receiving command of the *Eilat* two years before, Shoshan had been the navy's chief electronics officer. He knew from that tour of duty that Israel had as yet no effective measures to counter missiles. In the skirmish off Romani, he had initially kept his distance in case the Egyptian vessels were missile boats, which would find the relatively large silhouette of the *Eilat* an easy target. For the same reason, he ordered the *Eilat* this day—October 21, 1967—to turn away from Port Said while still a good mile and a half from Egyptian waters. According to intelligence, there were missile boats inside Port Said harbor.

It was now almost 5:30 P.M., and the eastern Mediterranean embraced the ship with its usual autumnal calmness. In five minutes there would be a routine sounding of battle stations as the sun prepared to slip below the horizon. Off-duty sailors lingered at the rails to watch the sunset or stare into the chameleon waters, which had now turned blue-black. This would be the last swing past Port Said on this patrol. In a few hours the *Eilat* would turn toward home.

"Green rocket to starboard."

The cry from the bridge jarred the sunset reverie. From the direction of Port Said, the starboard lookout had seen a flaring of greenish light. The glow turned orange-yellow, and from a roiling of smoke on the horizon a dark object hurtled into the sky. Shoshan swung his binoculars to starboard and saw a bright ball of light. It was not rising like a flare but wafting lazily toward them and trailing smoke. He saw it swerve slightly and knew instantly that he was looking at his nightmare. The missile age at sea was beginning, and he had less than a minute to try to save his ship and the two hundred men who sailed upon her.

"Alert," shouted Shoshan.

The cry was instantly repeated into the public-address system by the watch officer. "Alert" surpassed "Battle stations" in its degree of urgency, permitting gunners to open fire without further orders.

Sailors raced to their stations as the raucous klaxon urged them on. In the crowded corridors below decks, crewmen pressed against the walls to give gunners the right of way. Within seconds, the ship's gunnery officer on the bridge was calling the direction and range of the target over a bullhorn to the men at the guns.

"Engines full ahead," said Shoshan, keeping his binoculars fixed on the approaching missile. "Rudder hard left."

By increasing speed he was increasing maneuverability. Heading south, as it had been for the last minute, the *Eilat* was now broadside to the missile and offering its maximum profile to the missile's radar. In turning, the vessel would be presenting its narrow stern. As the helmsman put the wheel over, Shoshan spoke over the intercom to the radioman in the ship's command room.

"Inform headquarters that a missile has been fired at us."

A machine gun on the starboard side began an urgent clatter, but the anti-aircraft guns remained silent. None of the gunners had ever seen a missile before, and some believed the object approaching them to be a disabled plane. It was trailing smoke and flying at less than the speed of sound. By the time they could see it clearly, it was too late. A powerful explosion tore through the *Eilat's* starboard side just above the waterline.

For the first time in history, a ship had been hit by a missile, and the effect was devastating. One blow had been sufficient to reduce Israel's flagship to a drifting heap of scrap metal. More than a thousand pounds of explosives had detonated in a boiler room in the very heart of the ship. The adjacent engine room was destroyed, the ship powerless. Shoshan ordered all sectors to report damage and casualties.

Reports of numerous dead and injured began to stream in. All electricity was out. All radios were out. A fire was being fought amidships. Several gun positions had been knocked out. Many of the rafts and lifeboats had been destroyed. The ship was beginning to list.

"Missile to port!"

The cry by the port lookout froze movement. From the same direction that the previous missile had come two minutes before, a bright light was once more arching into the sky. The powerless ship was spinning slowly to the left as a result of the last order issued by Shoshan before the missile hit, but it had swung past the narrow-profile orientation and was now once again turning broadside to the missile, this time offering its opposite side. Without power, nothing could be done to arrest the drift. Several machine guns opened fire at long range, but the missile came on implacably.

With the calmness of someone reconciled to the fact that his life had already ended, Shoshan watched the missile approach in the last light of day. It passed within twenty yards of him as it dived toward the ship's waterline. The twenty-foot-long object had stubby delta wings and looked like a small pilotless plane. The blast holed the ship on the port side and staggered the men on the bridge. Looking down, Shoshan saw the deck amidships peeled back like a sardine can, with the ship's toppled funnel lying across it. The *Eilat* was now listing fifteen degrees to port.

Darkness closed on the stricken ship lit by flames and rent by the cry of wounded. The senior officers and noncoms in the engine room who led the damage-control operation in training exercises had all been killed, and it was necessary to improvise new teams in the darkness. Choking smoke filled many parts of the ship. With no power for water hoses, the crewmen tried to snuff out the fires with extinguishers. An ammunition locker near one of the guns exploded, killing a crewman. With shipboard communications knocked out, Shoshan had to shout his orders from the bridge or dispatch them by runner.

Slowly the reports streaming back indicated that the situation was stabilizing. Fires were being brought under control, and the bulkheads were holding. Shoshan began to feel the *Eilat* pulling itself together. The ship was still floating, and if help was quickly dispatched, rescue might be possible. Navy headquarters, however, was still unaware of their plight. The radioman had managed to establish contact after Shoshan's order but had given only the vessel's code name when the explosion severed communications. There was no reason for headquarters to think the break due to anything more ominous than communications failure. Shoshan ordered the communications officer to try to put together a working radio by cannibalizing parts from those that had been knocked out. Meanwhile, he turned to the work at hand.

The deck amidships had been ripped up so badly that to climb over the twisted girders in the dark to reach the stern was to risk one's life. A young ensign posted at the stern made his way forward across the toppled funnel to report numerous wounded and a dangerously weakened bulkhead. Shoshan issued instructions on shoring up the bulkhead and told the officer to report if it showed signs of giving way. If that happened they would have to abandon ship. An officer lifted a telephone at a gun position in the forward part of the ship and found that it was still in contact with one in the stern. Shoshan descended from the bridge to post himself at the forward gun.

Standing on the gun position with a bullhorn, Shoshan ordered all unwounded men in the forward part of the ship to assemble on the bow. Wounded were to be assembled in one place, he told them, and officers were to drill the men in procedures for abandoning ship. Anything that floated, including jerrycans and mattresses, was to be tied to the deck railings to be used instead of the demolished rafts if the abandon-ship order was given. The wind had begun nudging the ship toward Port Said, and Shoshan ordered anchors dropped to halt the drift.

Two hours after the missile attack, the communications officer managed to piece together a working radio. He tried alternate wavelengths to broadcast his message of distress.

"This is the navy ship *Eilat*. We are sinking and request assistance. Does anyone hear us?"

A shouted reply in Arabic was cut off as the officer switched wavelengths. His repeated calls were met by silence, and the hope that had gripped him began to fade. The radio's range was only twenty-five kilometers, and there could be no certainty that Israeli listening posts ashore would pick it up.

"To all units in Sinai, this is the navy ship *Eilat* requesting assistance. Does anyone hear us?"

Suddenly a deep, calm voice issued from the radio. "This is an army unit in Sinai. We have received you and transmitted your message. Help is on the way. Hold on."

"Are you hearing me now?" asked the communications officer.

"Affirmative."

"We are opposite Port Said, repeat, opposite Port Said. We have dead and wounded and are listing badly. We have been hit by missiles."

"I have received you and will transmit your message. Keep us informed of your situation. Help is on the way."

Over his bullhorn, Shoshan called on the crew to stop working for a moment. The moon had risen, and in its light Shoshan could make out the soot-blackened faces below him. Most of the sailors were just a year or two out of high school. They cheered when he announced that contact had been made with Israeli forces. Help would shortly be on its way, he said. From his knowledge of standing procedures, the skipper outlined a likely timetable for the rescue operation now that it was set in motion. He ordered the severely wounded to be immediately lowered onto rafts secured alongside, so that the rest of the crew could go over the side quickly when the abandon-ship order was given. The ship appeared to be settling at the stern, and the list had become more pronounced. It was clear they could not stay afloat much longer.

The armaments officer made his way to the stern to neutralize the depth charges and prevent their detonating when the men were in water. Code books were thrown overboard in weighted sacks, and sailors smashed secret electronic equipment with axes. At seven-forty the ensign in the stern reported that the bulkhead was beginning to give way. There could be no more clinging to the crippled vessel. Addressing the men on his bullhorn, Shoshan told them to distance themselves at least two hundred meters from the ship so as not to be sucked under when it went down. They would stay in groups led by officers and noncoms. It was imperative that they stick together, because the rescuers would not find them all if they were scattered. For orientation, they would swim away from the ship in the direction of the moon.

Shoshan looked up at the mast, tilted crazily against the night sky, and raised the bullhorn. "Abandon ship."

Jerrycans and mattresses tumbled into the water as crewmen released them from the railing and followed them over the side, a cascade of dark figures wearing life vests throwing up white splashes as they hit the water. The rafts with the wounded were cut loose. Shoshan remained on deck to make sure that no one alive was still aboard.

"Missile."

The shout came from the water. Shoshan turned quickly. High to the west, the bright malevolent eye was once more searching them out. The captain watched as the ball of flame descended toward the ship and hit the stern. The blast knocked him backward against the starboard rail. He could feel the rail pressing higher against his back as the ship perceptibly tilted. He threw away his bullhorn and slid down the ship's side. His feet hit the stabilizer fin so hard that when he rolled into the water he was unable to use his legs. Supported by his life preserver, he pulled strongly with his arms to distance himself from the ship.

The bow of the *Eilat* was projecting above the water in the classic pose of a sinking ship when he looked back. Around him, men were calling to one another. Suddenly, someone shouted "Missile." The Egyptians were again firing in pairs. Shoshan suddenly remembered a warning he had read in a seamen's journal to swim on one's back if there was a danger of underwater explosion, in order to avoid the blast's impact on the abdomen. As he turned over on his bruised back there was a loud explosion, and his body was pummeled by a powerful underwater blast that wrenched a cry of pain from him.

When he had recovered from the shock and looked about him, Shoshan found himself alone in the darkness. The *Eilat*'s bow had disappeared and there were no sounds to be heard except for the lapping of waves. His ship and the two hundred men he had commanded were gone. Only the fuel oil he could smell and taste suggested that they had ever been there. In the womblike embrace of the dark and empty sea, the instincts of command that had sustained him superbly in the critical hours since the first missile was sighted began to crumble before a primal sense of guilt over the fate of the men and the ship he had been entrusted with. He was suddenly gripped by fear and disoriented by shock, and his legs seemed like weights pulling him under. As he paddled, his arm struck something. In the moonlight, he saw that it was a dead sailor floating face downward.

Shoshan thought he heard the sound of singing in the distance. Uncertain whether he was dreaming or awake, he began moving in that direction. Again his arm brushed someone. "Who's that?" said a familiar voice. It was an officer who had joined the voyage on a training mission. He seemed badly wounded but could still swim. Supporting each other, the pair moved in awkward tandem toward the sound. As they drew closer, they could hear a chorus singing "We Shall Overcome" in Hebrew. The singing was coming from a group of sailors gathered around a raft bearing wounded. The men in the water hung on to the raft or to ropes attached to it. The officer in charge of depth charges was leading a singalong to keep up morale among the young sailors. The electronics officer, a strong swimmer, had given his life jacket to a sailor who didn't have one, and was circling the area to pull in men who might be drifting helplessly.

As Shoshan and the wounded officer approached, someone called out, "Who's there?"

"The skipper," said the wounded officer.

An exultant cry went up, and space was made by the raft for the two men. As they came alongside, a young sailor panicked, grabbed Shoshan for support, and briefly pulled him underwater. The sailor had no visible wounds but soon died, apparently from internal injuries. He was one of the many casualties caused by the missile that had exploded in the water.

An hour after the *Eilat* went down, rescue planes flew low over the survivors and dropped flares and rubber boats. The rescue scenario went almost exactly as Shoshan had outlined to his men earlier—first the planes, then the dark shapes of torpedo boats picking their way carefully toward the survivors, and finally the helicopters pulling men up on winches from the boat decks.

Shoshan was recognized as he was pulled aboard a rescue boat close to midnight. "We've got orders to fly you to Jerusalem to meet with the prime minister," an officer said. As a helicopter hauled him up on a sling, he felt a terrible pain in his back. A doctor gave him morphine and he was flown to a hospital in Beersheba. "You're not going anywhere," said the doctor who examined his X rays. "You've got a broken vertebra."

The general commanding the Sinai front was among the first to arrive at Shoshan's bedside. Hadn't Shoshan known, asked the general, that there had been intelligence information prior to the attack that the Egyptians were preparing to fire missiles? The emotions that had begun to well within Shoshan in the dark waters now exploded. Given that intelligence had known of a possible Egyptian launching, the whole tragedy could have been averted if only the navy had been informed. Seeing the agitation gripping Shoshan, the general ordered him removed from the crowded ward and placed in a private room.

The *Eilat* disaster was the worst the navy had ever experienced. Of the two hundred men aboard, forty-seven had been killed and more than a hundred wounded. Shoshan would soon recover use of his legs, and after a few months was given a new assignment as a base commander. Emotionally, however, his wounds had festered. After a few drinks at a cocktail party in celebration of his new appointment, the normally teetotaling Shoshan turned on the navy's senior commanders and began blaming them loudly for having permitted the *Eilat* to sail unprotected into the range of enemy missiles. "Murderers," he shouted. Fellow officers calmed him down, but the trauma of the *Eilat* had shattered him. A few months later, Yitzhak Shoshan, once one of the most promising officers in the Israeli navy, retired from active service.

What happened to the *Eilat* was more than a tragedy for those involved or the loss of the major warship of the small Israeli fleet. The sinking of a destroyer by a missile was an event that changed the nature of naval warfare as dramatically as the introduction of naval guns or the appearance of the first ironclads a century before. Projectiles fired from a small boat by operators viewing their target only on a radar screen had destroyed a ship ten times the size of the attacking craft.

The West had known of the existence of the Soviet sea-to-sea missile but had no idea of its accuracy or power. Three of the four missiles fired had hit their target, and the fourth had missed only because there was virtually nothing left of the ship sticking out of the water to hit. No weapon system like this existed in the West.

There was only one country in the world working on an answer to the Soviet missile boats. The country, as it happened, was Israel.

2
The First Escape

The two small craft with the spindly masts seemed out of place in the vastness of the naval arsenal in Cherbourg. They flew no flag, displayed no names, and bore no armament.

The vessels were the sixth and seventh in a series of twelve ordered by the Israeli navy. The first five had sailed for Israel since the sinking of the *Eilat* fourteen months before. But the small Israeli naval mission posted in Cherbourg was becoming increasingly pessimistic about the chances that the remaining boats would be permitted to leave after launching. An embargo on arms shipments to the Middle East imposed by President Charles de Gaulle on the eve of the Six Day War had not been applied to the unarmed boats being built in Cherbourg. Few people outside Cherbourg knew of their existence; in Cherbourg the local press deliberately refrained from mentioning them. However, with Paris's new pro-Arab orientation becoming increasingly blatant, the fate of the Cherbourg boats was no longer clear. Captain Hadar Kimche, the head of the Israeli naval mission, had begun seeing to it that freshly launched boats waiting for completion of sea tests had enough fuel to get away if an embargo seemed imminent.

Now, in the last days of December 1968, that moment seemed to have come. Israeli commandos had raided Beirut Airport three days after Christmas and destroyed thirteen planes in retribution for an attack on an El Al plane in Athens by Palestinians a few days before. No one had been killed in the Beirut raid, but the Israelis in Cherbourg feared Paris's reaction to this blow at the dignity of a country that had been a French mandate.

The feeling of unease was shared by Admiral (ret.) Mordecai Limon, a former commander of the Israeli navy now serving as head of the military purchasing mission maintained by the Israeli Defense Ministry in Paris. With his extensive political contacts, Limon had reason to believe that de Gaullian wrath might now be brought to bear on Cherbourg.

Telephoning Kimche on Wednesday, January 1, 1969, Limon relayed rumors he had heard that action might be taken against the Israeli boats. "Things are getting warm here," he said. Boat Number Six, which had been launched in November, had completed its trials and was scheduled to sail for Israel in a few days. Boat Number Seven had been launched only a few days before and had not yet been tested at sea. Speaking elliptically, Limon made it clear to Kimche that if Boat Number Six could be gotten away that night, it would be a good idea to do so. Kimche indicated his assent.

Assembling the crew and going aboard Boat Number Six to prepare it for sailing, Kimche left to his deputy, Commander Moshe Tabak, the delicate task of getting clearance from the French navy to leave port without revealing to them that the boat would not be coming back. At the operational level, this involved arrangements for opening a swing bridge that would let the boat out of the arsenal. At the quasi-diplomatic level, it was much more awkward.

Before the departure of each boat for Haifa, the Israelis would officially notify the French naval authorities. At a small ceremony in French naval headquarters in the harbor, Kimche would present the captain of the departing craft to the French admiral, and there would be mutual toasts. The Israelis had requested anchorage facilities in the arsenal while the new boats were being tested, for fear of a possible Palestinian attack in the unguarded civilian port. The French had generously obliged, even providing living quarters for the crewmen in the arsenal and supply facilities. To delude them now and run off with Boat Number Six on false pretenses was an unsavory act for the Israeli naval officer, who had developed warm personal relations with his French counterparts. But a review of the alternatives persuaded Tabak that his own feelings were of little consequence in the matter.

Telephoning Commandant Sardas, the French liaison officer with whom the Israelis dealt, Tabak said that the crew of Boat Number Six would be taking the vessel out again in the evening for a running-in exercise. This time it would be a long-distance test that would last forty hours. Captain Kimche would be joining the boat and there was a chance, if the weather was good and the test produced no problems, that the boat might continue on to Israel, rather than return and risk bad weather on its scheduled date of departure the following week.

"Oh, no, Commandant," said Sardas. "How would I explain that to my superiors?"

"If you want," said Tabak, "I'll explain it to them."

The boat's preparations were nearly completed when darkness fell. Its captain, Lieutenant Commander Yaacov Nitzan, told the radioman to inform arsenal headquarters that the boat would be leaving at 7:00 P.M. and to request that the swing bridge be opened at that hour. Tool kits left behind by shipyard workers who had been putting finishing touches on the vessel were still aboard when it slipped through the arsenal exit into the harbor.

High seas pursued the boat as it raced south at thirty knots. Nitzan had been assured that the boat would be easy to handle, but he could barely control its movements. The waves were moving at the same speed as the vessel, which was behaving like a floating cork. Hoping that increased speed would afford the boat a better grip, he moved up to thirty-seven knots, but the boat heeled over so sharply as it skidded down a wave that he feared it was going to broach. Nitzan throttled back to twenty-one knots and found that the boat responded well.

Nearing Cape Vincent, at the southern tip of Portugal, on the second night, Nitzan was informed of fifty-knot headwinds awaiting him if he turned the corner into the Mediterranean. He chose instead to wait out the storm in the lee of the cape. Once he had dropped anchor close to shore, he ordered the galley to prepare a hot meal for the exhausted crew.

The premature departure of Boat Number Six had taken by surprise Lieutenant Commander Shabtai Levy, the captain of Boat Number Seven. Each of the Israeli boats departing Cherbourg normally carried the captain of the boat that was to follow, so that he could familiarize himself with the boat's handling during the six-day run. Levy, who was in London when the boat left, boarded a commercial flight to Gibraltar to intercept the vessel on its first refueling stop.

The same storm that had forced Nitzan to seek shelter was battering

Gibraltar's airport as the British airliner carrying Levy approached. The pilot announced over the loudspeaker that because of the weather the plane was diverting to Algiers. The Israeli naval officer, who was wearing civilian clothes, asked a stewardess to speak to the pilot urgently. Upon learning Levy's identity, the pilot agreed to brave the storm and land at Gibraltar, rather than risk having his passenger taken into custody by the Algerian authorities.

In Cherbourg, shipyard workers who found the boat gone expressed their disappointment to Tabak at having been deprived of the farewell cocktail party that traditionally preceded the departure of each Israeli vessel.

"You haven't missed out on anything," he assured them. "We're going to have the party Friday on Boat Number Seven."

That vessel was still covered with an untidy clutter of cables and unfastened equipment, but tables for the celebration were set up in the boat's largest cabin. In a brief speech, Tabak praised the workers for having finished Boat Number Six on schedule. "As you know, the boat has gone out for testing. Captain Kimche has decided to continue with it to Israel. He reports all the systems functioning perfectly." Raising a glass, Tabak offered a toast: "To the life of the boat and to those that will come after it. May they reach safe harbor."

In the spirit of *bonhomie*, a foreman announced that he would come the next day to install heating on the bridge of Number Seven, which was to begin its sea trials on Sunday. Tabak's aversion to cold was well known in the shipyard. "I don't normally work on Saturdays," said the foreman, "but I will do it for you—providing, of course, that the boat will still be here."

Tabak joined in the guffaws. Gesturing at the exposed cables, he said, "Do you think we would sail three thousand miles in this?"

"Do I know?" replied the foreman with a Gallic shrug. "You people are capable of anything."

The frantic week was not quite behind Tabak when he arrived home that evening. He put in a call to Gibraltar to make certain about fueling arrangements for Number Six, spoke with London to confirm Levy's departure for Gibraltar, and contacted Haifa to inform naval headquarters of the latest developments.

These chores completed, he could at last turn to that snug harbor in which the Jewish people have ever been able to find brief solace in a stormy world—the Sabbath. Unlike most Friday nights, this time there were no guests for the Sabbath meal. His enjoyment of the quiet family meal with his wife, Esther, and their infant son was heightened by the prospect of the solid night's sleep that lay ahead.

He was still sleeping soundly the next morning at eight when the phone rang. "It's Mocca," said Admiral Limon, using the nickname by which he was known to intimates. "Do you remember the vacation in Israel that you asked for? Well, they've approved it. I'd be interested in your leaving as soon as possible."

Tabak had asked for no vacation but, groggy as he was, he understood that Limon was telling him to get Boat Number Seven away to Israel. The two had discussed a few days before the possibility of having to escape with Number Seven if an embargo seemed imminent, but in view of the boat's condition they had spoken only of taking it across the Channel to get it out of French jurisdiction.

"Are you sure they want me to take the vacation in Israel and not England?" Tabak asked.

"No, no, they want you to go to Israel, as you requested," said Limon. "You're needed there. Can you leave today?"

"I'll have to check some things—tickets and flight schedules. I'll try to make it today. I'll call you as soon as I know."

Hanging up, Tabak was not certain that he had understood Limon correctly. However, as his mind focused, he decided that he had. He telephoned an aide and told him to get to the crew's quarters immediately and make sure no one left. After dressing swiftly, he made his way to mission headquarters, the task before him unscrolling in his mind. The boats were normally tested hundreds of miles before being sailed to Haifa, and serious problems were often uncovered. Boat Number Seven would be risking winter storms on a three-thousand-mile journey with no testing at all. It would have to sail with a crew of twelve—all that remained in Cherbourg—instead of the normal complement of thirty, and its captain, Lieutenant Commander Levy, had flown to Gibraltar to join Number Six. Furthermore, it had a handicap none of the other boats had had. In order to test the boat's stability when armed, an unwieldy seven-ton dummy cannon had been secured to its deck.

On the street, Tabak saw a car carrying his chief machinist and two other sailors. He flagged them down.

"We're going to Paris for the day," said the machinist.

"Your plans have just been changed," said Tabak. "Get back to the boat and get it ready to sail. We're leaving today for Haifa. The French aren't to know about it."

Remaining behind to mind the shop would be Lieutenant Haim Shachak, the mission's supply officer. Tabak told him to get food aboard Number Seven and, if possible, to get customs clearance so that, legally at least, the boat would not be a runaway. The one legal requirement before departure, the Israelis had learned, was customs clearance, which attested that the foreign parts imported to France for the boat, like its German engine, were aboard the boat when it sailed. Informing the French navy of departure was merely a courtesy.

It was raining heavily when Shachak rang the customs officer's doorbell on the fringe of Cherbourg.

"Oh, Commandant, what wind has brought you?" asked the Frenchman in surprise, showing him in.

Shachak apologized for interrupting the official's weekend and said that an emergency had occurred. "You've probably heard about the raid on Beirut Airport," he said. "There's a lot of tension now in the Middle East, and the boat is needed there. We want to sail today and would like clearance. We need your help."

"But the boat is unarmed," said the customs officer. "What could you do with it?"

"We'll put a gun on it and patrol."

When Shachak quoted a passage from Jonah to reinforce a point, the customs officer's wife, who had joined them, responded enthusiastically. She was the daughter of a minister and was delighted at the opportunity to exchange biblical quotations with the Israeli visitor.

"Listen, Jacques," she said to her husband. "The commandant has come especially for you. Go with him."

The official dutifully put on his coat and accompanied Shachak.

There remained the important task of obtaining a weather map of the treacherous Bay of Biscay. Tabak assumed that Limon had understood that to be the meaning of his remark about checking timetables. Intent on avoiding Commandant Sardas because of the embarrassment over Boat Number Six, he went directly to the office of the arsenal's weekend duty officer, instead of going through the liaison officer. As he entered the room, Tabak was startled to see that the duty officer behind the desk was Sardas.

"What are you doing here?" asked the Frenchman warily.

"I've come to apologize," said Tabak, recovering quickly. "I heard you were duty officer."

Sardas's tense demeanor relaxed a bit. "You don't know how angry they were with me in Paris," he confided. "I was rebuked."

The two men chatted awhile, and then Tabak said, "We're having trouble with the propeller of Number Seven and want to test it. Can I get the weather?"

"No problem," said Sardas.

He went out to the meteorologist's office down the hall, then returned with a large map of the region. Tabak pretended to study the Cherbourg area, but out of the corner of his eye he carefully noted the barometric readings for the Bay of Biscay. He was relieved to see no troublesome lows.

Still missing from his weather picture was the area farther south, around Cape Vincent. For this he radioed Boat Number Six, which was still anchored there. Kimche reported that the wind had dropped sufficiently for his vessel to begin sailing for Gibraltar. In veiled language, Tabak indicated that they might be seeing each other sooner than expected.

Shortly before noon, the boat's chief petty officer informed Tabak that it was impossible to fuel the boat because the shipyard foreman and two assistants had arrived to install the heating system on the bridge. There was nothing to do but wait. The foreman would immediately have understood what was afoot if he had seen the boat being fueled for a long journey. Fortunately, the workmen were done in less than an hour, and fueling could begin.

As the day wore on, Tabak was increasingly troubled by a sense of unease over the operation. Contacting Haifa, he expressed his misgivings and asked whether the urgency was real. "If you're sure about the boat's seaworthiness," headquarters replied, "go."

By midafternoon, preparations were complete. Attempts to pry loose the dummy cannon had failed, and the boat would have to sail with it aboard. Tabak telephoned Limon in Paris. "I've got my tickets and I'll be leaving Cherbourg by train at four-thirty."

Limon wished him a good journey.

Tabak returned to the boat to find a new French duty officer taking a keen interest in the unusual Saturday-afternoon activity around the Israeli vessel. Tabak introduced himself and informed him that they were going out in order to test the boat's propeller. Could a sailor be posted to open the bridge at four-thirty? The duty officer assured him it would be taken care of. The bridge swung open at the designated time, and Tabak conned the boat out through the narrow opening.

The boat ran well across the relatively calm Bay of Biscay. With the excitement of the departure behind him, Tabak again began to be seized by doubts about the whole enterprise. Had it really been necessary? Had Limon perhaps overreacted? By running off in this fashion for the second time in three days—deceiving the French naval authorities again—were they not endangering the boats yet to be built? Ten hours out to sea, Tabak received a message from Haifa congratulating him on his rapid organization and departure. It eased his mind to know that headquarters was pleased, since presumably they knew something he didn't.

Limon had not overreacted. He had been informed on Friday by a senior French official that de Gaulle had decided to declare a total embargo in reaction to the Beirut raid. An order was to be sent later in the day from Paris to all customs offices to halt clearance of war matériel destined for Israel. The directive was being issued before a public announcement of the embargo in order to forestall any last-minute flight of matériel that Israeli machinations might contrive. Limon was able to persuade a French official to have the message to the Cherbourg customs office misaddressed to a district customs office in Normandy and dispatched only late on Friday. The directive would not be rerouted to Cherbourg until after the weekend.

Tabak was unaware of this as he rounded Cape Vincent and entered the Mediterranean. The sea was mountainous, but the wind was behind him. The low clouds around Gibraltar were so thick he couldn't pick up the rock on his radar. After entering the harbor, he tied up alongside Boat Number Six and stepped down from the bridge for the first time in forty-nine hours. Kimche was on the quay to greet him.

Leaving the two boats to sail on to Israel the next day under Tabak's command, Kimche flew to London and took the cross-Channel ferry to Cherbourg to face the French wrath.

"Oho, are they looking for you," said Commandant Sardas when Kimche telephoned him. Wearing a dress uniform for the confrontation, the Israeli officer was ushered into the office of the admiral commanding the arsenal.

Flanked by aides wearing severe expressions, the French officer remained standing and did not offer Kimche a seat. The Israelis had not acted "*avec l'honneur*," said the admiral. They had violated the French navy's hospitality and he was therefore obliged to ask them to leave the premises of the arsenal within twenty-four hours. Kimche was asked if he had anything to say.

"What would you have done in my situation?"

"That is not a question I am obliged to answer," said the admiral.

The tension eased somewhat as the admiral accompanied Kimche to the door, the official message having been delivered. As they parted, the admiral shook hands and said, "In the same situation, I might have done the same."

Outside the door, French officers were waiting to make arrangements for the transfer of Israeli property from the arsenal. Kimche asked for a twenty-four-hour extension, and this was readily granted.

The punishment was far milder than expected. The Israelis had feared banishment from Cherbourg, and even possibly a halt in further construction of the boats. They had been willing to risk it to ensure that at least Boats Six and Seven were in hand, because of their critical importance.

The boats of Cherbourg were not the conventional patrol boats they seemed. They were in fact among the most unconventional vessels afloat, platforms for a technology and method of warfare almost a decade ahead of any Western navy's. Israel was gambling the future security of its sea frontier and maritime lifeline on these frail-looking craft. They were the realization of a revolutionary concept that had emerged eight years before in Israeli naval headquarters almost as a passing thought.

3

The Maverick

The handful of naval officers on the air-force plane had told their wives that they would be gone for a week at sea on a training exercise. But their destination was as far from the sea as one could get in Israel. On landing at an airbase in the southern Negev they were helicoptered to a tent camp at the edge of the Large Crater, a massive moonscape in the heart of the rocky desert. They and the larger contingents from the army and air force had been brought to observe demonstrations of a new weapon devised by Rafael, the government's highly secret Authority for Weapons Development.

Israeli scientists had been working on a guided missile since 1954. Bringing explosives down upon an enemy by remote control while remaining outside the enemy's range was a tempting option for a small nation surrounded by numerous foes and seeking to overcome this numerical inferiority with the help of technology. Early experiments with remote-control boats and glider bombs had been encouraging.

Rafael was constricted by the secrecy that prevented it from working with foreign firms. Nevertheless, by sending its young scientists and engineers abroad, it attempted to keep abreast of significant developments in the world. Young as the country was, the scientific talent emerging was impressive.

The new nation's industrial base, however, was still that of the small colonial outpost it had been until the British departure in 1948. The

22

most distinctive armament developed in the War of Independence was an outsize mortar notable for the terrifying noise its shells made rather than its accuracy. Reinventing the wheel, as it were, the Rafael scientists developed the skills in metallurgy, aerodynamics, rocket propellants, and other disciplines to enable them within three years to create a guided missile called the Luz that flew twelve miles. It was directed onto target by radio signals sent by a forward observer manipulating a joy stick as he tracked the missile through large binoculars.

At the weeklong test in the Large Crater in November 1958, Rafael was attempting to interest the armed services in three different versions of the Luz—surface-to-surface, air-to-ground, and ship-to-ship—in the hope that they would support further development. Neither the army nor the air force expressed enthusiasm. The army saw little advantage in guiding an expensive missile onto a target when conventional artillery could do the job at much less cost. The air-to-ground version required launching from a slow-flying plane like a Dakota that would be too vulnerable to ground fire.

The navy, however, was intrigued. The Egyptians had acquired Soviet Skory-class destroyers whose guns far outranged those on the Israeli destroyers, the navy's largest vessels. The Luz, if mounted on destroyers, could outreach the Egyptian guns with a powerful warhead. Although still experimental, it was virtually the only hope the Israeli navy had of staying afloat in any confrontation.

The naval officers converging on the former monastery hospice atop Haifa's Mount Carmel late in 1960 had the sense of fresh beginnings that comes with a new commander, a feeling enhanced by the aura this one brought with him. Rear Admiral Yohai Bin-Nun, who had summoned them to Stella Maris, Israel's naval headquarters, had become a naval legend in Israel long before moving up the ladder of command.

As a young officer in the War of Independence twelve years before, Bin-Nun had led a small naval commando unit that had been outfitted with six one-man assault craft acquired in Italy on the war-surplus market. An Italian instructor accompanied the craft to Israel. He had participated in the two actions the assault craft had been used in during the war—a successful attack against British tankers in Crete's Suda Bay, and an unsuccessful foray into Malta's Valletta harbor when the British captured the raiders.

The craft were in effect manned torpedoes containing six hundred pounds of explosives. The operator sat in a small cockpit at the rear. The engine made little noise, permitting the craft to approach its target at night stealthily. Several hundred yards short of the target, the operator fixed the rudder with a special screw to ensure that it stayed on steady course, released the safety device on the explosive charge, and opened full throttle. At one hundred yards, he pulled a lever that ejected a wooden float to which he was stoutly lashed. A recovery boat waiting in the darkness would then dash in to pick him up. The operators wore bathing caps with an infrared light that was invisible to the enemy but could be seen by a lookout in the recovery boat using infrared binoculars.

Training had just gotten under way along an evacuated stretch of waterfront in Tiberias, on the Sea of Galilee, when the naval command ordered the unit transported by truck immediately to Jaffa, on the Mediterranean coast. The flagship of the Egyptian fleet, the *King Farouk*, had been sighted off Gaza with an accompanying minesweeper, and the special unit was to be used against them. Bin-Nun and his men had twenty-four hours in which to arm the craft and prepare for the attack. The Italian instructor worked with them through the night. A freighter that had been used to ferry illegal Jewish refugees from Europe in the prestate period was adapted as a mother ship because of its large afterdeck, which could accommodate the assault craft. Exercises to lower the craft into the water were carried out as the vessel headed south for Gaza.

Toward evening, Bin-Nun lay down for his first nap in three days. He was roused by a radioman who handed him a message. His eyes first noticed the signatory: Prime Minister David Ben-Gurion. The message was succinct: "Attack with all you've got."

Bin-Nun assembled his men on deck and outlined their attack formation, using carrots to represent the craft and their targets. Because of the random course they had been taking to mark time until nightfall, the captain of the mother ship was not certain of their location. One of Bin-Nun's men, however, had been a fisherman in the area. By determining the depth of the water from soundings, he estimated that they were about ten miles west of Gaza. Bin-Nun timed his attack so that the moon would just be rising behind the enemy vessels as he came into position.

Four craft were lowered into the water. Two would make the first attacks on the enemy vessels. One would be a recovery boat. Bin-Nun, in the fourth, would be the reserve force, attacking whichever ship needed a follow-up punch.

The sea was calm as they approached the enemy vessels. The two attack boats were four hundred yards from their targets when it became clear that they had been spotted. The Egyptians could be heard raising their anchors and getting under way. As gunfire was opened on the Israeli craft, Bin-Nun saw that the operator assigned to attack the minesweeper was mistakenly heading toward the King Farouk along with the other assault boat. The minesweeper, meanwhile, was beginning to gain headway, and Bin-Nun could see foam beneath its bow. He opened full throttle and headed for it.

The vessel turned directly toward him, offering only a narrow profile. Suddenly Bin-Nun was caught in the light of two searchlights. A large explosion off to the side told him the King Farouk had been hit, but he had no time to look. Machine guns and anti-aircraft guns had opened on him at fast-closing range, and the water around him splattered with shots. Completely blinded by the glare from the searchlights, Bin-Nun decided to aim between them. At one hundred yards, he pulled the ejection handle that should have sent the float against which he was leaning into the water. Nothing happened. Bin-Nun pulled harder and the handle came off in his hand. The rope around his waist, tying him to the float, was knotted too well for him to release it before impact. Bin-Nun climbed over the float and leaped into the water. He was dragged behind the speeding boat for a few seconds. Then the rope snapped, cutting a gash in his side but leaving him floating free. A few seconds later, there was a tremendous explosion. Although he was only some forty yards from the ship, he was not injured.

Bin-Nun's cap had been ripped off, but he was able to signal the rescue boat with a flashlight he had in his belt. As the boat came alongside, the lookout reached down and dragged him in. Around him Bin-Nun saw the sea full of Egyptian sailors drowning or swimming. Within minutes the other two operators were spotted by their infrared lights and were pulled aboard. Neither of them was injured.

Awarded one of the twelve medals for exceptional bravery issued in the war, Bin-Nun went on to lead the underwater commandos and then commanded a destroyer. His appointment as navy commander marked the first arrival of an experienced combat officer in that post. Although the navy had since become a professional force with conventional warships and captains who did not lose their bearings at sea, Bin-Nun still believed in the unconventional approach to warfare, particularly by a side that was outnumbered and outequipped.

To the meeting in Stella Maris, Bin-Nun had invited, in addition to headquarters staff, all flotilla commanders and a naval architect. The participants had been told that the meeting would last two or three days and that there was only one question on the agenda—the nature of the fleet that should be acquired in the coming decade.

The question was far from academic. The navy was a floating anachronism. Its backbone was three World War II destroyers—one of them captured from the Egyptians in a running battle off Haifa during the Sinai Campaign of 1956. These old British destroyers were outranged and outnumbered by the new destroyers the Soviets were supplying the Egyptians. Furthermore, the destroyer complement of 250 men made it too large a ship for a small country like Israel, with its limited capacity for absorbing casualties: the sinking of a single destroyer would be a national disaster.

The few other naval craft, including six torpedo boats and two submarines, did not much improve the situation. The navy might hope to provide protection for the Israeli coast but could not mount any offensive actions against the Egyptian and Syrian fleets or protect Israel's shipping lanes.

The navy's tiny budget reflected the General Staff's view of its marginal function. It was clear to all that Israel's fate rested on its air force and its ground army. Nothing decisive would happen at sea, one way or another. The nation's sparse defense funds would therefore not be spent on frills like modern destroyers but on tanks and planes.

Given these circumstances, what should the navy aspire to? Going around the table, Bin-Nun asked each man to address the subject.

Several schools of thought emerged. The commander of the destroyer flotilla advocated replacing the outworn vessels with newer ones of a similar type, so as to have a balanced navy with a capacity, however small, to perform a variety of missions, from surface combat to antisubmarine work. Most participants saw this as only perpetuating the navy's impotence, because none of these activities could be performed seriously. To continue picking up discards from other navies was not the answer to Israel's needs.

The commander of the submarine flotilla suggested abandoning the surface altogether to the much larger Arab navies and, except for a small coast guard, relying on an all-submarine fleet that would compensate for the Israeli navy's physical inferiority by stealth and serve as a vehicle for transporting naval commandos to targets.

Bin-Nun himself had in the recent past advocated an all-commando navy, which would attempt to cope with the Arab navies by "striking at source"—hitting their ships in harbor.

These suggestions were desperate attempts to find a meaningful role for a navy that could not afford ships. The commando suggestion was attractive. Naval commandos had the ability to penetrate enemy harbors, and their budget was minimal. Opponents of the idea pointed out that in any war the commandos would almost certainly be denied the major factor needed for success—surprise. Even if Israel were to open the war, it would doubtless be the air force that would deliver the first strike, and the air force would doubtless choose daylight. The commandos would not commence operations before darkness, by which time the war would be raging and the enemy on full alert.

As the discussion moved around the table, a fourth option was tentatively voiced by one of the participants. Noting the attempt being made by Rafael to develop the sea-to-sea version of the Luz, he suggested that the missile—if it should ever be perfected—be mounted not on destroyers, as was intended, but on small boats. Small craft could not carry large guns because of their powerful recoil, but they could serve as a platform for missiles, which had far less recoil stress. Such boats would require only small crews and therefore reduce the danger of large-scale loss of life. Not least, the boats would be relatively cheap to build. Enough of them might even be acquired to permit separate task forces for Syrian and Egyptian waters, a strategic option Israeli naval officers until now could only daydream about.

The suggestion was dismissed as futuristic whimsy by most of the officers at the table, who pointed out that such boats did not exist in any Western navy. But the idea would not go away. None of the other proposals offered any hope. The small-boat/big-punch concept did, if it could be proved feasible. The idea would float at the periphery of the navy's consciousness until, in 1962, Bin-Nun assigned his deputy, Captain Shlomo Erell, to undertake a serious examination of the concept.

Erell was the closest thing to a crusty professional sailor in the Israeli navy. Born in Poland in 1920, he was six when his family emigrated to

Palestine. He had become involved as a youth in the right-wing Betar movement and was imprisoned by the British in the Acre fortress for six months in 1938 for underground activities. The following year, with the outbreak of World War II, he joined the British merchant marine. The young sailor participated in the evacuation at Dunkirk and made the Murmansk and Atlantic convoy runs, surviving two torpedoings. By war's end, he was master of a small cargo ship on the Mediterranean. Afterward, he captained the Dead Sea fleet, salt-encrusted vessels carrying potash extracted from the mineral-rich waters of the inland lake four hundred meters below sea level. With the outbreak of Israel's War of Independence in 1948, he joined the fledgling navy and commanded several landing operations behind enemy lines. In the following years he commanded virtually every type of vessel in the navy and spent a year at the Royal Naval Staff College in England, where he was cited by the course commander as having a "fresh and original mind." But the idea that had surfaced at the Bin-Nun staff meeting as if of its own accord—the one he had been charged with probing—enchanted him as if he were a young ensign on his first watch as bridge officer.

If a marriage could be made between the Luz and a patrol boat, it would mean giving the tiny craft the punch of a heavy cruiser. The Luz warhead was as devastating as the eight-inch shells of the largest cruiser, its range was about the same, and its chances of hitting its target far greater if the guidance system worked. Israel could hardly think of acquiring a new 3,500-ton destroyer, let alone a 15,000-ton cruiser, but if this idea could be implemented Israel would have a fleet of 250-ton-cruiser equivalents that moved faster than any destroyer and could sink any ship that floated in the eastern Mediterranean. It was a fantastic notion, but it looked less fantastic the more he stared at it.

Erell did not accept the navy's role as a passive spearholder for the air force and army. Its elite commando unit, the most highly trained of all units in the Israel Defense Force, was the navy's pride. The commandos were capable of attacking coastal installations and of penetrating enemy harbors to strike at their fleets. The army and air-force officers on the General Staff liked to hear about such plans, which did not divert substantial budget allocations from planes and tanks.

However, Erell believed that the navy's destiny remained on the surface, carrying out the conventional tasks demanded of navies—defending coastline and maritime routes and attacking the enemy in his waters—even if this had to be done in an unconventional manner. Merchant shipping, upon which Israel depended for survival, was vulnerable once it passed Crete, for the last six hundred miles of the run to Israel. Air power alone, Erell was convinced, could neither protect shipping nor defend Israel's coasts from determined attacks by enemy warships. Lying out of range of Israeli planes by day, enemy raiders could run for the coast under cover of darkness and shell the coastal strip in which 70 percent of the country's population was squeezed and where most of the industrial infrastructure was located, including oil refineries and power plants. Even the outdated Egyptian destroyer captured in 1956 had managed to lob scores of shells in the direction of Haifa before being intercepted.

The Egyptian navy had lately been mustering large forces in training exercises a hundred miles north of Alexandria, from where they could either go for the shipping lanes to the west or dash eastward toward the Israeli coast. For Israel to abandon the sea would be madness. The navy's present path was a dead end, but the missile-boat concept offered a way out. Missile boats did not exist in the West, nor did sea-to-sea missiles. If Israel wanted them, it would have to create them. Late in 1962, Erell organized a think tank of several senior naval officers. In blissful ignorance of the difficulties that lay ahead, they began putting down on paper the outlines of the boat that had been circling at the center of Erell's mind.

The pair of missiles rested on launchers set up on a dirt track leading down to the beach. Hillocks a few meters on either side masked their bright-yellow noses from distant view. At successive firing commands, they lifted bravely into the air on a plume of fire and smoke and headed out to sea. A few hundred meters out, both plunged ignominiously into the water.

The site inside a navy base on the Mediterranean coast was code-named Nature Reserve, but Israelis participating in the tests called it Cape Canaveral. To ensure secrecy, adjacent beaches were cleared for a ten-kilometer distance before each firing, and a patrolling airplane ensured that no boat was within twenty-five kilometers. A torpedo boat cruised offshore at every firing to pick up floating remains of aborted missiles. The crew was ordered below during the tests to keep the secret from them; only the captain and a security man from Rafael remained topside to fish out debris.

The land version of the Luz had achieved a fair measure of reliability up to a range of twenty-seven kilometers. The artillery corps had organized a Luz battery, but the naval version was proving extremely problematic. Rafael scientists were able to determine, from fragments of a missile engine retrieved after three days of diving, that metal failure was to blame for exploding engines.

The main problem, however, was visibility. Smoke from the missile's exhaust obscured the bright flares in its tail. Repeatedly the missile missed because the aimer, squinting through binoculars, could not see it in the heavy smoke caused by the humidity's effect on the exhaust emissions. Despite the discouraging results, however, the navy urged Rafael to press on.

The morning sun was already heating the tents at the edge of the Large Crater in the summer of 1961, and canvas flaps were raised in supplication for a vagrant breeze. A new missile test was being staged by Rafael for an interservice audience, but launchings were not scheduled until late afternoon, and Ori Even-Tov lay on his cot in the enervating heat waiting for the time to pass. It was the first Luz test he would be witnessing and, he presumed, his last. The thirty-five-year-old engineer had joined Rafael a few months earlier, after a decade in the United States, and was already planning to leave. He found the plant's atmosphere stifling. Interesting projects were going on there, and the personnel were first-rate, but each research team operated in total ignorance of what the others were doing. At the American defense firm where he had worked, there had been constant interchange among the scientific and engineering personnel. At Rafael, such interchange was blocked by what Even-Tov saw as obsessive security-mindedness and bureaucratic turf-guarding. He was convinced that research and development could blossom only where ideas could be juggled in free barnstorming sessions. He himself had formulated a totally new approach to the Luz guidance system that would eliminate the need for the joy stick, but he found the high priests at Rafael, as he referred to them, unresponsive.

Even-Tov glanced across at the naval officer sharing the tent. He had been thinking for some time of the possibility of making direct contact with the navy, the service most likely to be interested in his idea. But it was not clear how, as a brand-new hand in an R&D organization top-heavy with engineering talent, he could gain a serious hearing from the navy command. His tentmate was only a lieutenant commander, but the navy was small and he presumably had access to the top brass.

Even-Tov decided to launch.

"I don't think the Luz is ever going to work as a sea-to-sea missile," he said.

As the naval officer knew, Rafael was trying to find a new fuel that would eliminate the smoke problem. Even-Tov said he didn't think they would succeed. But even if there were no smoke, trying to guide a missile onto target from a rolling ship with binoculars and a joy stick was fusing modern missile technology to a bow-and-arrow guidance system. At night there could be no aiming at all. He had his own idea, said Even-Tov, for an autonomous guidance system that would permit the missile to seek out the target by itself, by day or night. The naval officer was giving him his full attention.

At the American firm where he had been working, said Even-Tov, he had been manager of a project involving the development of an un-manned minisub for cutting the cables of sea mines. The sub had been fitted with a sonar altimeter that would permit it to follow the contour of the sea bottom at a fixed height. Although the vessel had never be-come operational, the altimeter had proved workable. Even-Tov was convinced that the same principle could be applied to the Luz. An altimeter would keep the missile at a fixed height above the water with-out relying on a fallible human controller. As for steering horizontally onto the target, radar could be inserted into the missile, as in existing ground-to-air missiles. By the time they emerged from the tent, Even-Tov was confident that his idea would percolate up from the desert proving grounds to navy headquarters atop Mount Carmel.

Testing of the sea-to-sea version of the Luz, initially carried out from launchers on the Mediterranean shore, was shifted to the destroyer *Jaffa*. To preserve secrecy, all hands were sent below whenever the cover was to be stripped from the launchers, which had been installed on deck the previous night by Rafael technicians. The crewmen had been told that the containers held special illumination rockets. Moving at high speed, the destroyer launched its missiles at a canvas target pulled at the end of a long towline by a torpedo boat.

Six chief petty officers had been trained on simulators to serve as missile aimers. Despite their best efforts, the tests invariably ended in failure. A new fuel had been acquired from France, but it merely produced black billows instead of white, leaving the missile completely hidden from the aimer. Attempts to outflank the smoke by placing the aimer on a helicopter or a scout boat, tracking the missile from an angle, produced no better results. A number of test firings were held in 1961 and 1962 with totally negative results, the missiles striking anywhere up to a thousand meters off target. Despair gripped the Rafael scientists and the navy command, and a halt was declared in all further sea testing of the Luz.

Ori Even-Tov was at his desk in the Rafael plant near Haifa when the guard at the gate telephoned to announce a visitor.

"This is Hyman Shamir of Israel Aircraft Industries," said the visitor on the guard post phone. "Is it possible to meet with you?"

"Come on in."

"I'd rather meet you outside," said Shamir. "Please don't tell anyone I'm here."

It was drizzling when Even-Tov stepped outside. Shamir was waiting for him in the courtyard. The two men shook hands and sat on a bench, despite its dampness.

"I understand that you have some ideas about a new guidance system for the Luz," said Shamir. "Could you tell me about it?"

Almost two months had passed since the conversation in the tent. Its contents had not only percolated upward in the navy hierarchy but also been passed on to the most ambitious firm in the thin ranks of Israeli military industries. The Israel Aircraft Industry (IAI) had been established a decade before as a maintenance facility. Its founder was Al Schwimmer, an American aircraft-engineer who had acquired surplus airplanes for Israel in the critical days just before and during the War of Independence. At Prime Minister David Ben-Gurion's personal request, Schwimmer had settled in Israel to establish an aircraft-maintenance infrastructure. Schwimmer's ultimate objective, however, was to manufacture planes. Meanwhile, he was out to develop his firm's own engineering infrastructure.

Before the approach was made to Even-Tov, his background was checked out. Born in Jerusalem, he had not finished high school, being swept up in the armed struggle culminating in the War of Independence. He had served as a platoon commander in the prolonged battle for Jerusalem and stayed on in the army until 1952, when he traveled to the United States, at the age of twenty-five, to pursue his education. He graduated from Columbia, obtained an engineering degree at Drexel, and became a project manager at a large defense plant outside Philadelphia.

At Rafael he had the reputation of being brilliant but ornery, a bane for his superiors, who found it difficult to confine him to any fixed path. He professed contempt for the practice of Rafael's top scientists, many of whom taught at Haifa's Technion, to publish papers on their research. R&D work the world over, he maintained, was practiced by bright minds who preferred complicated solutions to simple ones because there are more learned articles to be generated that way. He himself reveled in the label of "garagenik" bestowed upon him by his colleagues, denoting a dirty-handed problem-solver. For all his unconventionality, however, he was accepted as an exceptional engineer with sometimes startling insights.

As they sat in the Rafael courtyard, Even-Tov outlined his approach for Shamir. When he was done, Shamir asked, "Would you be willing to work on this project at the IAI?"

"I'd be willing to work on it in a clothing factory," said Even-Tov. He had already given notice to Rafael that he would be leaving to return to America when his year was up. Determined efforts by management to dissuade him had failed.

Even-Tov's arrival at the IAI plant abutting the international airport at Lod in the late autumn of 1961 was low-key. Shamir conducted him to a room he himself had been using as an office and turned it over to him. The IAI official promised all the staff and space Even-Tov needed as the project developed. Wishing him well, he left Even-Tov alone in the room to survey his empty desk.

4
Journey to Germany

The last time Yitzhak Shoshan had encountered the German military, he had been a boy of ten scrambling over the rooftops of Brussels in 1940 with his family, to escape a roundup of Jews. It was surrealistic now to be sitting as an Israeli naval officer in the German Defense Ministry in Bonn.

The future commander of the *Eilat* and another Israeli naval officer had come to Germany to inspect the Jaguar torpedo boat. It was the end of December 1960 and they had already visited several European countries to view similar craft, traveling by night train to save the navy hotel expenses. The staff meeting with Admiral Bin-Nun on the navy's future had occurred a few months before, but the small-boat/big-punch concept was still only a theory. Israel, meanwhile, had an immediate need for new torpedo boats.

The Germans were in civilian clothing, except the admiral at the head of the table. At one point Shoshan posed a technical question about the Jaguar no one could answer. "I'll call someone," said the admiral.

He spoke into a phone and a uniformed naval lieutenant strode into the room, his cap under his arm. The officer had blond hair and a scar on his face, and he was old enough to have served in the war. He clicked his heels, saluted the admiral, and barked his salutation.

Shoshan felt a hot flush over his body followed by a sense of bloodless cold. Swept by nausea, he begged leave and hastened from the room. In

34

the toilet he vomited and shivered uncontrollably as sweat soaked his shirt. When he returned to the meeting room, the lieutenant was gone and a younger officer was waiting to respond to the earlier question. Shoshan glanced at the admiral and sensed that he had understood.

The next day the two Israelis were taken to a port on the North Sea. The squadron commander who received them aboard a Jaguar, Korvetten Kapitän Noodt, was a veteran seaman with a warm face and an easy manner. Noodt told his guests that they had the run of the boat and could see everything except the code books. Although the captain had fought in the war—the Israelis immediately noted his limp—Shoshan took an instinctive liking to the man. As the squadron put out to sea, Noodt related that he had been a naval cadet in the same port when World War II broke out. He had been wounded on a torpedo boat and hospitalized, then transferred to submarines, but the war ended just as he was to sail on his first mission.

At lunch Noodt said he understood there was a problem about kosher food. Wincing at the prospect of again facing the potatoes and hardboiled eggs being pressed upon them by the fastidious Germans, Shoshan said, "Well, there's not really much of a problem." German punctiliousness prevailed, however, and two kosher lunchboxes were produced.

The Jaguar had begun life in World War II as a *Schnellboot* (S-boat), harassing Allied shipping in the North Sea and the English Channel. It was a healthy craft, Shoshan saw, with room for considerable armament and electronic apparatus. Although it was not very comfortable for the crew, it was powerful and built for fighting. The captain was able to control the vessel effectively from the bridge. At Shoshan's request, Noodt executed squadron maneuvers to demonstrate the ease with which the boats could keep formation.

From Germany the Israeli officers traveled to England to see a British torpedo boat and write their final report. It was Christmas Day and Shoshan, forgetful of the customs of the gentile world, vainly scoured the streets of central London in search of an open restaurant. On returning to the Israeli embassy, he drafted his report. He was lukewarm about the other boats they had seen, but of the Jaguar he wrote, "This is a ship of war."

Ori Even-Tov was outlining his idea once again, this time in naval headquarters in Haifa. Facing him and Hyman Shamir across the table were

Captain Erell and the navy's top technical officers. Erell was an eager listener. When an electronics officer flanking him attempted to demolish Even-Tov's presentation on technical grounds, he was signaled into silence by a discreet kick beneath the table from the deputy naval commander. The officer on the other side of Erell was likewise kicked in the shins when he laughed at the paltry sum Even-Tov suggested would be necessary to develop the weapon.

"We need their help," Erell told his aides after the visitors had left. "The IAI is a good horse to run with. What we can't push they can push."

Erell found a sympathetic ear when he called on the director general of the Defense Ministry, Moshe Kashti, to request funds for a feasibility study by the IAI. Although the General Staff preferred investing the limited defense funds available in proven armaments purchased off the shelf abroad, Kashti and his boss, Shimon Peres, believed it imperative to divert some of these funds to the development of a military industry at home. Israel's political isolation demanded this, and so did the desire to develop a modern industrial infrastructure.

Even-Tov was summoned by Kashti to spell out his proposal. "What would you need to develop this missile?" asked Kashti.

"I've got to design it first. And for that I'll need a few people and a year."

"You'll get it."

Returning home with a beard and degrees acquired during five years of advanced studies in London, the young mathematician wondered whether any challenging work would be available for him in Israel, with its limited technological infrastructure. When he inquired at Israel Aircraft Industries, he was told that there was a job opening up that would possibly require someone with his background, which also included studies in electrical engineering. He was led down the hall and shown into a large office where a solitary figure sat behind a desk. Ori Even-Tov set down the textbook he had been reading and chatted briefly with the new arrival. Even-Tov, who had arrived three weeks before, had asked for two things—a mathematician and a set of basic American textbooks on airborne radar and allied fields. Now he had both.

The two men closeted themselves in the office for the next few weeks, poring over the books like students cramming for an examination, pausing occasionally to exchange comments and make notes. Ground-to-air and air-to-air missiles employing radar to home in on targets were operational in the West, but Israel was not privy to their secrets. What was available was textbook theory, and this the two men now digested. When they had finished, Even-Tov had a clear vision of his direction. It was one never taken before.

He proposed using an altimeter to have the missile fly just a few meters over the sea surface. This would make it a difficult target for an enemy to spot with his own radar in time to take evasive action or shoot it down. The warhead would also strike near the waterline. Radar could not guide the missile on such a low-level flight, because the reflection of the waves—"sea clutter," in electronics jargon—confused the sensors. Radar could, however, be used to home in on the target on the horizontal plane while the altimeter kept the missile at a predetermined height. Even-Tov's proposal to split the guidance system by using both an altimeter and radar in order to create a sea-skimming missile was a major innovation in missile technology.

He was fortunate in having in hand existing hardware—the Luz—with sound aerodynamic features and a reliable warhead. The problem was that it had not been designed as a homing missile that tracked a target on its own, but as an optically guided missile steered by impulses sent from the ground to its tail. The cone, instead of housing a rotating radar antenna, as in air-to-air missiles, was packed with 150 kilograms of high explosives. To redesign the Luz in order to shift the warhead farther back and put the radar in its place would have entailed a budget allocation and a delay that would probably have doomed the project.

Even-Tov elected to solve the problem cheaply with stationary antennas projecting from the missile's sides. It was a solution that any radar expert would have told him could not succeed, for clear mathematical reasons. Even-Tov was not acting in defiance of these opinions but in ignorance of them. The textbooks he had read did not allude to stationary antennas because of their obvious unfeasibility. The calculations he and his assistant arrived at had shown him that a fixed antenna of a missile fired in the general direction of the target would have enough lateral vision—about five or six degrees—to track a ship whose relatively slow speed would not permit it to reach the radar's blind zone before impact.

There was no computer in Israel capable of checking these calculations except one at Rafael, which would never grant Even-Tov access. With the navy footing the bill, Even-Tov flew to Italy. The computer results there confirmed that the missile should fly with its dual control system and its fixed antenna, if Even-Tov had made his calculations correctly and the laws of physics held.

Even-Tov and his assistant were shifted from their bookish retreat to a large workshop and provided with a small staff of engineers and technicians to begin building a prototype. Their work had hardly begun when they learned that they were already behind. The Soviet Union had developed its own missile boats—the first in the world—and had begun supplying them to Egypt.

The Soviets had conceived their missile boats in the 1950s to deal with a problem at the margin of the superpower confrontation—the prospect of an American carrier task force approaching the Soviet coast and launching nuclear strikes against the nation's heartland. Until their own fleet was strong enough to confront the Americans on the high seas, the Soviet naval command proposed to deal with the carrier threat by developing a seaborne missile with a powerful warhead.

It had been the Germans who had introduced guided weapons against ships when they began attacking Allied convoys in 1943 with radio-controlled bombs. The Russians, technologically the most backward of the major Allied combatants in the war, had been advanced in rocketry research in the 1930s and resumed this avenue of development following the conflict. They were assisted to a limited extent by captured German rocket scientists—lesser luminaries left behind after the Americans had transported the cream of the German rocketry program to the United States.

By 1957 the first sea-to-sea missiles in the world were mounted on a number of Soviet destroyers. Dubbed Scrubber, the missile had a hundred-mile range, but its performance was evidently less than satisfactory. Two years later the Soviets introduced the Styx missile—much shorter in range but capable of being fired from small vessels with a high degree of accuracy.

The Styx was not a sophisticated sea skimmer like the missile Even-Tov had envisioned, but it packed a five-hundred-kilogram warhead capable of causing havoc even to an aircraft carrier. Its range of forty-five kilometers meant that the vessel firing it could stay out of gun range of any major warship. About ten kilometers from its target, a small radar in the Styx's nose was switched on. Picking up the echo of the target on the sea's surface, it glided toward the target on the track of its own reflected beam.

The missile was installed on a converted torpedo boat called the Komar. The Soviets conceived these small missile boats as an extension of their shore batteries, rather than as independent operators. Sent out in swarms, a sufficient number would evade air attacks, the Soviet planners hoped, to get within striking distance of the carriers.

By 1962 the Soviets had begun distributing Komars with their two Styx launchers to Warsaw Pact allies and friendly countries like Egypt, because a more advanced missile boat, the Osa—armed with four launchers and with better seakeeping qualities—was already in the pipeline to the Soviet fleet. The appearance of the Styx in the eastern Mediterranean stunned the Israeli naval command and lent sudden urgency to their own missile program. Admiral Bin-Nun decided that the time had come to seek government backing—and money—for the missile-boat concept.

The admiral requested an interview with Shimon Peres, the dynamic young deputy defense minister. Although Prime Minister Ben-Gurion held the defense portfolio, it was Peres who effectively ran the ministry. Bin-Nun knew him as a ubiquitous troubleshooter for the prime minister, frequently traveling abroad on secret diplomatic missions, and as a technocrat intent on building up a modern industrial infrastructure in Israel. It was Peres who had developed the arms link with France in the mid-1950s that brought Israel the planes, tanks, and artillery used to win the Sinai Campaign in 1956. He had done it by circumventing diplomatic channels in order to cultivate French political figures in and out of power. Employing both political argument and appeals to sentiment, he had persuaded them to supply arms to Israel even at the risk of Arab anger. This was the first break in the near-total embargo imposed on Israel by major arms suppliers since the state was created in 1948, a period during which large amounts of arms were reaching the Arab countries. From France, Peres would also obtain reactors for nuclear research in Israel.

At their meeting, Admiral Bin-Nun said that the navy could no longer continue as a collection of floating hand-me-downs. The refitted

Arab navies could strangle Israel's maritime lifeline and bombard its coast. The answer—the only answer Israel could afford—was the missile-boat concept. There was still no operational missile to counter the Styx, but Bin-Nun expressed confidence that one would be developed. If the navy could obtain six missile boats, it would scrap all its other surface vessels. The first step was to acquire a suitable torpedo boat from abroad to serve as a missile platform. The boat the navy believed most suitable was the German Jaguar, which Shoshan and his colleague had reported on two years before.

Peres responded immediately. "You have my blessing and you'll get the money."

Bin-Nun, who had been braced for a lengthy exercise in persuasion, was surprised by the quickness with which Peres had grasped the concept, and his readiness to commit funds.

The money did not exist in the defense budget. There was, however, another source—the Federal Republic of Germany. The opening to Germany had again been forged by Peres himself. A year after the Sinai Campaign, he had driven through the December snows of Bavaria for a secret meeting with Germany's defense minister, Franz-Josef Strauss, at the latter's small-town home. The constricting arms embargo had been broken by France, but it was imperative to widen that lifeline, and Peres had decided to cross forbidden ground.

The emotional chasm that lay between the two countries was unbridged by diplomatic ties. Ironically, it was Israel that was interested in such ties and Germany that was hesitant. Ben-Gurion believed that beleaguered Israel's national interests demanded diplomatic relations with Bonn. Germany feared that such ties would lead the Arab states to sever diplomatic relations with Bonn and establish them with East Germany instead.

After a lunch served by Mrs. Strauss, Peres outlined Israel's military needs in the face of massive Arab arming, and Strauss discussed the danger of Soviet penetration into the Middle East. At the center of their five-hour discussion was the relationship between the Jewish state and the country that had murdered six million Jews. Peres suggested that Germany would take a significant step toward acknowledging its responsibility for that past by furnishing Israel with arms for its survival, doing so without publicity to avoid Arab ire, and without payment. Israel was as poor in resources as it was rich in enemies.

Strauss expressed agreement. He saw in such an arrangement, if approved by his government, a step toward Germany's moral reacceptance into the Western world. Endorsement of his position would come two years later from German Chancellor Konrad Adenauer in his historic meeting with Ben-Gurion in the inappropriate elegance of New York's Waldorf-Astoria Hotel. Meeting in March 1960 in a gilded room filled with ghosts, the two elderly statesmen agreed that there could be no reconciliation between the two peoples—at least not in this generation—but that postwar Germany and the state born out of the ashes of the German Holocaust must find a way of relating to each other without forgetting the past. When, in the course of their far-ranging discussion, Ben-Gurion asked if Strauss's pledge to Peres had his backing, the chancellor replied, "Yes, that is right."

The next Federal Republic budget would include a $60-million item for "aid in the form of equipment." The recipient and the type of equipment were not specified. The entire amount was in fact earmarked for Israel over a five-year period and included items such as jet trainers, trucks, helicopters, and field guns. Following Bin-Nun's conversation with Peres two years later, the list would be adjusted to include six Jaguar torpedo boats.

It was as a provincial in search of guidance that Captain Shlomo Erell called on naval commands of NATO countries at the beginning of 1963. He was seeking reassurance from veteran continental navies that Israel had not struck off with its missile-boat concept into some futile dead end. Within the Israeli General Staff the notion of the tiny navy, with its total of fifteen years' experience, attempting to formulate an original type of warfare based on a weapon system that did not yet exist anywhere in the West seemed absurd. Erell himself, on more than one restless night, was less than certain that they were wrong. Endorsement of the concept by European navies would, Erell hoped, lend the program legitimacy in the eyes of the General Staff. He also hoped to enlist a continental partner in the project—a move that would provide both technical backing and reassurance.

He found neither. The Europeans were dismissive of the notion of missile boats as a response to the Soviet Komars. In any major confrontation, they pointed out, their own role within the NATO framework was limited to fringe assignments, such as convoy escort duty and antisubmarine warfare. Confronting the Soviet fleet was a matter for the American navy—in particular, the American carrier task forces. American naval air power would deal with the Soviet missile boats before the latter could get into effective range of the Western fleets. No one was interested in working with the Israeli navy in developing an answer to the Styx.

The Soviets had conceived the sea-to-sea missile in the face of overwhelming American naval strength, but the United States saw no need for such a weapon. At the end of World War II it had more than a hundred aircraft carriers and more than two dozen battleships. Its navy was unchallengeable by the Soviets or any combination of powers. The U.S. navy had in the late 1940s toyed with the development of a sea-to-sea missile, the Loon, based on the German flying bomb, but it was soon abandoned. When a sea missile, the Regulus, was introduced in 1954, it was as a strategic weapon with a nuclear warhead designed for land targets hundreds of miles away. The appearance of the Styx did not alarm the American naval command. The missile was primarily designed for defense against American carriers, but these could strike against Soviet targets from 750 miles offshore. Soviet missile boats would have to come out almost all that distance before they reached firing range, running the gauntlet of air attack all the way.

It was the appearance of the Komars in Cuba in 1962, the same year they arrived in Egypt, that turned the American navy's attention to countermeasures. At the request of the Atlantic fleet, the navy experimented with converting existing surface-to-air and air-to-air missiles for ship-to-ship purposes, but the results were unsatisfactory. Lacking the sense of urgency that had already impelled Israel to seek its own answer to the Styx, the Americans would let the problem ride for almost a decade.

To the extent that there was an attempt among European navies to think about the problem in the early 1960s, it focused on the idea of fast missile-boat killers that would be too small a target for missiles to hit. These boats would close on the missile boats and destroy them with gunfire.

This reminded Erell of the response at the beginning of the century to the emergence of torpedo boats. Because torpedoes were self-propelled and had no recoil—in effect, underwater missiles—they could be fired from small boats. Their powerful warheads made them a gerous threat to the capital ships that ruled the sea. To counter the threat, the destroyer was developed. These shallow-draft and highly maneuverable vessels, less vulnerable to torpedoes, would screen the main fleet from torpedo-boat attacks. At a later stage, they were armed with torpedoes themselves for offensive operations as fleet destroyers.

Israel, thought Erell, could not afford a conventional approach. Small, fast attack boats might prevail against Soviet missile boats if the missiles weren't very accurate, but the Israeli navy needed a multipurpose craft that could take on destroyers in surface actions, hunt down subs, stay at sea for extended periods on escort duty, and provide close-in shore bombardment. There was nothing in the naval arsenals of the West that met those specifications. Or in the East, for that matter. The Soviet vessels, which were basically platforms for missile launchers, were not capable of other missions. To produce a boat tailored to its needs, Israel, despite its lack of naval tradition, had no choice but to dare to be original.

The cry of outrage from Rafael at being informed that the sea-to-sea version of the Luz was being transferred by the Defense Ministry to the IAI under Even-Tov was prodigious. His superiors had been so angered at his leaving that they had vowed to prevent him from finding work in Israel. When Even-Tov wrote to Rafael to request data on the Luz's aerodynamic performance, he received a wire from Professor Ernst David Bergmann, Rafael's top scientist, informing him that he had no need for the data since Rafael was the sole military R&D enterprise in the country. Peres ordered the data turned over. Most of the information eventually was, but on one occasion a naval officer found it necessary to "borrow" data on the Luz from an army ordnance base after determining when the officer in charge of the records would be out to lunch.

Even-Tov had asked for a year in which to formulate his plans, but well before then there was peremptory knocking on the gate of his ivory tower. The appearance of the Styx, the anxiety of the navy, and the angry reaction of Rafael were piling pressures on the IAI to produce some tangible results, and Hyman Shamir had begun looking over Even-Tov's shoulder. In a display of temperament that was to mark his way, Even-Tov had a falling-out with his patron, but was permitted to carry on.

By the end of 1962 he had completed his plan and submitted it to

Shamir in two thick volumes. A few weeks later Even-Tov was invited to Peres's office in the Defense Ministry in Tel Aviv. Even-Tov carried a copy of his report to the meeting. "You don't think I'm actually going to read that?" said Peres with a smile as his guest entered. Even-Tov noticed that a copy of his report already lay on the deputy minister's desk. Alongside it was another report, in a black binder. Peres identified this as an analysis of Even-Tov's proposal prepared jointly by the air force and Rafael at his, Peres's, request. Its conclusion, he said, was that the project was totally unfeasible. The analysis had made use of data supplied by Even-Tov himself to prove that it was mathematically impossible for the missile to perform as designed.

"How am I going to make a decision?" asked Peres rhetorically.

What he would do, he said, would be to send Even-Tov to France to meet with senior engineers at three of that country's leading aeronautical plants. The French engineers would provide objective appraisals, said Peres, and he would make his judgment after hearing their opinions.

The trip to France was not an encouraging one for Even-Tov. At two of the plants the engineers' verdict was a resounding negative. The chief engineer at the third plant, a White Russian, had plainly studied the two reports carefully. He questioned Even-Tov closely about the unconventional solutions he was proposing. "I believe it can work," he said finally. "But it won't take five years and five million dollars, as you estimate. It would be more like twenty years and fifty million dollars."

It was with considerable trepidation that Even-Tov returned to Israel for his second meeting with Peres. His faith in his vision had not diminished, but the weight of outside opinion against him appeared overwhelming. Peres, however, surprised him. On the basis of the one quasi-positive French report, Peres said he was authorizing the program to continue.

Tenuous as the missile program seemed, it remained the most hopeful option for the navy. If it were junked, there would be no choice but to face either costly re-equipping of the navy or its abandonment as a serious military arm.

A romantic aura had surrounded Israel's naval arm since prestate days, but it had never achieved the status of hard-nosed professionalism earned by the army and the air force. A motley collection of small freighters, an icebreaker, and other castoff vessels had been acquired by the underground Haganah to transport illegal Jewish refugees from Europe to Palestine after World War II through the British blockade. With the establishment of the state, many of these vessels were rigged with old guns and commissioned into the newly established navy.

During the War of Independence the boats participated in several indecisive engagements with Egyptian vessels and provided occasional gun support for Israeli troops operating along the coast. The only serious naval encounter was the attack by the one-man assault craft led by Yohai Bin-Nun, which sank the Egyptian flagship and badly damaged its minesweeper escort.

The first commander of the navy was an American Jew, Paul Schulman, who had graduated from the U.S. Naval Academy and served in the American navy during World War II. He was succeeded at the end of the War of Independence by an experienced army officer, Shlomo Shamir, who was seconded to the navy in order to reorganize it. One of Shamir's first decisions was to dispatch officers to foreign naval academies in large numbers for courses lasting several years. With their return, the navy's officer corps, hitherto based on veterans of the merchant fleet, began to take on a new professionalism.

This reshaping of the navy's command structure in the mid-1950s was not matched by the ships put at its disposal. Although the converted refugee transports gave way to real warships, these were few and antiquated. When the missile boat concept was brought to Peres, he realized that it was the only viable option for the navy. As long as Even-Tov's proposal offered a thread of hope for keeping the option alive, Peres would go with it.

5
Gabriel

Shlomo Erell had larceny in his heart when he flew to Germany in March 1963. Much argument had been used to persuade the Israeli General Staff and the German authorities that it was necessary for him to make the trip.

The equipment Germany had been supplying the Israeli armed forces under the secret agreement with Strauss, most of it imported from the United States and other countries, had been happily taken "off the shelf" by the Israeli army and air force. They had learned over the years to avail themselves quickly of arms sources as they became available, before political considerations stopped the flow again. Erell had argued that the Jaguars could not be shipped without modifications if they were to be utilized efficiently, because the warm eastern Mediterranean differed from the stormy North Sea, for which the Jaguar was designed. What Erell had in mind, however, was not minor modifications but an essentially new boat. The technical officers he had assigned to the missile-boat think tank had already determined that the Jaguar had to be altered if it was to serve as a missile platform. If the German arms deal could not be taken advantage of to acquire a suitable boat, Erell knew, there was unlikely to be another opportunity.

Erell's request to visit Germany was initially rejected by the German authorities, who feared that the Arabs would learn of the secret deal. Peres tried to discourage him but Erell insisted and the Germans finally relented on condition that Erell come alone and maintain the lowest of profiles.

At the German Defense Ministry, Erell met with senior officials of the technical division to spell out his "modifications." The boat Israel wanted, he said, required a range of one thousand miles and a top speed of at least forty knots. In addition to antisub torpedoes it would carry ship-to-ship missiles, rapid-firing guns that could be used against either planes or ships, sonar equipment for sub hunting, and very advanced radar, plus detection and communication systems so advanced that destroyers several times the size of the Jaguar did not carry them. The boat must have good seakeeping qualities and be capable of fighting independently or in formation. In other navies, concluded Erell, this was a small vessel, but for Israel it would be a capital ship.

The silence that followed Erell's presentation was finally broken by the head of the technical division, Dr. Ments. Leaning forward, he said bemusedly, "*Ja, ja,* very interesting, Captain. But tell me, don't you want a grand piano in this boat, too?"

Erell's request to meet with the builders of the Jaguar, the Bremen shipbuilding firm of Lurssen Brothers, met with foot dragging. The authorities, he discovered, had not informed the shipyard that the client was the Israeli navy for fear the secret would get out. He would fly to Germany several times before he could convince the Defense Ministry that fulfillment of Germany's commitment required direct contact with the shipyard. When permission was granted, after a year, he flew back to Germany with Commander Haim Shahal, a naval architect who had been a prime advocate of the missile-boat concept at the initial meeting with Bin-Nun. At Lurssen there was an immediate meeting of minds. Shahal had brought only a two-page outline of the boat's desired characteristics instead of the thick volume such specifications normally occupy. But the firm's chief naval architect, Herr Waldemuth, immediately grasped what the Israelis, for all their inexperience, were getting at.

Calculating estimated weights of the planned systems and the space they would occupy, Shahal pointed out that they could not fit onto the Jaguar as it existed. Would it be possible, he asked, to stretch the vessel 2.4 meters by inserting two more of the frames that formed its hull, in order to give a total length of forty-five meters?

Waldemuth made his own calculations and said, "We can do it."

The Jaguar was a wooden boat, so built to elude magnetic mines in the shallow waters of the Baltic. The Israelis wanted their six boats built of steel, because they hoped eventually to produce similar boats themselves, and wooden shipbuilding involved more difficult technology. Rearrangement of the boat's internal partitioning would also be required.

Waldemuth responded warmly to the Israeli requests and established a close working relationship with Shahal, who would make frequent visits to Bremen to be party to the design process. Whatever irony the Israelis may have felt working with a shipyard that had been part of the backbone of the German naval production during World War II was outweighed by the obligations of the present.

With its new technology, the Luz had acquired a new name—the Gabriel.

An Israeli engineer posted to an Italian electronics firm working on the missile's radar had mentioned to a Canadian engineer employed at the firm the need for a code name to be used in telexes being exchanged with Israel: it would not do to be mentioning missiles openly. The Canadian noted that the firm named its export products after either saints or angels. The Israeli thought an Old Testament angel would be more appropriate for an Israeli missile than a New Testament saint, and the Canadian suggested the first angel's name that flew into his head.

The missile itself had yet to fly. Its first test came in mid-1964. It was a test of the altimeter, with right-left steering remaining for the time being in the hands of an aimer with a joy stick. The test was held on the coast, south of Ashdod. A lighthearted air of expectancy hung over the beach as the countdown got under way. Members of the General Staff were there, as well as the navy brass, top Defense Ministry officials, and a somber delegation from Rafael, whose members did not exchange a word with Even-Tov.

Six missiles facing seaward were lined up neck to neck like a pack of well-trained pointers patiently waiting to be unleashed at the target on the horizon. The launchers rested on the back of command cars. At the launch command, the first missile arched into the sky and plummeted straight into the sea. Hoots and raucous whistles burst from one edge of the crowd. Even-Tov looked over and saw the source to be the Rafael contingent. The second missile duplicated the flight of the first; so did the third. Even-Tov called a halt. There was no point in firing the other three missiles before it could be determined what had gone wrong.

Deputy Chief of Staff General Yitzhak Rabin approached Even-Tov and asked, "*Nu*, what's going to be?"

"We'll be ready to try again in three months," said Even-Tov.

The deadline was impossibly short but Even-Tov met it. Meeting it was his only accomplishment. Again three missiles went up, only to abort aimlessly into the sea. The enthusiasm that had sustained Even-Tov's team from the beginning gave way to a sickening sense that this may have all been an extravagant indulgence. Moshe Kashti, normally benign and supportive, turned to Even-Tov and said astringently, "Ori, we'd also like to see it work occasionally."

General Rabin came up and asked, "*Nu*, now what's going to be?"

Even-Tov's seemingly limitless self-confidence wavered, but only slightly. "We'll be back," he said. "But we'll need nine months this time."

Rabin nodded. "Okay, we'll wait."

In his office the next day, Even-Tov calculated the length of lifeline he had left. He plainly had a problem. The project was unlikely to survive another failure, and there were already opponents arguing that the Defense Ministry should cut its losses and scrap it immediately. He hoped the telemetry readings sent back from the missiles during their aborted flights would provide clues as to what had gone wrong, although the readings from the first test, three months before, had plainly not unlocked any secrets.

Even-Tov was interrupted in his cogitations by one of the technicians, Yaacov Becker, who asked if he might speak with him. Becker had joined the project four months earlier. "I don't think the missile is going to work unless we repackage the altimeter," said Becker. On a staff top-heavy with engineers and scientists, Becker's role was a minor one—he had been dealing mostly with telemetry readings from instruments aboard the missiles in flight—but Even-Tov had been favorably impressed by his sound instincts and gifted hands.

Since the Luz had not been designed with an altimeter, the only convenient space that could be found for it was around the exhaust pipe in the missile's tail, which it circled like a bagel full of printed circuits. It was an awkward configuration, and Becker said the altimeter design was simply not robust enough to withstand the blastoff and flight.

"Do you have any proposals?" asked Even-Tov.

"Give me a few days," said Becker.

Becker had had only a vocational-school education, but he had gained much practical experience working on gadgets for military intelligence before joining IAI. The plan he placed on Even-Tov's desk the next week called for dividing the printed circuits on the "bagel" into separate wedges, each a plug-in module that could be removed independently, to make it easier to adjust the instrument during the testing period. Such plug-in units were still unknown in Israel. Also, the altimeter would be cast in aluminum to make it rigid.

Although the proposal was sketchy, Even-Tov recognized the work of a craftsman—a fellow "garagenik." He summoned the two senior engineers and outlined Becker's proposal. Both objected that it was unworkable and said they would rather resign than pursue it.

"In that case your resignations are accepted as of now," said Even-Tov. It was not clear whether their objections were to the specific design or to its proposal by a low-grade technician.

Even-Tov summoned Becker and informed him that his proposal was accepted and that he, Becker, would head the altimeter project. He would have thirty men under him and all the equipment he would need. "You've got less than nine months," said Even-Tov. "Run."

The entire plan would run, seven days a week. In all of 1964, Yom Kippur was the only day that the key men on the project did not report for work, although Even-Tov and a few others came in even then. Workdays routinely ran for twelve or fourteen hours, and the engineers leaving the modern, windowless plant to which the project had been shifted were sometimes startled to find that night had come; sometimes even come and gone. For some, the marital strain induced by this schedule would lead eventually to divorce proceedings.

Even-Tov swept them along with a leadership consisting of radiant confidence in the ultimate success of the project, and his own ability, time and again, to resolve with unconventional insights problems that had seemed to doom the entire project. His temperament did not permit him to pause long over any breakthrough, the dangling threads being tied together by his aides. This suited them in any case: they preferred to have him plunging forward, for fear that if he took a second look at any design element he would attempt to improve it, stalling all momentum. The impossible deadlines he fixed were somehow met.

Becker, charged with the most critical aspect of the project, took to sleeping on a cot in the workshop. He was no stranger to rough sleep. His family had been evacuated from eastern Poland in 1939 by the Soviets and had spent the war years in Siberia before making the arduous trek to Israel in 1948.

In addition to the packaging, Becker also conducted extensive field tests of the altimeter rigged beneath a jet trainer flown by an IAI test pilot. At no small risk, the pilot would take his hands off the controls and let the altimeter hold the plane as low as fifteen meters above the water.

It was during one of these tests that Becker discovered why at least some of the missiles had aborted. As the plane thundered over the telemetry van on the shore at Rishon Le-Zion and headed out to sea at three hundred meters altitude, Becker saw that telemetry instruments on the altimeter were indicating that the plane was only two meters over the water. Not until the plane descended did the altimeter begin to give true readings.

The reason was deduced afterward. Height was measured by having one antenna bounce an electronic beam off the water below, to be picked up by the other antenna. Above a certain level, however, the signal was too weak to bounce; the receiving antenna instead began picking up signals from the broadcasting antenna directly across the body of the missile, two meters away. Since the missile was programmed to fly at fifteen meters, it attempted to rise above the two-meter altitude it was recording, but the false signal persisted until the missile could no longer rise, instead falling into the water like a stone. Once the problem was understood, the circuitry was redesigned, but there was no certainty that this had cured the Gabriel's altimeter problems.

The French naval proving grounds were on an island shared with a nudist colony. Yitzhak Shoshan, who had been among the crop of young Israeli naval officers sent to France in the early 1950s for training, met one of his French classmates from that period when he visited the proving grounds in 1964 with an Israeli naval mission. The French navy was experimenting there with a sea-to-sea missile connected to a wire by which an operator guided it onto target as he focused through binoculars. To the Israelis, this looked like a primitive version of the Luz, and its range was much shorter. Shoshan and his former French classmate repaired to the bar, where, over drinks, the Frenchman said that he was aware that the Israelis were concerned about the Styx and felt that the French navy should be worried, too. "I've tried to persuade my colleagues that the Styx and the Komar are dangerous," he said. "The only way we can counter them is by developing a missile of our own. But my colleagues just don't see it."

Uri Harrari descended from the plane in Switzerland carrying a case filled with small pieces of aluminum piping, like a plumber responding to a housewife's call. His mission seemed, even to him, almost as innocent as that as he rode into the nearby city and checked into a hotel.

An expert in precision mechanics, Harrari had joined the Gabriel team just a few weeks before, after hearing that the IAI had a group of madmen working around the clock in a remote corner on a top-secret project. The notion had appealed to him, and he was promptly accepted by Even-Tov and Becker, who were looking precisely for someone like him—a master craftsman who could shape metals.

Even-Tov had thought that he could create the Gabriel's guidance system by marrying the altimeter they were developing with a small radar bought off the shelf from a foreign firm and fitted into the missile. In tests, however, the radar had proved disappointing, and Even-Tov had daringly decided to try to develop the necessary radar technology in Israel from scratch.

Harrari's was a key role. It was for him to shape the metal tubing through which the radar's microwaves would pass. This had to be done to an extremely high degree of precision so that, despite the pipes' numerous twists, the cross-section was constant—otherwise the waves would be distorted. Neither he nor anyone else in Israel was familiar with the procedure. After Harrari had achieved some crude success in bending microwave tubing and in joining, or braising, tube sections, Even-Tov suggested he travel to Europe to learn what more he could. Neither man was thinking in terms of industrial espionage.

A prominent European firm had agreed to let Harrari consult with its chief chemist. After spending three profitable days, Harrari moved on to a plant in another West European country, where an engineer responded readily to Harrari's questions and demonstrated braising methods in the plant's laboratory. On the second day the engineer took Harrari aside.

"Look, Mr. Harrari, I know what you're doing. A child can see it.

This braising is for radar components, isn't it?" Studying Harrari's face, he said, "Don't worry. I want to help you. I want to help Israel. I am going to send you to a place where you will learn a lot. You won't be able to be there for more than a few hours—maybe half a day, maybe a day. A friend will meet you at the gate. You will not identify yourself to anybody else. With your blond hair you can easily pass for a European. If they find out who you are, my friend and I will be in serious trouble."

Harrari boarded a train the next morning for a town in another part of the country. A taxi took him to the gate of a huge plant with high fences and a profusion of armed guards. His contact was waiting for him at the gate. After fitting Harrari out with a visitor's badge, his host led him into a windowless room plainly intended for security briefings. "Because of the high degree of secrecy around here," he said, "visitors are not obligated to identify themselves once they're inside. So, if anybody asks you where you're from, don't tell them, and don't tell anyone your name. Just say you're here at my invitation. I'll walk with you a bit, but then one of my assistants will accompany you. Don't tell him anything, either."

The next four hours were a revelation for Harrari. The plant was engaged in advanced weaponry development, and its scale was immense—huge hangars with mockups of warships and planes bristling with electronic gadgetry. What Harrari was looking for were examples of braising, and these he found in plenty. To his informed eye, even a casual glance or a few words with a workman spoke volumes. Periodically he would enter a men's room, where he would feverishly make notes on a small pad.

The normal method for delicate work like microwave tubing involved a costly braising procedure that the hard-pressed Gabriel project was unlikely to sustain. In reading the professional literature, however, Harrari had learned of another form of braising, furnace braising, that was far cheaper. The problem was that furnace braising was a crude process not used for microwave tubing anywhere in the world. What Harrari had now learned would enable him to adapt furnace braising to his needs.

On the train back to the town where he was staying, Harrari was virtually shaking from excitement as he completed his notes. He was deeply touched by the risks his European acquaintances, Christians all, were taking, out of sympathy for Israel.

From Paris, Harrari sent a detailed report to the IAI. When he returned to Israel a few days later, anticipating an enthusiastic welcome, he encountered instead a furious Even-Tov.

"Do you realize that you should be put in jail right now?" shouted Even-Tov as Harrari walked into his office. "Do you know what the security laws are? You penetrated a top-secret installation of another country without authorization." When the harangue was over and Even-Tov had calmed down, he nodded in the direction of the workshop. "Now, get back to work, you bastard," he said affectionately.

Captain Erell, who knew that the future of the navy rested on the Gabriel, had to content himself with reassurances from the senior navy officer attached to the project that the missile would in the end fly. There were plenty of experts in the defense establishment eager to point out the unlikelihood of that eventuality.

For Erell and Bin-Nun, the entire program was an enormous gamble. There was no certainty that any of the major components would work on their own, let alone together. It was an open question whether the Gabriel would be any more effective than the Luz; the crucial electronic systems on the boats were a bold leap into the unknown; the boat platform being designed in Bremen was as new and untried as the German diesel engines that had been decided upon. Even the deck gun, seemingly the most conventional of elements for a naval vessel, was an innovative and problematic weapon.

The navy chiefs did not burden the General Staff by spelling out the risk factor for fear that this would doom the project to instant demise. A wordless conspiracy had emerged between the navy and the fledgling military industries, which had come to recognize the missile-boat/Gabriel project as an opportunity for breaking out of the Third World mold into the forefront of high technology. The danger of failure was downplayed for the foot-sloggers at GHQ, in effect, hoodwinking the armed forces command about what the navy was getting into. As Erell would put it to his colleagues: "We're stealing horses."

With the Gabriel in danger of going the way of the Luz, it was vital to get expert outside opinion on whether the system was workable. The plan shown the French aeronautical engineers by Even-Tov had been theory; now there were hard data from the telemetry readings that could either support or destroy that theory. The computers had provided answers, but Even-Tov could not be certain he had asked the right questions.

A foreign systems engineer who had been subjected to a careful but discreet security check was invited to visit the IAI plant as a consultant, was given a desk, and spent several days going over Even-Tov's figures. He was not asked to provide any input into the missile program, but to confirm the calculations that had been made. When he finished, he looked up and pronounced his benediction: "It should work."

6
Falling Leaves

The lights burned late atop Mount Carmel. The brightest talents in the navy had been assembled by Captain Erell at Stella Maris in a highly secret project code-named Shalechet ("Falling Leaves"). Their mission—to reduce the grand vision of the missile boat to tangible dimensions. What armament and electronic systems were to be put into the boat, how were they to be designed, how were they to be integrated with one another? There were no precedents to follow and no textbook answers.

The team, which would eventually number several hundred men, was broken into subgroups, each charged with a specific design aspect. How many masts could accommodate the dense electronic demands? What kind of engine would be powerful enough to provide forty knots but small enough for this size boat? What procedures would enable seamen in the midst of a battle—not just technicians in laboratory conditions—to fire the missile and hit?

The questions seemed endless, and each solution carried with it new problems. How can missiles be launched from the small deck without endangering the crew manning the gun nearby? How can the sensitive electronics of the missile be protected from the corrosion of sea spray? What to do about the mutual interferences—electronic, noise, electromagnetic—among systems located near one another? How to prevent the missile from being struck by a wave as it is launched in rough seas?

Israel's military industries, stretching into new areas of technology, were able to provide some solutions. International catalogues of military hardware proved useful—a plotting table was ordered from Holland, a depth gauge from Sweden. However, key elements, like radar and the fire-control system, which would aim the gun and missiles, had to be developed abroad, since Israel did not yet have the know-how. Navy and IAI teams were posted at plants in Europe to work with foreign engineers on their design and production.

It was the biggest and most complex industrial enterprise ever undertaken by Israel, and the navy's fear of being overtaken by a war drove it with a sense of urgency. Most of the officers chosen for the initial Shalechet team were torpedo-boat men, considered more innovative than their colleagues on destroyers. The project's expanding scope would oblige the navy to triple the number of men passing through its officers' course.

The Shalechet team leaders met regularly to report on progress and thrash out differences. Sitting around the table in Stella Maris, each became an advocate for his system. Search radar, which scanned the sea for enemy ships, and fire-control radar, which guided the missile onto target, vied with each other for higher position on the mast; gun and torpedo tubes elbowed each other for choice position on deck; sonar argued against being thrown overboard in order to save weight. When no compromise could be reached, the Shalechet chief would decide, and sometimes the decision would be left to the navy commander. A wooden mockup of the boat was built, so they could see how its systems might be fitted together.

For most of the men involved, this would be the greatest adventure of their lives. A backward navy in a country of three million with no sophisticated industrial base had taken upon itself to shape a major weapon system that no other country in the West possessed. Officers who had sailed in nothing but antiquated castoffs found themselves plunging through uncharted waters at the frontier of military science. It was an exhilarating experience, given an edge by the knowledge that the war contingency being planned for was not theoretical but a life-and-death reality that more than likely waited around some nearby corner. In this effort, as with the Gabriel, challenge evoked ingenuity, technical daring, and in more than one case something approaching genius. The young officers overseeing the systems being built in foreign plants overcame their initial diffidence and began demanding changes from the veteran continental engineers, who more than once expressed skepticism about what they were being asked to do.

The flow of information in Shalechet was constant—from everyone to everyone—and the pace manic. Tests were constantly being set, reports presented, contracts for components signed, meetings scheduled. Work went on every day until close to midnight, sometimes beyond. This pace would last for years, laced for all with moments of despair, when it seemed mad to have attempted the enterprise, when it seemed a piece of chutzpah—indeed, hubris—that must end in farce if not tragedy. As the pieces slowly began to be fitted together, these crises gave way to a sense of having embarked upon an epic voyage of discovery. Looking about him, Erell was convinced that no major power had ever put as much energy into the design of a battleship.

Straw boss of the teams developing the weapons systems for much of this period was Aviah Shalif. The engineering officer had grown up in Jerusalem with Ori Even-Tov and Yohai Bin-Nun. Wiry and acerbic, he could deftly lay a tangled problem bare and propose a solution. His ability to make quick decisions and keep things moving forward mattered more than the relative merits of the technical approaches he had to choose between. Shalif was not a believer in ideas whose time has come. Big ideas, he knew, have to be fought for if they are to survive against the natural counterpressures they arouse in people who regard them as unfeasible because they are outside these people's experience. He fought, often ruthlessly, and there were no pauses for agonized reflections as long as he was in the picture. It was Shalif who formulated, in a document of several hundred pages, the comprehensive "logic" of the weapon system, showing how all the elements were linked and how they affected one another. This was an excruciating task, carried out without the aid of a computer, which he had not yet learned to use.

Visiting one of the leading electronics firms in Europe in search of assistance in developing a radar, Shalif and an electronics officer listened to a lengthy exposition on a new instrument the firm's engineers said had just been developed. When they left the building, Shalif said to his colleague, "They haven't got a radar."

"You're crazy," said the electronics officer. "We've just seen the whole logic of the system on the blackboard, and they explained the components."

"Those solutions are flimsy," said Shalif. "They're full of air. I don't think they've actually got one of these things operational."

When the Israelis asked to see the radar, they were told that security prevented this as yet. Israel turned instead to an Italian firm, and Shalif would later learn that his original hunch about the nonoperational status of the first firm's radar had been correct.

Virtually nothing in the system was taken off the shelf, beginning with the elongated, metallic version of the Jaguar itself. Some of the stormiest sessions in Shalechet revolved around the gun. Even in the missile age, there was clear need for a gun. Some targets are too small to waste a missile on. There are suspect boats that might be stopped by a shot across the bow, or into the hull, without crossing the point of no return involved in firing a missile that would destroy, rather than just stop, the target vessel. There are shore targets to be hit and planes to be defended against.

The original specification called for 40mm guns, conventional armament for ships of similar size, and this was the gun installed on the first six boats. However, the Israelis learned that the Italian firm of Oto Melara was developing a lightweight version of a much more potent 76mm gun. Its range was triple that of the 40mm gun and its shell much more powerful. In addition, it could be loaded from below decks, a blessing in stormy waters, and its larger shells could be fitted with proximity fuses whose buckshot spread multiplied their effectiveness against aircraft. The gun was still in the testing stage and was so riddled with technical bugs that Germany, the only other country to have expressed interest, had rejected it. Shalif, at the head of the pro-76 school, prevailed over Shalechet's 40mm faction, which preferred a weapon that was proved and of lesser weight. Israel would have to introduce more than a hundred changes in the gun system before it would become a reliable weapon, but the modified 76 would open the strategic coastal installations of the Arab states to a formidable new threat. Many navies would subsequently adopt the 76mm gun.

To cram all the systems into a tiny platform required compactness and multipurpose uses. Critical space and weight were saved by the brilliant idea of having the fire-control system, which aimed the mis-

sile—a highly sophisticated linkage of radar, computer and consoles—
do double duty by serving the gun as well, instead of having a parallel
system. Riding the new wave of miniaturization permitted by the dis-
placement of vacuum tubes by tiny transistors, the Shalechet team created smaller shipborne systems than those existing in any other navy at
the time. No sonar for the detection of submarines was small enough to
be fitted onto boats this size. But at the direction of the Shalechet planners one was developed abroad. The planners' crowning achievement
was the Combat Information Center (CIC), the below-decks war room
from which the boat commanders would direct the battle. The radar
screens, consoles, and communication equipment in the crowded CIC
constituted a state-of-the-art command center more advanced than
those to be found even on contemporary cruisers. Information coming
in from sensors on the boat itself and from outside sources like planes
or other ships would be instantly analyzed and displayed to provide a
real-time picture of the battle zone and clear options for action.

In 1966, General Rabin, now chief of staff, visited Stella Maris for a
briefing on the project. He was plainly impressed by its daring and
originality, but he gave the navy chiefs clear warning that if their gamble was unsuccessful the General Staff would not simply shrug its
shoulders. "We don't understand the navy in the General Staff, and I
can't say whether this project is justified or not. This is the first time the
navy is building a fleet according to its own needs and its own plans. I
hope you're right. Otherwise we will have to draw some very sad conclusions." All those present understood that these conclusions would
probably be to reduce the navy to a coast guard and leave defense of
the shipping lanes to the air force.

The Shalechet planners in Haifa were constantly aware that their
accomplishments would be futile if the team at Lod, eighty miles to the
south, failed to develop a reliable missile. Without it they would be left
with a gunboat—fast and sophisticated, but no match for the Styx.

The third test of the Gabriel was held in 1965 on a secluded stretch of
coast south of Haifa. Patrolling planes and vessels kept boats out of the
area. Even-Tov had met the nine month deadline he had set for himself.
The large crowd of observers who had sorted themselves out along the
beach and on the dunes looked funereal. Even-Tov saw the Rafael contingent standing apart on a hillock. As the controller began the count-

down by intoning over the loudspeakers, "Three minutes to firing," Becker took shelter in a ditch near the launcher. "Three, two, one, launch." The first missile leaped from the back of the command car, arced into the sky, and fell like a stone into the water. A heavy sense of *déjà-vu* engulfed the onlookers, while despair gripped the members of the Gabriel team. Two years of prodigious labor seemed about to end with another sterile splash.

"Launch."

The second missile reached the top of its trajectory and began plummeting toward the sea. Suddenly its dark shape seemed to halt in midair and hang suspended. It was several seconds before Even-Tov realized that the missile had not stopped but had leveled off and was heading out to sea. Cheers of joy and relief exploded along the beach as the others realized it, too. Men pounded one another on the back and waved their arms heavenward. The aimer was so flabbergasted that he forgot to direct the missile onto target with his joy stick, but it did not matter: the altimeter worked. The crowd erupted again as the next missile leveled off at the predetermined altitude and was guided directly onto target. Even-Tov instinctively swiveled toward the hillock, but the Rafael contingent had disappeared.

The arrival of the German emissary at Ben-Gurion Airport in March 1965 boded ill. Defense Ministry officials in Tel Aviv had been bracing themselves for such a visit since the Arab states had learned of the arms deal with Israel and publicly threatened to break relations with Bonn unless it was abrogated. The nightmare of the take-it-off-the-shelf-and-run school had materialized.

In Jerusalem, the emissary said that Germany intended to honor its obligation to Israel, but only by supplying it with the money to purchase the agreed-upon items elsewhere. As for the boats, Germany could, regrettably, not go ahead with their construction, which had been scheduled to start in a few months.

Erell was unwilling to settle for the money. He insisted on the plans and the license to use them as well. The Germans were unwilling to furnish them since such a step could compromise them with the Arabs. The Israeli Defense Ministry began to pressure Erell to take the money and find another shipyard. Erell stood fast. It was inconceivable, he said, that the past two years' labors should have been for naught. Without the German plans and license, more years would be wasted in starting from scratch—a waste that could leave the navy helpless when war came.

The German emissary flew back and forth several times in an effort to overcome this final impediment to the shutdown of the German arms pipeline, but Erell refused to budge. Peres, submitting to the political necessity of concluding the episode, finally insisted that Erell accompany him to Rome to arrange for the purchase of Italian patrol boats as a substitute. They arrived to find the Italian government likewise reluctant to enter into an arms deal with Israel. They were still in Rome when a senior naval officer in Haifa telephoned Erell to call his attention to an article in the current issue of the prestigious British naval publication *Jane's,* noting that Lurssen had cooperated with a French firm in producing patrol boats. Such a connection might make it palatable for the German government to permit the plans and license for the modified Jaguar to be made available to the French shipbuilding company, thought the officer. Erell grabbed at the idea.

Mordecai Limon, head of the Defense Ministry's purchasing mission in Paris, was summoned to Rome by Peres to be briefed. He conferred with the French shipbuilders upon his return and reported that they were eager to take on the project and had well-placed connections in Germany that would make it possible to have the plans and license for the modified Jaguar transferred. The location of the shipyard was Cherbourg.

7
Cherbourg

For a town that had lain squarely across the road to Armageddon, Cherbourg offers few remembrances of war. Its port was the principal supply funnel for the Allied armies following the D-Day landings twenty miles down the Normandy peninsula. The harbor facilities had been destroyed by the Germans but, as was not the case in the other major ports on France's Atlantic coast, most of its buildings and old charm had survived, due to the forbearance of the Allies, who wanted the town as intact as possible.

The military figure who dominates the waterfront atop a high bronze horse is not a hero of that grim struggle but Napoleon, who had chosen Cherbourg as a naval port because of its strategic location at the midway point of the Channel separating him from his English enemies. Although the English come now on cross-Channel ferries in pursuit of cheese and wine, the naval arsenal founded by Napoleon continues to produce ships of war for whatever contingencies history may provide. Since the beginning of the century it has been France's main shipyard for submarines and, for much of this time, Cherbourg's chief employer.

The second-largest employer in 1965 was the private shipyard founded by Félix Amiot, who, at the age of seventy, was about to enter a new and momentous phase of his rich life. It was his firm, Les Constructions Mécaniques de Normandie, that the French defense authorities had recommended to Israel. Amiot had begun designing airplanes

63

in his teens, before World War I, and by the time of World War II he was one of France's major airplane manufacturers. During the German occupation his firm was obliged to produce parts for Junker bombers. For this he was barred by the government, following the war, from returning to the aircraft industry. Returning to his native Cherbourg, he turned to shipbuilding. His firm became a major enterprise that at its height employed fifteen hundred workers. A feudal figure who took a personal interest in his employees' health and family affairs, Amiot combined peasant shrewdness with technological innovation and a surprising vein of sentimentality.

Following the initial Israeli approach, Amiot invited Shimon Peres and Admiral Bin-Nun to his home, near Paris. In the late afternoon, while they walked through the wooded grounds of his large estate, the industrialist's eyes teared as he spoke of having hidden Jewish children during the war. In Israel, to which Amiot flew for final negotiations, he was invited to a home dinner by the Israeli naval officer serving as his escort. Amiot kept pressing him about the future he foresaw for his three young sons. At Amiot's request, the officer took him into the children's room to see them sleeping.

Work on the Israeli vessels got under way in the shipyard in the summer of 1965. A small contingent of Israelis took up residence in the town, to monitor the boats' construction and to test them after they were launched. The contingent would grow to thirty or forty men when the time approached to sail the boats to Haifa. Uncertain of their own expertise, the Israelis asked the French navy to provide technical supervision of the construction program.

The Israelis were delighted by Cherbourg. With a population of only thirty thousand, it had a cheerful, small-town atmosphere, but the amenities such as restaurants and shops were of a scale to service a large suburban area and transchannel traffic. Although the great transatlantic liners no longer sailed from Cherbourg, there were several ferries a day to British ports. The weather was like that of the nearby Channel islands, changeable and bracing. "We have the four seasons here every day," Cherbourg residents liked to say. Napoleon had proposed cutting a canal through the peninsula, which would have made them islanders in fact. Although attached to Normandy, the Cherbourgians, shielded by a low range of hills, felt remote from the seat of power in Paris.

The boat contract had a powerful impact on the town's sagging economy. The Israeli sailors were at first housed in barracks in the arsenal and ate alongside French ratings. Bachelor officers were quartered in an officers' club outside the base, and family men rented apartments. In their free time, the Israelis frequented restaurants and cafés overlooking the inner harbor, where the fishing boats anchored, or the square, where flower markets were held three times a week. They were intimidated by French cooking and seafood, and some would stick for a long time to bread and salads. Only after repeated looks of distress on the faces of waiters did the men learn that one ordered white wine with fish and red with meat. The Israeli sailors of North African origin, who spoke French, soon had girlfriends. The others wasted little time in finding tutors. Following their ejection from the arsenal, the Israelis were lodged in the Hôtel Tourville, on the waterfront, adjacent to the Amiot shipyard.

The Israelis discovered soon after their arrival that there was a small Jewish community in Cherbourg. Before the war there had been forty families, many of whom had come from Eastern Europe in the late 1920s hoping to board the weekly Cunard or German liners that used to sail from Cherbourg to the United States. When Washington tightened its immigration laws, these families had stayed on. The Germans expelled the Jews from the strategic town when they captured it in 1940, and after the war only a handful returned. There were now ten families in all, and half the men had married Christian women. Nevertheless, there was a strong communal feeling, even though there was no rabbi or synagogue. The fifteen children would be gathered twice a week to hear a talk on Jewish subjects from Dr. Michel, a dentist whose grandfather had been a rabbi, or Jacques Prelman, one of the few Jewish merchants to close his store on Yom Kippur. On Sundays they would watch together a television lecture by a rabbi broadcast from Paris.

Warm relations were quickly established with the Israeli contingent. One of the Israeli wives began teaching Hebrew and Jewish culture to the children, and the local families would join the Israelis for the Passover seder and for Yom Kippur prayers led by a rabbi sent down from Paris.

The first of the Saar ("Storm," in Hebrew) class boats, as they were called, was launched on April 11, 1967. The German design team came down from Bremen to join the maiden sailing. The occasion merited a spiraling round of toasts among the Germans, the French, and the Israelis, and most of the men aboard the boat were several sheets to the wind by the time the motors were ignited. As the boat eased past the breakwater into the English Channel, the Israeli officer conning the craft kept it under tight rein. The powerful thrust of the four engines was beyond anything he had ever handled.

The Germans were impatient at the caution. "Let us take over," urged Herr Waldemuth, the German naval architect. The Israelis relinquished the wheel and the engine room to the German team. Gunning the motors, Waldemuth took the boat up past its thirty-knot cruising speed to its forty-knot tactical speed—the speed at which it would maneuver in combat. The small craft leaped through the water, and they were soon off Southampton. A large Cunard liner, one of the *Queens*, was emerging from the British port. Laughing exultantly, Waldemuth ran the updated S-boat in wide circles around the British liner, as if finding himself in a quirky replay of history, before handing the controls over to Captain Binyamin Telem, head of the Israeli team.

Telem, too, had been born a German. His father was a psychiatrist in Dessau until Telem's brother came home from school one day in 1933 with his shirt ripped and a swastika painted on his back. The family wasted little time in moving to Palestine, where the elder Telem established a mental hospital in Haifa. "Binny," as he would be called, enrolled in Nautical High School after completing his elementary education. In 1947 he served on a gunrunner smuggling weapons from Europe past the British blockade. After the founding of the state, he commanded torpedo boats and a destroyer before being sent to England for a course at the naval staff college in Greenwich. He had been serving as commander of the destroyer flotilla when he was posted to Cherbourg. Respected for his professionalism and liked by his colleagues for his amiable nature, Telem was destined for high rank. As he gripped the wheel of the Saar, he felt that the boat could do it all— move fast and turn fast while remaining stable.

The Israelis had welcomed outside help on this first run of the Saar, as they had with the boat's design and the French navy's supervision of construction. But they were learning every day and gaining in self-confidence.

The first of the Saar boats was subjected to ten thousand miles of punishing sea tests. The most troublesome problem was the tiny holes that developed in the propeller at high speeds. It would be Amiot himself who came up with a solution after the problem had baffled his engineers.

Erell, who succeeded Bin-Nun in 1966, persuaded the General Staff to double the order for missile boats, a move that would permit the navy to cope simultaneously with the Egyptian and Syrian fronts. The cost of each boat would be about $2.5 million, a runaway bargain even when that price was doubled by the electronic systems and armaments. About eight such boats could be built and armed for the price of a single conventional destroyer, Erell argued, and each of the missile boats would be many times more lethal than a destroyer.

Although little more than a score of men were at first assigned to Cherbourg, the Israeli navy was psychologically anchored there and in the European electronics and armaments plants where other elements of the system were being developed.

Strategic intelligence forecast that there would not be a war before 1970, by which time the first missile boats should have replaced the aging warships in the Haifa naval base. However, this evaluation had not reckoned on war by miscalculation. In mid-May 1967, a month after the first Saar was launched, Egyptian President Gamal Abdel Nasser moved his army into Sinai, and Israel began to mobilize its reserves. Erell would not be diverted by the mounting tension from what he saw as the navy's top priority—preparing its missile fleet. Toward the end of May, he ordered one of his senior officers to leave for France, as planned, in order to check components for the missile-boat radar. "Forget what you've been hearing about war plans," said Erell. "This situation is going to end soon, one way or another, but our work on the boats has to go on." The navy entered the Six Day War, its officers would come to say, with its head in the 1970s and its feet in the 1950s.

On the morning of June 5, Israeli planes skimming over the sea deliberately rose into radar view as they approached the Egyptian coast. Their sudden appearance on coastal radar screens allowed the Egyptian pilots just enough time to get to their planes and begin warming them up for takeoff. The warm engines made perfect targets, as the Israelis had calculated, for the heat-seeking missiles fired by the planes, which roared over the airfields moments later. On the ground, Israeli armored spearheads broke through the hard outer ring of Egyptian defenses and began to race for the Suez Canal. So quick was the ground movement that the Israeli seaborne attack planned behind the enemy lines at the Sinai coastal town of El Arish for the first night of the war was canceled.

Attempting to make itself felt, the navy pulled a number of contingency plans from the drawer, but almost all were aborted. Six naval commandos who penetrated Alexandria harbor from a submarine were captured without having found their targets. Admiral Bin-Nun came out of retirement to lead a commando raid on a Syrian port, but it was called off at the last moment.

The one attack pressed home was the tragic torpedo-boat attack on the United States intelligence-gathering ship *Liberty*, mistakenly identified as an Egyptian supply vessel. Unknown to the Israelis, the vessel had sailed into the war zone on June 8, the fourth day of the war, to monitor battlefield communications. On that day, naval headquarters in Haifa ordered three torpedo boats to sail from Ashdod harbor to check reports that El Arish, captured by the army three days before, was being shelled from the sea. The explosions and smoke in El Arish had in fact been caused by an Egyptian ammunition dump that detonated. However, as the torpedo boats approached the area, their radar picked up a target to the west, moving away from El Arish. Presuming it to be an Egyptian warship, naval headquarters called for an air strike to slow up the seemingly fleeing vessel.

Two Mirages were directed to the area, and the lead pilot reported seeing no flag. The ship had two guns on the forecastle and was clearly not Israeli. *Liberty* crewmen would firmly maintain afterward that the American flag was being flown, but the Mirage pilot's report was taken at navy headquarters as confirmation that the ship was an Egyptian vessel trying to reach Port Said. Ordered to attack, the planes set the vessel afire with strafing runs. The smoke thickened when another plane dispatched to the scene dropped a napalm bomb on the *Liberty's* deck.

The son of Admiral Erell, Udi, was an ensign aboard one of the torpedo boats. He could see the smoke from a long distance as the boats raced at top speed toward the scene. As the vessel came into view, Erell's skipper scanned an identification book containing pictures of the ships in the Arab fleets and consulted with the commanders on the other boats. The squadron commander concluded that the ship was the

Egyptian supply vessel *El-Quseir*. Ensign Erell, looking over his skipper's shoulder at the picture and glancing up at the burning vessel, fully agreed, even though he would later recall that the mast in the picture was not positioned identically with the mast of the target vessel. Frustrated at the navy's inactivity while the army was overrunning Sinai and the West Bank and the air force was scoring its spectacular victories, the navy command had been hoping to find an enemy ship that would enable it to get in on the war. At last it seemed to have found what it was looking for.

Nevertheless, the squadron commander sought to confirm the vessel's identity before attacking. When the Israeli signalman flashed the message "What ship?," Udi Erell saw the response flickering through the smoke four miles away—"AAA," the signal meaning "Identify yourself first." That same signal had been flashed, the Israelis were aware, by the Egyptian destroyer challenged off Haifa during the Sinai Campaign in 1956. Americans on the bridge of the *Liberty* would later state that the signals flashed were the ship's name and its international call sign, not what the Israelis believed they saw. Even with binoculars, Erell could make out no flag. The squadron commander ordered his boats to commence torpedo attacks. The vessels peeled off to make their runs and fired five torpedoes. Only one hit home. The boats raked the burning ship, now dead in the water, with their guns.

Fire was halted when one of the officers reported seeing the identification markings CTR-5 on the ship's hull, markings that were not those of an Arab vessel. Notified of this, Haifa ordered the squadron commander to pick up survivors and definitively establish the ship's identity. The Israelis found the water full of green paper, which seemed to have been thrown overboard. Drawing closer to the burning vessel, they were able to make out a flag. It was not opened by a breeze and could not immediately be identified, but it was clearly not Egyptian. Udi's boat was bobbing in the water next to one of the other boats as the officers studied the vessel. His captain, lowering his binoculars, looked over at the captain of the boat alongside and pointed toward the third boat, some distance away, which carried the squadron commander. The captain then wordlessly pointed toward the insignia of rank on his shoulders and made a gesture as if pulling them off. The meaning was clear—there had been a terrible foul-up and the squadron commander would probably have to pay.

Udi saw a splash of red on the flag and heard a report being sent back to Haifa that the vessel might be Russian. The report caused shock and consternation when passed on to General Staff headquarters. The shock was not abated when the torpedo-squadron commander reported half an hour later that he had identified the vessel as American.

Thirty-four American crewmen were killed in the attack and scores wounded. Israel would pay $13 million in compensation and express its profound regrets. However, many in the American military hierarchy would persist in seeing the attack as a deliberate attempt by Israel to prevent the Americans from learning about its war plans, even though the war was virtually over on both the Egyptian and the Jordanian fronts when the ship was attacked.

In Israel itself, the nonperformance of the navy in the Six Day War was hardly noticed amid the general jubilation, but the navy seethed with frustration. Telem, who returned from Cherbourg in time to lead a destroyer sortie off Port Said on the first night of the war, was so disgusted at the navy's lack of preparation that, in protest, he refused to wear his epaulettes. Three times, missions ordered by Erell were blocked by the General Staff on the grounds that the war was already effectively won. Erell pleaded in vain that it was vital for the navy's future to start a combat tradition. The ambush off Romani a month after the war, in which two Egyptian torpedo boats were sunk, was seen by some as a release of naval frustration.

The embargo imposed by de Gaulle on arms sales to the Middle East on the eve of the war remained in effect for those countries that had been involved in the fighting. For Israel, it meant the blockage of fifty Mirage fighter-bombers already on order and the end of the special relationship that had led to France's becoming Israel's major arms supplier. The planes that had destroyed the Arab air forces in the Six Day War were all of French manufacture. The Paris-Jerusalem relationship had been nurtured by the Algerian War, which had placed France at odds with the Arab world. De Gaulle was now seeking a way back into that world after having boldly cut the Algerian knot.

The embargo did not affect the boats being built at Cherbourg. As construction of each vessel finished, it would be taken over by the Israeli mission for sea tests. At a "christening" ceremony before launching, the wife of a dignitary would unveil the boat's name plaque. After being reviewed by Telem, the crew would clamber aboard and the vessel would be pushed on its cradle into the water. As the boat bobbed free, Moshe Tabak, in charge of sea trials, would start the engines and take the boat out on its first shakedown run.

For the launching of the first boat on April 11, 1967, Amiot brought guests from Paris by special railway car. The vessel would not legally be Israeli property until defects discovered during sea tests were corrected and the boat was officially accepted by the Israeli navy. During the testing period, the boats would fly only the pennant of the shipyard.

The most important test was the measured mile. A bonus was paid to the shipyard for each tenth of a knot the boats could achieve above forty knots. The French navy had set up two pairs of tall poles for its own testing on the hills surrounding Cherbourg. Taking the boat up to its maximum speed, Tabak would stand on the bridge with a stop-watch. As the first pair of poles came into alignment, he started the timer. He stopped it as the second pair came into alignment a mile away. The test would be made three times in order to balance out the currents.

Running down the northern Normandy coast, Tabak would some-times study the indentation of the low-lying peninsula and conjure up the morning, more than two decades before, when five thousand ships hove to in these waters in the openings hours of D-Day. Never far from such thoughts for the Israeli sailors was the tragic fate of European Jewry during the war, and their own role in the armed forces of the Jewish state born out of the ashes of Holocaust.

In the spring of 1968, Telem was recalled to Haifa for promotion to deputy naval commander. His place in Cherbourg was taken by Cap-tain Hadar Kimche, who had been serving as commander of the sub-marine flotilla. Born in Kibbutz Ein Harod in the Jezreel Valley, Kimche had been an infantryman in the War of Independence and was severely wounded fighting an Iraqi force in the Jordan Valley. Invited to join the newly organized naval commandos upon his release from the hospital, the young kibbutznik began a new career, which would in-clude ten years as an underwater sailor before his posting to the missile-boat flotilla. Paris seemed to be restaging the French Revolution when Kimche arrived from the airport: the streets swarmed with demonstrat-ing students and workers, and he had difficulty getting to the train station for the final leg of the trip to Cherbourg.

Lieutenant Peleg Lapid waited nervously in front of Rome's Excelsior Hotel. The young electronics officer, destined eventually to head the navy's EW (electronic warfare) program, had been visiting the Italian factories that were producing components for the missile-boat system. He was surprised at the sudden order to proceed to the Excelsior to meet Admiral Shlomo Erell. A man in civilian dress emerged from a limousine in front of the hotel, and it was a moment before the lieutenant recognized him as the navy commander. Erell attempted to put him at his ease: "Let's walk up the Via Veneto and look at girls."

They sat at a sidewalk café, and Erell asked Lapid what he would drink. The flustered lieutenant, unaccustomed to the cafés of Europe, said he didn't know what to order. "How about a lemon drink?" said Erell. "Two citrons, waiter."

After they had sat for a while watching the passing parade, Erell began to spell out his vision of a future missile navy. It was a vision Lapid would recall years later for its daring and prescience.

Erell had created the future for the Israeli navy, but he would himself be overtaken by the present. The navy's bleak performance in the Six Day War, the sinking of the *Eilat* thereafter, and the tragedy of the Israeli submarine *Dakar* (mysteriously lost at sea with a crew of sixty-nine in January 1968 on its maiden voyage from England) created an aura of misfortune about this period not tempered in the public mind by knowledge of the new navy being built. Disagreement with the General Staff over his proposals for the navy's future decided Erell's fate. In September 1968, less than three years after assuming command—having served less than half the term of his predecessor—Admiral Shlomo Erell stepped down as O/C Navy.

Half a year after Erell's departure, on April 7, 1969, two of the Saar boats that had already reached Israel put out from Haifa Bay. The deck of one was crowded with observers, including members of the General Staff. The deck of the other, the *Haifa*, was empty except for curious white pods resembling large garbage bins.

A brief sailing brought the destroyer *Jaffa* in sight. Until a few months before, it had been Israel's flagship. Now it lay anchored in the open sea, with no one aboard, awaiting its fate. If the test about to be undertaken was a success, there would no longer be any need for destroyers in the Israeli navy. At a firing command, one of the pods opened to reveal the cone of a missile—the first Gabriel with a live warhead to be fired. The deck of the *Haifa* had been cleared, for fear of an accidental explosion. There was a brief spurt of flame and the missile shot upward. It arced over, dove toward the sea, and straightened out in the direction of the *Jaffa*.

The observers on the accompanying boat soon lost sight of it, but half a minute later there was a flash aboard the destroyer, followed by the sound of an explosion. A second missile was fired and hit the *Jaffa* amidships. The derelict destroyer slid slowly beneath the sea, carrying with it a naval era.

It had taken just eight years and $11 million to develop the Gabriel—more than the five years and $5 million Even-Tov had initially predicted but far less than the twenty years and $50 million the French aeronautics engineer had conservatively estimated. Even-Tov would estimate that in the United States the Gabriel's development costs would have reached $150 million.

Israel's navy had become the first in the West to enter the missile age. It had been able to do it, Erell would say, because of the ignorance and lack of tradition that had permitted the navy, the military industries, and the government to embark blithely on an undertaking that would have intimidated more experienced countries capable of foreseeing the immense difficulties involved.

It would soon become apparent that, despite Israel's breathtaking victory, the Six Day War was not the war to end all wars in the Middle East. The sinking of the *Eilat* four months after the war was an expression of Egypt's determination to recoup its losses. Unreconciled to Israel's possession of Sinai, the Egyptians opened a war of attrition along the Suez Canal, with massive artillery bombardments and commando incursions. The countdown to the next major conflict had begun.

THE ESCAPE

8
The Plot

The diplomatic corps in Paris filled the elegant reception hall of the Elysée Palace in a horseshoe formation on the first day of January 1969. At the open end, Charles de Gaulle prepared to welcome the diplomats to the president's traditional New Year's reception. As the most veteran foreign diplomat in Paris, Walter Eytan, Israel's ambassador for the past eight years, stood next to the papal nuncio, who was always doyen of the diplomatic corps, regardless of his length of stay.

The nuncio was the first to speak, delivering good wishes to the French leader on behalf of the entire diplomatic corps. When de Gaulle stepped forward, he astonished the diplomats by departing from the bland well-wishes traditional for the occasion and pointedly rebuking Israel, although not by name, for its raid on Beirut Airport a few days before. In a cutting voice, he condemned "exaggerated violent acts like those that were just committed by the regular army of a nation on the civilian airport of a peaceful country and traditional friend of France." Colleagues close to Eytan, who was standing just a few paces from the president, thought they saw his otherwise impassive countenance flush.

Israel was formally notified five days later that the embargo imposed on the Mirages in June 1967 was now extended "to all arms." The Israeli and French press were vague about particulars, citing only spare parts for aircraft. There was no mention of boats. Except for the Cherbourg press, the media were in fact unaware of the boats' existence. The two Cherbourg newspapers had kept silent in order not to endanger an important factor in the local economy. Publicity might even bring a Palestinian raid on the port. Limon's forewarning that the embargo would reach out to Cherbourg had enabled Boats Six and Seven to get away. A decision now had to be made regarding the last five boats. The embargo applied only to their shipment to Israel, not to their manufacture. Should Israel go ahead with construction or invest the money elsewhere? The Defense Ministry and navy decided to proceed, in the hope that, despite de Gaulle's ire, the embargo would be lifted by the time the vessels were ready to sail. It was a hope that echoed the old Yiddish story of the Jew who staved off a pogrom by accepting the prince's challenge to teach his dog to sing within a year or die. "A lot of things can happen in a year," the Jew reassured his family. "Maybe the prince will die, maybe I will die, maybe the dog will learn how to sing."

Just three months later, the prince indeed stepped off the stage when a referendum ordered by de Gaulle was defeated, leading to his immediate resignation. French officials had been assuring the Israelis that the embargo would be lifted quietly one morning when de Gaulle's fit of temper had dissipated, but as the weeks passed under his successor, Georges Pompidou, it became evident to the Israelis that they were up against high policy, not just personal pique. On July 10, Pompidou gave a press conference in which he reaffirmed the embargo on the grounds that there had been no political changes in the Middle East to warrant a change of policy. Observers felt that Pompidou, a former director/general of the Rothschild Bank, who had not accompanied de Gaulle to England in the war or been involved in the resistance, chose to remain faithful to his predecessor's policy even if he did not entirely concur, because he wished to be perceived not as a Rothschild valet but as a true heir to de Gaulle. Pompidou left open the return to a "selective" embargo, which would presumably permit export of equipment other than the Mirages, but this, he said, "would depend on the situation."

By midsummer, Limon and Israeli naval officers were increasingly focusing on an activist solution. They bandied the idea of having the shipyard sell the boats to another navy, which would then sell them back to Israel, but upon examination it seemed unlikely that any country would risk endangering its relationship with France by participating in such a ruse. The possibility was even examined of abandoning the embargoed boats altogether and acquiring a patrol boat developed by the United States as a response to the Komars supplied to Cuba. The American PGM-class craft had a top speed of fifty knots and was intended to close on the enemy missile craft by speed and maneuver to destroy it with gunfire or torpedoes. The aluminum-hulled vessel was similar in dimension to the Saar, but it proved to be unsuitable for the open sea.

The more the Israelis examined the problem, the more it became evident that if the navy was going to be prepared for the next military round with the Arabs there was no choice but to get the five boats out of Cherbourg, even without the blessing of Paris. After all, the boats belonged to Israel, which had ordered them, provided the design, and given a down payment. They were in effect being hijacked by France, in violation of written contracts, for the crudest reasons of national self-interest, painted over by lofty rhetoric about the search for peace.

Rich in adversity, Israel had long since learned how to proceed by the obscure byway when the high road was impassable. In the chaos of postwar Europe, operatives dispatched by the small Jewish community in Palestine had created an underground railroad that brought out two hundred thousand concentration-camp survivors and other displaced persons across closed borders, through the Iron Curtain, and over snow-covered mountain passes to ships that would carry them to their new homeland. They created parallel networks to bring out the Jews of the Arab world. From Europe and the United States they smuggled sufficient clandestine arms, from Sten guns to flying fortresses, to hold off and then defeat the five Arab armies that invaded Israel on the day it was born.

In numerous operations, the emissaries of the state-in-the-making and then of the young state itself had learned the measure of both discretion and boldness. They had used flags of convenience, false documents, false uniforms, and, when all else failed, a frankness that disarmed. They used money when they had it and chutzpah when they didn't. Their adventures were breathtaking in their scope and audacity—while an emissary in postwar Poland was arranging the opening of a border-crossing point for Palestine-bound Jews with a Russian general who believed that the Polish-born Palestinian represented the

Polish government, an emissary in New York was dealing with Mafia figures and industrial tycoons as he acquired the machinery to create the base of an arms manufacturing industry in Israel. This daring and imagination had not been lost with statehood, even though most of the secret agents inevitably became bureaucrats. Israel's vulnerable beachhead on the hostile shores of the Middle East—and on the often hostile shores of the international body politic—meant that it would still periodically have to resort to its wits, rather than abide strictly by rules that securer nations can permit themselves.

Only a few months before, Professor Enrico Jacchia, director of nuclear safeguards for the European Community, had discovered to his amazement that two hundred tons of uranium had disappeared from a plant in Belgium, despite the precautions taken to prevent unauthorized transfers.

The uranium had been shipped from Antwerp by a German chemical firm that had purchased it, ostensibly to be processed by a Genoa firm prior to being used in conventional chemical processes. At the request of both the German and Italian firms, Euratom—the EEC agency monitoring uranium movements—permitted the shipment, although regulations forbade uranium's export from EEC countries without elaborate approval procedures. Since it was going from one European country to another, Euratom agreed that it need not be considered an export even though it was going by sea.

It was only months later, after both the German and Italian firms failed to file routine notices that the uranium had reached Italy and been sent on to Germany, that Euratom became uneasy. Investigators discovered that the uranium had never reached Italy. When the small German firm declined to give details of the uranium's whereabouts, on the grounds that it was a private business matter that lay outside Euratom's mandate to probe, the agency accepted that it did not have the legal teeth to press the matter and let it die quietly, for fear of embarrassment. It would be nine years before it would come to public attention as the Plumbatt affair—the name Plumbatt had been stamped on the 560 drums filled with uranium "yellowcake" that had been placed aboard a beat-up freighter, the *Scheerberg A*, in November 1968. The vessel, which had been acquired by a Liberian shipping company set up three months before in Zurich, sailed for the Mediterranean but never reached Genoa. According to reports published years afterward in the

West, its cargo was transferred at sea to an Israeli freighter guarded by two gunboats. These reports alleged that the Plumbatt uranium had been converted to weapons-grade plutonium in Israel's nuclear plant in Dimona and been used to create the warheads of Israel's nuclear armory.

No official evidence, however, ever linked the Plumbatt uranium with Israel. Professor Jacchia would write admiringly that the evasion of Euratom's supervision in the Plumbatt case was a demonstration of exceptional legal skill. "It made it possible for the imaginative mind of the diversion authors to operate in perfectly legal manners until the crucial moment—the exit of the *Scheerberg* from the port of Antwerp—when the captain could freely sail his ship not to the port of Genoa but to its real and previously planned destination. It was a nonviolent, intelligent interpretation of the Euratom Treaty's procedural rules."

Ever since the expulsion from the arsenal following the escape of Boats Six and Seven, the Saars had been moored in the transatlantic basin of Cherbourg's civilian port where the great ocean liners used to dock. Since dwindling passenger services had been shifted to Le Havre, the huge basin was largely empty except for transchannel ferries to England. Despite the embargo, the boats were unguarded. Motorized police patrols checked the basin a few times a day against a terrorist attack, not to make sure the Israeli vessels were still there.

To the handful of men pondering a solution to the Cherbourg embargo, the simplest answer was a quasi-commando operation in which crews would slip into town one night and make off with the boats. Such a snatch-and-run operation was proposed by Limon to Defense Minister Moshe Dayan in midsummer. The answer was a firm negative. Prime Minister Golda Meir, with whom Dayan discussed the proposal, did not wish to endanger relations with France because of some boats. The message from Jerusalem was clear—nothing illegal must be done that could be used as an excuse by Paris for severing the already tense relations.

This reply did not unduly discourage Limon. The distinction between something legal and something not illegal may be no wider than a lawyer's comma, but in the right circumstances that might be wide enough to drive a missile-boat squadron through.

In July, Limon called on Ambassador Eytan to inform him that there had been a proposal to run off with the boats but that it had been vetoed by Jerusalem. The diplomat was relieved to hear that the idea had been dropped. The new French president, he felt, should be given a chance to change policy. This was the last time the subject would come up between the two men. There was little love lost between Eytan, a consummate diplomat who never gave newspaper interviews, and the freewheeling ex–naval commander who virtually ran his own diplomatic shop out of his offices a few blocks away from the embassy. Limon was the one member of the Israeli purchasing mission to have diplomatic status.

One night, one of his numerous acquaintances, journalist Jean-Claude Servan-Schreiber, rang his doorbell to pass on a message from the chairman of the National Defense Committee of the French Assembly, Alexandre Sanguinetti—"Why don't the Israelis just get on their boats and go?" Sanguinetti had made a similar comment to Amiot, during the visit of a parliamentary delegation to the Cherbourg arsenal, when he had seen the Israeli boats tied up in the basin. To be sure that his view reached Limon's ears, Sanguinetti asked Servan-Schreiber to speak to him directly.

Limon lightly turned the suggestion aside, asserting that Israel still hoped that the French government would change its policy. He did not think it politic to reveal that he and his colleagues were already trying to figure out how to relieve the French of the embarrassment of the embargoed boats.

That subject had headed the agenda of "Binny" Telem when he visited Cherbourg in August on his way back from the United States to Israel. He crossed from England by night ferry to Le Havre, and Moshe Tabak drove through a foggy night to meet the admiral at 6:00 A.M. Kimche had left for Israel to begin organizing the first seven boats into an operational flotilla, and Tabak was in charge in Cherbourg. As they drove through the French countryside, he and Telem ran through the options. The remaining boats were coming off the production line on schedule every two or three months. Three were already in the water; the fourth would be launched in October and the last in December or January.

If, as they presumed, Jerusalem's reservations about running off with the boats would be overcome, the principal problem was fueling. More than three thousand miles lay between Cherbourg and Haifa, and the

Saars would have to refuel twice on the way. Until now, they had fueled at Gibraltar and at Sicily. But on a breakout there could be no entering of ports, for fear that the French would seek to impound the boats. Tabak suggested augmenting the fuel supply with inflatable rubber fuel-tanks that would be distributed above and below decks. Telem told him to pursue this line further.

After the mission's naval architect determined that the rubber fuel tanks would not destabilize the boats, Tabak visited several French factories before he found one that could undertake the project. What was wanted, he explained, was fuel tanks for desert use. They would be transported on trucks and would have to be able to withstand considerable shaking and heat. Tabak was in civilian dress and although the factory executives knew he was an Israeli military man, they did not know he was from the navy. As production of the tanks got under way, Tabak became increasingly uneasy about the entire idea. The boats would be powder kegs, with disaster requiring no more than a stray spark. In his communications with Telem in Haifa, Tabak urged that some other solution be found if possible.

As flotilla commander, Kimche would make periodic visits to Cherbourg, stopping off in Paris to meet with Limon. Kimche did not think it possible to escape with all five boats: the French would likely place tight security around the quay once all the boats were in the water. The chances were much better with only four boats, he believed. Limon, however, thought it possible to get away with all.

Although Limon was now a civilian, he had become the pivotal force in the situation, because of his French contacts and his standing in the Israeli defense establishment and among his former naval colleagues. His diplomatic status would have inclined him away from a grossly undiplomatic adventure like the one he had proposed, but his awareness of the boats' revolutionary importance—something not fully understood in Jerusalem—and the pressure of his old naval comrades pushed him into the key role. The navy itself could not, because of its nature as a military organization, undertake the political wheeling that would be necessary. Nor, because of its status, could the embassy in Paris. Limon, however, was perfectly positioned—by his job and by his background.

At twenty-six he had become commander of the two-year-old Israeli navy. Despite his youth, there were few Israelis as richly experienced at sea. His family had emigrated to Palestine from Poland when he was ten, and he went off to sea seven years later as a deckhand on a Norwegian tanker. In World War II he served in Allied merchant fleets making the Atlantic and Murmansk runs. As a member of the sea arm of the Haganah underground in the postwar years, he commanded refugee ships running the British blockade to Palestine. These voyages sometimes ended in violent encounters with British boarding parties and internment in Cyprus. Limon escaped twice—once by leaping into Haifa Bay and swimming to safety, once by hiding until the boarding party had taken the passengers off. On his third voyage he was captured and spent several weeks in Cyprus.

It was as a young admiral that he met his future wife, Rachel, while she was doing her two years of obligatory military duty. Retiring from the navy at the age of thirty in 1954, he studied business administration at Columbia University in New York and returned to Israel to serve as deputy director general of the Defense Ministry. In 1962 he was sent to Paris as head of the ministry's purchasing mission, which was acquiring for Israel the bulk of its foreign armaments, particularly warplanes. An introvert by nature, Limon had a ready ability to win friends once the curtain of his reticence was penetrated. The balding, pipe-smoking former admiral had become highly successful in his quasi-diplomatic role, in which his primary task was to cultivate contacts in political and defense circles. His home on the Left Bank was regularly visited by figures from the French establishment, and the parties organized by his attractive wife drew a wide range of personalities.

The Cherbourg embargo had cast Limon back into a key role in the navy's affairs. As other options fell away, he began to focus on the idea of selling the boats to a foreign shipping company, which, unlike a foreign government, could be in a position to sell them back quietly to Israel. This meant selling them for civilian purposes. The question was what civilian purpose these high-powered craft could plausibly serve. Since the French authorities had to approve the sale if the boats were to depart from Cherbourg legally, the cover story had to seem reasonable. Some World War II corvettes and similar warships had been converted for passenger and transport use, but small, four-engined patrol craft capable of forty knots were another matter.

The one potential category that came to mind was oil-prospecting companies. Such quirky big spenders might conceivably be willing to purchase overpowered craft to run supplies to oil rigs. Limon consulted with an old friend, Mordecai Friedman, head of an Israeli oil-exploration company, Netivai Neft, which had been exploiting the oil in the Gulf of Suez since Sinai had fallen into Israeli hands. Friedman not only encouraged the idea but also suggested to Limon a Norwegian shipbuilder he knew as a possible front. The suggestion intrigued Limon. A Greek or an Italian front for the operation might not lull suspicion. A Scandinavian address was perfect cover—respectable and remote—for Mediterranean mischief.

The Norwegian was Martin Siemm, director of the Akers Shipbuilding Group, the largest shipbuilders in Norway. His firm had built more than a score of tankers, refrigerator ships, and other vessels for a Haifa shipping firm, and he had a minority interest in an oil pipeline being constructed from Eilat to Ashkelon. During World War II, Siemm had been one of the leaders of the Norwegian underground. He had visited Israel a few months after the Six Day War and was struck by the dynamism of the country built up by Jewish people who had survived the same dark forces he had fought. During a visit to Sinai he met Friedman. The two men took an immediate liking to each other and maintained contact in the ensuing years, even though they had no direct business dealings with each other. Friedman was convinced that Siemm was a friend of Israel who would be willing to help rescue the boats from Cherbourg.

The more Limon mulled it over, the more the Norwegian option looked reasonable. There seemed no other way of getting the boats out of France as long as Jersualem refused to permit running off with them. Limon raised and then dismissed the idea of the boats' actually sailing to Oslo after being sold, in order to affirm the legality of the enterprise, and then quietly making their way to Israel over the course of time. If five warships arrived in Oslo harbor, even unarmed, their presence would inevitably raise questions. It would not take much scratching to expose their quasi-legal cover, and France would ask to have the boats impounded. Once the boats had legally departed from Cherbourg harbor, there would be no choice but to run for it. With the launching of the last boat just two months away, it was time to make the move.

Mordecai Friedman was in London on a business trip in October when the phone rang in his hotel room. It was Limon calling from Paris.

"I've got to meet with you, Motti," said Limon. "It's urgent."

"How urgent?"

"Immediately. I want to fly over on the next plane."

"I've got tickets for the theater tonight," said Friedman. "I can skip it or you can join me. I'll leave a ticket in your name at the box office if you like."

Limon agreed to the theater rendezvous. If he made his connections, he might even get there before the show started. At the theater, Friedman eyed the cabs pulling up outside as curtain time approached, but when the last of the crowd started filing in, he followed. A few minutes after the curtain went up, a tall, familiar figure slid into the empty seat next to him and whispered "*Shalom.*"

At intermission, the two men went into the lobby, where the chain-smoking Limon gratefully lit a cigarette.

"What's up?" asked Friedman.

Limon casually glanced around him through the cigarette smoke he had exhaled. "I want you to contact your friend in Oslo tonight and arrange a meeting between him and us—if possible for tomorrow morning."

The two Israelis stayed on to see the rest of the show and then took a cab to Friedman's hotel, where the oilman put a call through to Siemm's home.

"Martin, something important has come up," said the Israeli. "I can't talk to you about it on the phone, but I'd like to see you as soon as possible; in fact, I'd like to fly to Oslo tomorrow morning. I have a friend who would be coming with me."

"If it's that important," replied Siemm, "I'll meet you partway. Let's meet in Copenhagen."

Limon nodded when Friedman transmitted Siemm's offer. It was agreed to meet at Copenhagen Airport for lunch. Limon preferred not to drive into downtown Copenhagen because of the off chance that he and Siemm might be recognized by someone who could later recall their meeting.

Siemm was waiting for them in the arrivals hall when the Israelis got there, and he greeted his friend warmly. Friedman introduced Limon to the tall, distinguished-looking Norwegian. In the airport restaurant they sat at a corner table, well away from other customers. As the Israelis began their presentation, it quickly became apparent to Siemm that they had not come to discuss a business deal.

The Israel Defense Force urgently needed the five boats being arbitrarily embargoed by the French in Cherbourg, explained Limon. The nation depended on the navy to safeguard its lifeline in the event of war, and the navy was depending on these vessels.

The French, said Limon, were eager to rid themselves of the problem. "If they get an offer from anyone, they'll be happy to give us back our money." What was needed was a fictitious purchaser. If Siemm would agree to undertake that role, the problem could be elegantly resolved, with harm to no one and with immeasurable benefit to Israel's cause.

As for the cover story, Friedman told Siemm that if he was asked about why he had purchased the boats he could offer a reasonable explanation: "It's true that these aren't the kind of boats you would order built to service oil rigs in the North Sea, but they have one advantage that any businessman in urgent need of service boats can recognize—they're available."

The Israelis were not offering any compensation to Siemm for his participation, and the danger to his most prized possession—his good name—was clear. But Friedman saw Siemm's face brighten as he grasped the stakes involved and the ploy being spelled out. The Israeli oilman was certain that the proposal had sparked in Siemm recollections of his underground years, devising stratagems to outwit the enemy.

"I'm willing to help, but I can't decide on this myself," said Siemm. "I've got to consult with some others first. Give me forty-eight hours." The three men took leave of one another and boarded the next planes for Oslo, Paris, and London.

Two days later, Siemm telephoned the Paris number Limon had given him and in innocuous phrases let the Israeli know that he was prepared to proceed.

Limon had not informed his superiors in the Defense Ministry of his Norwegian probe until he knew that he had Siemm's cooperation. In a letter to the ministry sent October 30, he outlined his move. The preferable time for implementing the plan, he suggested, would be on Christmas Eve, when French alertness would be at its minimum.

The reply from the ministry was a total dampener: "We have weighed your suggestions and come to the conclusion that it is impossible at this time to consider them."

Limon, however, had not waited. On November 3, a letter drafted by him had gone out over Siemm's signature to Amiot, setting the game in motion. Upon receiving the ministry's negative reply, Limon telephoned General (res.) Zvi Tsur, a former armed-forces chief of staff serving now as special assistant to Defense Minister Dayan. Limon's assistant, listening in on an extension, heard Tsur express fears of the political-diplomatic fallout from such an operation. "All right," said Limon, "if you think we don't have to do it, I won't do it." Putting the matter in those terms placed the responsibility on the other end of the line for rejecting what the men in the field thought the best solution. Tsur softened his position. "Okay, you can proceed with your planning. But, meanwhile, I'm not telling Golda." Limon was confident that the authorities in Israel would realize soon enough that his proposal was the only feasible option.

Payment for the boats had been halted by the Israelis as a means of placing pressure through Amiot on the French government. Unlike the case of the fifty embargoed Mirages, which had been paid for by Israel before clampdown, only 30 percent of the cost of the embargoed boats had been advanced. The payment freeze made the embargo not just an Israeli problem and a matter of high politics but also a French problem of the nitty-gritty kind that politicians instinctively understand—a matter of jobs and possible votes. A shutdown of Amiot's production line would throw hundreds out of work and have an impact on the rest of Cherbourg's economy as well. Cherbourg was a strongly Gaullist town, and its mayor, Dr. Jacques Hébert, who also served as a deputy in the National Assembly, pressed vigorously in Paris for the embargo's end. Amiot, who had mortgaged much of his private holdings to obtain financing for continuation of the project, called on several ministers and even had ten minutes with de Gaulle himself. He argued that he was not building warships, only hulls. It was not right, he said, to impose an embargo on goods after a contract had been signed in good faith. His arguments, however, were to no avail.

It was necessary for Limon to confide his plan to Amiot, since his cooperation was essential for the legalistic flanking action being plotted. It would also be up to Amiot to see to it that the last boat was launched by mid-December so as to be ready for a Christmas sailing. The seventy-five-year-old industrialist responded enthusiastically to the plan. A tentative go-ahead had also come from Dayan, although a final decision would have to be made by Prime Minister Meir.

The letter Amiot received early in November over Siemm's signature bore the letterhead of the Starboat Oil and Shipping Company in Oslo. It expressed an interest in acquiring four to six fast boats for assistance in offshore oil exploration. The boats had to be capable of doing thirty-five knots and taking strong seas, have reliable diesel engines, be able to carry fifty workers and twenty tons of equipment. They were needed quickly, within no more than three months. Did the shipyard have any such vessels available? The return address was a post-office box number in Oslo. Starboat and Oslo were printed in large letters. In tiny letters there was also a Panamanian address. Starboat was in fact a Panamanian registered company, a status that could speedily be arranged by any Panamanian embassy. The only Norwegian connection was the post-office box and the man who had signed the letter, Ole Martin Siemm. The name Starboat was unknown in French shipping circles, but Siemm's impressive biography was listed in business reference books.

Amiot promptly contacted General Louis Bonte, director of international affairs for the Ministerial Delegation for Armaments—in effect, the Defense Ministry's chief arms salesman. Bonte had been closely following the affair of the embargoed Israeli boats. Whatever its political wisdom, the embargo was clearly a nuisance for those charged with promoting the export of French armaments. The boats cluttering the quay in Cherbourg were an embarrassment in themselves—nothing could be done with them as long as Israel did not relinquish ownership—and were a poor advertisement for French reliability as a supplier. The offer reported by Amiot could neatly resolve the problem, if Israel could be persuaded to drop its claims to the boats and accept its money back. The Israelis had so far stubbornly refused to do so with regard to the fifty embargoed Mirages, but the astute, Jesuit-educated Bonte, a former air-force test pilot, thought it might be possible to persuade them to accept payment for the *vedettes*.

Meanwhile, Amiot wrote to Siemm that he had four boats that met Starboat's specifications and a fifth boat that would be launched shortly. The boats had been ordered, he wrote, by a foreign purchaser who was "having difficulty taking delivery." The boats would answer Starboat's needs if the present owner could be persuaded to waive title.

Limon was prepared for Bonte's call when it came. The French official informed him that an offer had been received from a foreign firm for boats whose specifications appeared to match those of the boats being built in Cherbourg. The French authorities were willing to consider approval of the sale if Israel would waive its rights and accept a refund. Would it do so?

Limon did not pretend to be surprised by the offer. Monsieur Amiot, he said, had already spoken to him. "Personally, I'm opposed to it," said Limon. "These are our boats. We've paid for them and we need them." The decision, however, was not his, and he would pass the offer on to the Defense Ministry in Tel Aviv.

Limon had deftly inserted the sting. The French authorities were the ones pressing for the deal, rather than Israel. He decided to let that pressure build up. Several days after their initial conversation, an anxious Bonte called again. "Have you heard anything from Israel?"

"Not yet," said Limon. "I'll contact you as soon as I do."

Limon let several more days pass before calling Bonte. "They've acted against my advice and decided to let the boats go," he said. "They're just fed up with the whole business."

The Israeli approval came just in time for Bonte to add the boat sale as a supplement to the agenda of the November 18 meeting of the Interministerial Committee on Arms Exports. No arms sale could be consummated until the committee decided that it was in France's national interest. The detailed agenda for the November 18 meeting listed deals that France's thriving arms industry had struck around the world. At the bottom of the last page, the names of three countries were listed under the heading of "new business"—China, Finland, Norway. Unlike the case with the rest of the items on the agenda, no details were given of the proposed new business.

The meeting was chaired for the first time by General Bernard Cazelles, a genial artillery expert with a distinguished career who had been appointed by de Gaulle as secretary general at the Defense Ministry half a year before. The committee's frequent meetings are normally chaired by a junior official, but twice a year the secretary general himself presides, and at the request of a subordinate, Cazelles had agreed to take over the November 18 meeting.

When the final items were reached, Bonte's assistant outlined their nature with brevity, including the helicopters being sold to Finland and the *vedettes*, or patrol boats, to Norway. The absence of printed details and the sketchy oral presentation left some of the participants believing that the boats were destined for the Norwegian navy. There was no mention of the Starboat Company. Cazelles asked if Israel had agreed to the sale, and Bonte replied affirmatively.

Would the contract include a non-reexportation clause forbidding the Norwegian purchaser from reselling the items to another country? asked Cazelles.

"That is generally the case with this kind of contract," replied Bonte. Following that brief exchange, the sale was unanimously approved. When Foreign Minister Maurice Schumann later read the report of his ministry's representative on the committee outlining the sale of the Cherbourg boats to Norway, he wrote on it: "This is an excellent transaction that should serve as a model. Bravo."

The deal was in fact too good to be true. As the paperwork began to percolate routinely through the bureaucracy, more and more officials directly involved began to sense that there was something not quite aboveboard in it. The Starboat Company was an unknown name, but no one had bothered to check out the post-office box in Oslo. No one publicly questioned the logic of using high-powered warships to deliver lengths of pipe and cases of beer to oil rigs, although the question was being asked unofficially. Some officials guessed and winked. Some turned an eye. All saw it as an elegant solution to an awkward problem. Some saw it as a way of getting at Defense Minister Michel Debré, a principal advocate of the embargo. According to one knowledgeable French source, some thirty middle-level officials were to become aware of the fictitious nature of the sale, and a secret meeting was even held on the matter within one of the ministries involved. Some ranking Israeli and French observers would find it difficult to believe that the entire French government had not been aware. No evidence of this has ever emerged, however, while existing evidence indicates the contrary.

Limon, for his part, was careful not to compromise any of his French contacts. All were acting in their country's interests as they saw them, or in their own bureaucratic interests, not as agents of Israel. The Israeli needed a keen understanding of the workings of the French bureaucracy not to overstep the line. Virtually every French official, from general to customs agent, protected his flanks by keeping a personal dossier containing copies of documents showing that he had acted according to the book.

One key official was a Corsican named Jacques Marti who headed the customs division dealing with boat exports. When a lawyer for the Amiot firm came to him a few weeks after the interministerial committee's approval of the sale, to request his signature on the customs clearance, Marti carefully scrutinized the document. It listed the country of destination as Norway and the intended use of the boats as "servicing offshore oil installations." The Amiot lawyer tried to look blasé. Despite the committee's decision, Marti had the power to investigate if he suspected something amiss.

"Norway, eh?" said Marti. "These boats are headed for Israel, aren't they?"

The lawyer saw no point in trying to brazen it out. "Yes," he admitted.

"In that case," said Marti, lifting a pen, "I'll sign." He objected to the embargo, liked Israel, and felt that it should get the goods it had ordered and paid for.

Despite the benign conspiracy that had grown up around the boat "sale," the danger of discovery remained constant. If, by accident or intention, the fictitious nature of the deal were brought to the attention of nonconspirators in the police or any ministry, or if it would reach the press, the situation could explode instantly, with extremely unpleasant consequences for all concerned.

As the preparations began to mount around him, Captain Moshe Tabak in Cherbourg saw little hope of the complicated operation's coming off. It needed only a slip of the tongue or the curiosity of some government clerk to stop it in its tracks. "We're doing great work, Ester," he said to his wife one evening, referring to the two years of effort invested in the last five boats, "but I'm afraid it's all going to be for nothing."

Captain Amnon Tadmor, master of a small freighter belonging to Israel's national shipping company, Zim, had just left Marseilles for Israel when the message arrived from his home office in Haifa—"Appointed command *Lea*." The *Lea* was a freighter slightly larger than the one he was on. Tadmor was puzzled at the unexpected transfer. On tying up his ship in Ashdod port, he found the *Lea* moored alongside. As soon as he boarded, he understood that something unusual was afoot. Fuel lines led to five pumps freshly installed on the aft deck. This would allow simultaneous fueling of five boats. Merchant vessels were not fueled at sea, so a naval operation of some sort was indicated. Tadmor himself had served in the navy for fifteen years and had experience at fueling at sea, which he presumed was why he had been selected for his new command.

"They're waiting for you at navy headquarters," the outgoing captain of the *Lea* told him.

First there was a brief change-of-command ceremony to be performed. Tadmor inspected the ship, checked its papers, counted the money in the safe, received reports on water and fuel supplies, ordered the ballast sounded, lingered in the galley to get a good look at the cook, and met with all department heads. These chores done, he drove north to Haifa.

The room at navy headquarters was crowded with a score of Zim officials and navy officers. Commander Ezra Karshinksy—known to all as Karish, "Shark" in Hebrew—came forward to greet him. The captain of the first Saar to be launched in Cherbourg and commander of the first Saar squadron, Karish had been assigned the task of organizing the logistics of the Cherbourg escape from the Haifa end. After informing Tadmor of the operation, he explained that the fleeing boats would be refueled twice along the way from mother ships. The *Lea* would be the first, taking up position on the Atlantic side of the Straits of Gibraltar. A second ship would be in position in the Mediterranean. Tadmor was not told which ship or what position, and he did not ask. The *Lea*'s additional fuel supply would be carried in its ballast tanks. These tanks normally carry seawater to provide the ship with stability, and there is no way to discharge their contents except underwater. However, Zim's workshops had altered the ballast tanks' structure so that they could serve as a fuel reservoir that could be pumped out from the deck.

During the next few days, the *Lea* practiced new fueling techniques at sea with some of the missile boats from Karish's squadron. Sailing along like a mother hen, she dropped her floating fuel lines into the water to be hauled in by the men in the naval vessels. The lines were heavy and it was exhausting work. Tadmor discovered that there was a serious communication problem between his crew and the navy crews. Although all his men were Israeli, the common language for commands and nautical terms in the merchant navy, which often carried foreign crewmen, was English. The sailors aboard the navy vessel did not understand much of what was being shouted at them from the deck of the mother ship. The training program was extended informally to include Hebrew-English nautical equivalents.

The second fueling ship was the car ferry *Dan*, which normally plied between Haifa and Europe with tourists. It had been laid up between seasons in Haifa. Large fuel tanks requisitioned from an oil company were installed in the parking area below decks, and a crew was formed from reservists mobilized for the mission and regular navy personnel. Chosen as captain was Yosef Dror, a former submarine commander who had been living in his kibbutz since retirement from the navy. At his briefing by Karish, Dror was told that he would be taking up position in the central Mediterranean.

A cover story had to be created for the refueling exercises. The sailors were bound to be curious and, left to their own devices, they might even begin guessing in the right direction. The explanation offered proved satisfactory—the refueling technique was being developed, the sailors were told, in case the Saars had to be dispatched from Haifa in the future on long-range missions.

The breakout operation would require the dispatch of eighty crewmen to Cherbourg to reinforce the forty already in place. The Saars in Haifa were stripped of their best men, over the protests of the boat commanders. The young crewmen, most of whom had never been abroad, were photographed for passports and told to stand by. Bachelor officers were preferred over family men, because of the possibility that some mishap might mean internment in French jails.

The freebooting operation Limon had been running out of his hip pocket on the Continent had begun to take on the structured, all-options-covered dimensions of a military operation. Navy headquarters had even given it a name—Operation Noah. All these preparations were being made with the understanding that the operation might never be carried off, since the government had not yet given its approval. Formal approval would in fact never come. The first message Limon received in writing to indicate—indirectly—that the political authorities were in any way party to the escapade was a coded telegram from the Defense Ministry on December 15 asking about the flags the boat would fly and other politically sensitive points. But he did not have in hand any document stating clearly that he was acting on behalf of the government. This was not, he knew, an oversight. If anything went awry, he was sure it would be his head that would roll.

The escape of the boats had in fact not been brought up for discussion, in either the Cabinet or the General Staff. But in a meeting with Defense Minister Dayan and Chief of Staff Haim Bar-Lev two weeks before Christmas, Mrs. Meir had finally given her permission to proceed. A detailed operational order was issued by navy headquarters on December 14, covering logistics, setting departure dates for the fueling ships, and citing radio frequencies to be used by the naval and merchant ships involved. It also established security procedures in accordance with the operation's top-secret classification, including cover stories for the crews flying to France and the documentation they would carry. The order named Hadar Kimche as commander of the operation.

Despite all the preparations, however, the success of the operation depended on events in Paris and Cherbourg beyond Israel's control.

9
Hocus-Pocus

As the countdown quickened, Moshe Tabak was keeping a close watch on the heavens. The sun and moon would be in their monthly alignment on December 16, which meant a tide three feet higher than usual. It was only when the sea was at this height that the shipyard could launch its boats. If the date was missed, it would be another month before Number Twelve could be floated. Tabak had been pressing the shipyard to launch by the 16th, but as the date approached the foremen insisted that they needed another few days to work out problems with the last engine installed. It was only Amiot's personal intervention that got the boat launched on time. The final touches were put on the engine after the boat was in the water, a procedure that struck the yard workers as lunatic. With the memory still fresh of his voyage a year before in untested Number Seven, Tabak pushed Number Twelve through stiff paces and discovered a crack in one of the fuel tanks, which was quickly repaired.

In the four and a half years since the Israeli naval mission had been established in Cherbourg, there had been no mention in the press of its existence. The two local newspapers had honored Amiot's request not to publish anything about the boats or the embargo and the French government had never made public mention of the subject. Local reporters attended the launchings of each *vedette*, and talked at the receptions with the Israeli naval personnel, but wrote nothing. Outside of

96

Cherbourg, the French public—indeed, the Israeli public—was ignorant of their existence. The secrecy would be undone one week before the planned breakout by a British reporter.

French Defense Minister Debré had arrived in Cherbourg December 12 with a large entourage to participate in the launching of France's second nuclear submarine, the *Terrible*. Following a press conference in the naval arsenal, Mayor Hébert took advantage of the minister's presence to repeat his objection to the embargo of the Israeli boats and to point out the danger of a Palestinian raid on their anchorage. Was there any solution in the offing? he asked. To the surprise of local reporters who had lingered to hear the conversation, Debré replied that there was, one that would be satisfactory to all parties. He was referring to the Starboat sale but did not elaborate.

The veteran British correspondent Anthony Mann of the *Daily Telegraph* had not attended the submarine launching, but he telephoned afterward to a stringer in Cherbourg—a local newsman working as a part-time correspondent for out-of-town newspapers. In passing, the stringer mentioned the colony of Israelis living in Cherbourg, a reference apparently inspired by the Debré-Hébert exchange. Mann perked up at the mention of Israelis and asked what they were doing in Cherbourg. To his astonishment he learned that they had been there for years to oversee construction of a series of gunboats and that these boats had been embargoed by de Gaulle. The apparently secret Israeli presence was intriguing, and so was the embargo, but the story still lacked the timely peg that would make it news.

This came a few days later, when Mann's Cherbourg stringer called to inform him of the launching of the last Israeli boat. Mann's story appeared in the *Telegraph* the next day, headlined "France Holds On to Gunboats for Israel." Although buried on page 17, it was enough to cause despair among the Israelis involved in the affair. The story even reported, "It is understood that some Israeli naval personnel will return home on Christmas Day." The statement was innocent enough. The stringer had heard that some of the Israeli families in town had declined invitations to holiday parties because they would be returning to Israel. There was a periodic turnover of Israeli personnel in Cherbourg, and Mann was not hinting at any imminent breakout of the embargoed boats. Nevertheless, his report stunned Limon and his colleagues. They feared that the article would focus so much attention on them that the entire operation would have to be aborted. But the follow-up did not come—not in the French press or anywhere else. The Mann article had in fact not been the first mention of the boats. Two weeks before, an annual publication put out by the French navy, *Combat Fleets*, had reported that five high-speed, missile-firing Israeli patrol boats were under arms embargo in France. That article did not mention Cherbourg or the presence of Israeli crews, and although it was summed up in a brief wire-service dispatch, it received scant notice.

Meanwhile, preparations for the breakout continued. It was not a simple matter to undertake in secrecy a quasi-military operation when the boats were in plain view in the center of a busy civilian port, with ferryboats docking alongside and apartments overlooking the quay. The boats would have to leave fully loaded with fuel for the first stage of their journey, but filling their tanks with fifty tons of oil would make the vessel sink perceptibly in the water. This could alert the French to the possibility that the Israelis were planning to embark on a long voyage. The solution arrived at was to take the boats out every day for "testing" and idle beyond the horizon for several hours. Upon returning they would take on the amount of fuel that would normally have been expended in high-speed runs. The boats thus sank lower in the water each day, but at an imperceptible rate.

An unexpected problem manifested itself one morning early in December when a *gendarme* presented himself on the quay and asked to speak to the officer in charge. Residents of the nearby apartment buildings, he said, were complaining that they had been disturbed the previous night by the sound of engines. The Israeli officer explained that a generator had been started up to provide heating for crewmen aboard. The *gendarme* accepted the explanation, which happened to be true, but the incident troubled the Israelis. If a single generator had caused a stir, what would happen on Christmas Eve, when each of the five boats ignited four powerful engines? Would this not waken the neighborhood and lead to immediate calls to the police and the French naval authorities? The Israelis decided on a Pavlovian approach. Generators were started up each of the nights that followed, first one, then two, then more. They were positioned with their exhausts facing the town. For the first few days the police came to pass on complaints, but then they stopped coming. Either the neighbors had learned to live with the noise or the police with their complaints. As one of the *gendarmes* had said, "As long as the windows are closed in winter it can't be too bad."

Parallel to the field preparations, the cover operation was weaving its complex cloak of legal obfuscation. At the request of the French authorities, Limon had sent a letter to Amiot on December 8 formally waiving Israel's claims to the boats. Siemm came to Paris to sign an agreement with Aimot whereby Starboat would refund the money to Israel directly rather than pay Amiot and have the latter return the money to Israel. This would spare Amiot the threat of subsequent prosecution for illegally transferring money abroad if the fictitious nature of the deal were uncovered and an angry government were looking for revenge. Siemm sent Amiot a letter on December 17 asking him to inquire of the Israelis if they would be willing to have their crews sail the five boats to their first destination, since there was little time to train Norwegian crews in the operation of the high-powered craft. This letter—which, like all the others, was drafted by Limon himself—provided an explanation, if one was demanded, of why Israeli crews were aboard the boats after the transfer of ownership. The formal sale did not take place until December 22 in Paris, with the participation of Siemm, Amiot, and Limon. Two contracts were signed in Amiot's office in Paris—one formally canceling the original contract by which Israel had purchased the boats, and another by which Starboat purchased them from Amiot at the same price.

The coup came the next day, when the parties met again to put their signatures to a series of secret documents that undid everything they had signed the day before. This time Siemm signed a contract with his old friend Mordecai Friedman as head of the Netivai Neft oil-exploration company, in which Starboat agreed to lease to Netivai Neft five boats that would assist in the search for oil in Israel's offshore waters. The lease was for three years, with an option to renew for three years. Somewhere in the fine print was a sentence giving the undersigned purchaser the option to purchase the above-mentioned boats within three months of delivery. In other words, the boats whose sale to Israel had been banned by the French government and whose sale to Norway had been approved were now being leased by the Norwegian purchaser to an Israeli company that would shortly have the right to purchase them outright. Unlike the contracts signed the day before, this agreement would of course not be shown to the French government—not unless the boats' arrival in the eastern Mediterranean became an issue requiring legal explanation.

Limon signed a letter to Siemm nullifying the contract of December

22 in which Siemm had undertaken to pay Israel for the boats. "We disengage you," said the letter, "from all contractual responsibility." Amiot and Limon jointly signed a document stating that the contract nullification signed by Limon on behalf of the Israel Defense Ministry's purchasing mission on December 22, wherein Israel waived its rights to the boats, was itself nullified, and that the original contract for the boats signed by Limon and Amiot in 1965 was still in effect. Siemm signed a letter to Netivai Neft notifying it that the leasing deal was nullified because the boats were the property of the Israeli government. These internal documents were designed as reassurances among the parties that none would ever attempt to make claims against the others on the basis of the fictitious dealings.

Thus, in a dazzling display of legal hocus-pocus, Limon had effectively brought the boats through the French embargo; on paper at least he had done it "not illegally."

The boats now had to be gotten away before the French started reading between the lines.

The Israeli destroyer *Eilat*, first victim of the naval missile age. *Bamahane*

Admiral Mordecai Limon upon his appointment as navy commander. *Israel Government Press Office*

Hadar Kimche, after promotion to admiral. *Bamahane*

Top right: Limon (in dark glasses) with French and Israeli naval officers and wives of French officials at a launching ceremony at Amiot shipyards. *Haim Shachak*

Right: Félix Amiot, flanked by wives of Israeli naval officers, addresses the Israeli naval contingent in Cherbourg at a festive dinner at his estate following the launching of one of the twelve boats built in his shipyard. Such dinners were a regular postlaunch event. *Moshe Tabak*

Right: The crew of one of the missile boats at a parade prior to a launching. At high tide the vessel would be pushed stern-first on a wooden cradle along tracks running out into the harbor, until it floated free. *Moshe Tabak*

Left: A newly launched boat, festooned with flags, ignites engines as it floats free of the cradle, not visible below the surface. *Moshe Tabak*

Four of the five last boats tied up in Cherbourg after the launching of the fourth, still flag-bedecked, in October 1969. The last boat would be launched two months later. *Haim Shachak*

Commander Moshe Tabak, who supervised the sea testing of most of the boats, unveils the plaque for the last one, the *Hetz*, launched December 16, 1969, nine days before the flight of boats from Cherbourg. Because of the desire to maintain a low profile as the breakout neared, the Israeli contingent dispensed with the usual ceremony with invited guests and with women unveiling the plaque. The unveiling was left to Tabak, the longest-serving officer in Cherbourg, in an informal setting. *Moshe Tabak*

Société d'Armement Maritime
et de Transports
2 5, rue de Montevideo
PARIS 16e.

DEMANDE D'AUTORISATION D'EXPORTATION
DE MATERIEL DE GUERRE

Pays de destination
          NORVEGE

Désignation du Destinataire
          STARBOAT, S.A.
          Oil and Shipping Services
          P.O. Box 2578 Solli - OSLO 2 - Norvège

Nom, Profession et Adresse

    a) - de l'Expéditeur
          Société d'Armement Maritime et de
          Transports - 26, rue de Montevideo
          PARIS (16e).

    b) - du Pétitionnaire
          Société d'Armement Maritime et de
          Transports - 26, rue de Montevideo
          PARIS (16e).
          Monsieur MAURICE - 870.08.77

Date de la décision concédant
l'autorisation de vente
          0.84409/DMA/DAI/42 DR
          du 3 Décembre 1969

Nom et adresse du Transitaire
          Agence Maritime DESHAYES & Cie
          20 bis, rue Alfred Rossel
          50: - CHERBOURG

Désignation du matériel exporté

    a) - Nature
          5 Vedettes Rapides auxiliaires aménagées
          en bateaux de servitude pour les instal-
          lations de forage en mer. (non armés militairement)

          Déplacement moyen essais : 219,500 t
          Déplacement en charge   : 240,000 t
          Jaugeage brut total   : 239,000 t
          Jaugeage brut   : 221,000 t

    b) - Modèle
          Coque acier

    c) - Nombre
          Cinq

d) - Nomenclature détaillée   Feuilles d'armement à bord des Vedettes

e) - Déplacement lège   198,400 tonnes

f) - Valeur en US Dollars   2,025,000 US$ par navire No. 405.000 U.S

g) - Bureau de Douanes où
    l'opération sera effectuée   50 - CHERBOURG

h) - Date d'expédition   Avant le 31 Janvier 1970

i) - Motif de l'expédition

Date, Signature et cachet du Pétitionnaire

PARIS, le 8 Décembre 1969

SOCIÉTÉ d'ARMEMENT MARITIME
ET DE TRANSPORTS
26, Rue de Montévidéo
PARIS-16e

Avec acquit-à-caution garantissant l'arrivée
à destination et la mise à la consommation

Autorisé 4848

Paris, le 18 DEC. 1969
Le Chef du Bureau E/4
Par autorisation
Le Secrétaire d'Administration

J. MARTI

5 Vedettes
ff 3011 o du 23-12-5

The request for the export license for the five last Cherbourg boats gives their destination as the Starboat Company in Oslo. The entry under "Nature" cites their intended use as servicing offshore oil installations. The departure date is given as "before January 31, 1970." The customs official who signed the document, J. Marti, surmised that the boats were destined for Israel, not Norway.

RECONNAISSANCE DU SERVICE DES DOUANES

DÉTAIL DE LA VÉRIFICATION (2)

Dénombré .... colis

Fait ouvrir : colis n°

　　　　　　colis n°

　　　　　　colis n°

Fait sonder : camion ⎫
　　　　　　　　　　 ⎬ n°
　　　　　wagon ⎭

Prélevé .... échantillons sur colis n°

CERTIFICAT DE VISITE

Bon à exporter

Le　24. 12. 69

L'Inspecteur,

VU (2)　　passer à l'étranger

embarquer sur

À l'exception des colis ci-après

A

Certificat de Visite. The certificate granted by a Cherbourg customs agent on December 24, 1969, a few hours before the boats stole away. The agent's verification that all the material imported to France for the boats' construction was installed in the vessels was the last document needed to make the departure "not illegal."

CONFIDENTIEL DÉFENSE

R.G. CHERBOURG
- n° 9 -

AuB

20 Décembre 1969

- NOTE DE RENSEIGNEMENTS -

Objet : Matériel militaire à destination d'Israël.

Les Etablissements AMIOT de Cherbourg (constructions navales) ont été chargés de construire une série de vedettes garde-côtes pour le compte de l'état israélien. La dernière vedette de cette série vient d'être mise à l'eau.

Actuellement, cinq de ces vedettes sont mouillées dans la darse transatlantique du port de Cherbourg. Elles font l'objet des mesures d'embargo sur le matériel militaire à destination d'Israël.

Selon des renseignements qui nous sont parvenus ces vedettes quitteraient prochainement Cherbourg de "façon légale". Elles feraient l'objet d'une vente fictive à un pays de l'Europe du Nord et gagneraient Israël par la suite.

adressé au DCRG
Paris
le 20 -12-69

A confidential French police memo five days before the boats' secret departure notes that the last of the five embargoed boats has been floated. "According to the information we have received, these vessels will soon depart from Cherbourg in a 'legal fashion.' They are the object of a fictitious sale to a Northern European country and will subsequently reach Israel." This report, however, apparently did not reach Paris before officials left on their Christmas holiday.

ORIGINE			EXPÉDITION				RÉFÉRENCE		CLASSEMENT	
DÉPARTEM.	POSTE	COTE SOURCE | SERVICE	NATURE	DATE	EXEMPLAIRES NOMBRE | N°	ENREGISTREM.	ENREGISTREM.	DATE	CATÉG.	DOSSI
50	2	2		31.12.69	11	736				

PIÈCES JOINTES	OBJET	DESTINATAIRES	
		MM. LE PRÉFET	1
		LE DIRECTEUR DES R.G.	3
		le Sous-Préfet	1
	Vedettes israéliennes	S.R.R.C.	2
		S.D.R.G.	2
		Archives	2
	− Cabinet −		

TIMBRE A L'ARRIVÉE

RÉSUMÉ

Celles-ci sont parties tous feux allumés. Les passeports de la colonie israélienne de Cherbourg auraic été régularisés tous les trois mois par l'Ambassade d'Israel à Paris.
Réactions diverses.

ENREGISTREMENT

DIFFUSION

1. Selon un témoin oculaire du départ des ved tes, le 25 Décembre, ces dernières sont parties tous feux allumés et à plein régime comme avaient l'habit de de le faire les équipages de ces vedettes lorsque celles-ci sortaient en mer pour effectuer leurs essa Ce témoin n'a pu préciser si ces vedettes avaient em prunté la passe Ouest ou la passe Est du port.

2. D'autre part, selon un renseignement que nous n'avons pu encore vérifier, le chef de la missi permanente israélienne opérait tous les 3 mois un ra sage des passeports des Israéliens présents à Cherbo et les faisait parvenir à l'Ambassade d'Israel à Paris. Cette dernière faisait régulariser les passeports.

COTE D'EXPLOITATION

CLASSEMENT

OBSERVATIONS

3. Les journalistes de la presse parisienne, des radios périphériques et de la Télévision italienn étaient présents le 30.12.1969 à Cherbourg.

Ils ont réalisé des enregistrements auprès des personnalités suivantes :

− M. HEBERT, Député-Maire de Cherbourg, qui a réaffirmé son hostilité à l'embargo.

Interviewé par le correspondant de l'RAI, le docteur HEBERT a, sur le mode ironique, traité de la concurrence entre les Chantiers Amiot et les chantier italiens, rappelé que les Italiens devaient armer

...../...

A secret police report by the Renseignements Généraux to the French Cabinet holding a special meeting on December 31, 1969, to discuss the flight of the Cherbourg boats. It quotes an eyewitness as saying that the boats left with all lights on, as when departing on routine test runs. The report cites "the ironic manner" in which Dr.

les vedettes qui sont parties et mentionné la qualité
des vedettes construites à Cherbourg.

- M. MICHEL, Président de la Chambre de Comme
de Cherbourg, qui a indiqué que s'il y avait des respons
bles, "c'est dans les Ministères qu'il faut les recherche
et a exprimé son inquiétude de voir retomber "sur un
lampiste" les conséquences de l'opération.

- M. LEVEQUE, transitaire en douane, qui a
effectué les transactions en douanes pour le compte de
la Société AMIOT, qui a réaffirmé la régularité de toute
les opérations effectuées à Cherbourg.

4. Dans le chapitre des réactions, notons l'
envoi d'une lettre de M. MARIGNY, secrétaire fédéral du
P.S.U. au journal local "La Presse de la Manche". Dans
cette lettre, M. MARIGNY s'étonne que "La Presse de la
Manche" n'ait abordé le problème des vedettes que le lun
29 décembre, puis il rappelle la position du P.S.U.
concernant l'embargo.

La rédaction de "La Presse de la Manche", sou
la signature de M. GIUSTINIANI, Directeur du journal,
répond assez sèchement à M. MARIGNY, en faisant état d'u
accord tacite passé entre la maison AMIOT et les représe
tants de la presse locale, ces derniers ayant accepté de
faire preuve de discrétion sur le problème des vedettes
israéliennes, pour ne pas "gêner la principale industrie
privée de Cherbourg".

A ce sujet, il faut préciser que les journali
tes locaux n'ont eu connaissance du départ des vedettes
qu'en fin d'après-midi, le 26 décembre.

M. LEMESLE, correspondant d'Ouest-France, a
passé l'information à son journal dans la soirée, et à
l'Agence France-Presse dont il est le correspondant,
seulement après minuit pour laisser à son journal la pri-
meur de l'information.

Il semble que "La Presse de la Manche" ait eu
également cette information, mais que ce journal ait res-
pecté l'accord passé avec la maison AMIOT.

Pour expliquer ceci, il faut mentionner que
M. GIUSTINIANI, Directeur de "La Presse de la Manche", a
des relations personnelles avec M. Félix AMIOT.

Hébert, the mayor of Cherbourg, referred to the episode
in interviews with the media, and notes his opposition to
the embargo. It notes that the editor of *La Presse de la
Manche,* the Cherbourg newspaper that had refrained
from mentioning the boats' existence, was personally
connected to the shipyard owner.

RÉPUBLIQUE FRANÇAISE

DIRECTION GÉNÉRALE
DE LA SURETÉ NATIONALE

CHERBOURG LE 29 DÉCEMBRE 1969

COMMISSARIAT CENTRAL
DE POLICE DE CHERBOURG

N° **15 0 5 4**

LE COMMISSAIRE PRINCIPAL
COMMISSAIRE CENTRAL DE POLICE DE CHERBOURG

à

Monsieur le SOUS-PREFET de CHERBOURG

OBJET : A/S des Vedettes Israéliennes.

    Conformément à vos instructions, j'ai l'honneur de vous rendre compte de ce que les Vedettes Israéliennes ne faisaient pas , en cette période, l'objet d'une surveillance toute particuliére.

    Cependant les patrouilles de routine de surveillanc de la voie publique, la nuit, avaient pour consigne de passer sur le quai pour s'assurer s'il n'y avait rien de suspect dan les environs du point d'amarrage des Vedettes.

    Le nombre des passages des patrouilles était varia suivant les servitudes, de une à trois (quelquefois quatre) par nuit.

    La nuit du 23 au 24 décembre quatre passages ont é effectués aux heures suivantes : 23 h.30 - I h. - 3 h. 30 et 5 h.30.

    La nuit du 24 au 25 décembre, deux passages ont ét effectués aux heures suivantes : 23 h. et I heure (le person a été ensuite requis pour différentes interventions au "Casin et au " Club")/

    Informé à 17 heures , le 25 décembre, par les ser vice des Renseignements Généraux du départ des Vedettes Isr liennes, je n'ai pas jugé utile de vous prevenir, sachant que les faits avaient été déja portés à votre connaissance.

LE COMMISSAIRE PRINCIPAL
COMMISSAIRE CENTRAL.

R. CAMBOULIVES

Mod. 6431

The report by the Cherbourg police chief to the sub-prefect of Cherbourg after the government launched an inquiry into the boats' escape. He notes that police patrols made routine checks of the pier at which the Israeli boats were tied. On the nights before their flight, four checks were made, including at 3:30 and 5:30 A.M. On Christmas Eve, however, the latter two checks were not made, because the patrol had to deal with problems at two night spots.

Top right: A sailor aboard the first of five boats arriving from Cherbourg prepares to throw the line as the boat docks at Haifa. *Israel Government Press Office*

Above: The commander in civilian dress on the bridge of *Starboat Two* gives docking orders as his vessel moors in Haifa. *Israel Government Press Office*

Top left: Photographers' floodlights illuminate the Saars upon their arrival from Cherbourg on New Year's Eve, 1970. *Israel Government Press Office*

Above: Captain Ezra Karshinsky (Karish) faces the press in Haifa upon his arrival with the Cherbourg boats. Reporters were led to believe that he was the commander of the operation. The true commander, Captain Hadar Kimche, remained incognito for security reasons. *Israel Government Press Office*

10
Countdown

The *Lea* had weighed anchor December 15 with a cargo of phosphates for European destinations and eight navy men jammed into the crew's quarters along with the regular crew. The newcomers included radiomen, a diver, and mechanics who would join the Saars at the rendezvous point. The ship's radio was normally manned for only one watch, but the additional radiomen would permit round-the-clock monitoring. Five days later, the *Dan* sailed out of Haifa harbor.

The first of the crew members detailed to Cherbourg would not leave Israel until a few days before the boats' scheduled departure, in order to reduce the risk that the tripled Israeli presence would be felt in the town. The men were to travel in small groups, with orders to draw no attention to themselves and to sit apart on the plane.

To prevent their inadvertently leaking the escape plan, the sailors had been told that an agreement for release of the boats was imminent. It was, they were warned, a delicate matter that could be wrecked by publicity. They were thus made aware that discretion was required without being alerted to the true nature of the operation.

Lieutenant Haim Geva, assigned as navigation officer on the command boat, had been told that he would lead the first contingent of eight crewmen to Cherbourg. His group was to fly to Germany and rent a minibus. Other groups would fly to other European countries and do likewise. A few hours before the boats' departure time, according to the plan, their vehicles would converge on Cherbourg.

A week before Christmas, Geva was summoned by Karish.

"Listen, Haim, there's a change in plans. You and your group are leaving tomorrow, and you're flying straight to Paris. From there you'll take the overnight train to Cherbourg. I'll be going with you."

"We don't have our passports yet," said Geva.

"You'll have them by tomorrow," said Karish.

That night Geva and his men, all supplied with passport photos, were driven to the Interior Ministry office in Haifa, which had been opened especially to issue them passports. Early the next morning, they boarded a scheduled El Al flight to Paris. They were dressed in civilian clothing topped by heavy civilian windbreakers, purchased for them in a downtown Haifa store, against the cold of Europe. Each sailor carried a uniform in his luggage, in the event that circumstances dictated assuming a naval identity. Also in their luggage were batteries, walkie-talkies, and spare parts needed by the boats in Cherbourg.

Lieutenant Commander Gadi Ben-Zeev, who was to command one of the boats, was aboard the same flight. At Orly Airport in Paris, the French-speaking officer led the group to the passport-control line. The French immigration official studied Ben-Zeev's Israeli passport and glanced past him at the young men in blue jackets lined up behind him. "What kind of group are you?" he asked.

"Students," said Ben-Zeev.

"Come off it," said the passport officer, who knew that the bronzed and purposeful faces before him were not for cloistered studies destined.

When Geva presented his passport, the passport officer addressed him in a language that was as startling as his question. "Are you military?" he asked in Hebrew.

"No, why do you ask that?"

"Because the passports are all numbered consecutively, you've all got fresh haircuts, and you're all wearing the same kind of jackets."

Geva called out to the sailors who had passed through and were waiting for him beyond the control officer, "Everyone who's finished, leave the airport." There was a chance, he felt, that some might get away before the *gendarmes* closed in.

"Take it easy," said the passport officer, and identified himself as a

Moroccan Jew who had lived for some time in Israel. "You've done nothing illegal. But you ought to tell your superiors about this."

If the operation had been mounted by the Mossad, such mistakes would doubtless have been avoided, but the navy was unschooled in conspiratorial techniques, particularly at border-crossing points far from the sea.

Karish, who was aboard the same flight, came through the arrivals gate lugging a suitcase heavy with radar parts. He saw Kimche waiting in the crowd and started toward him, but the flotilla commander deliberately walked past without offering any sign of recognition.

In Paris, the men made their way to the offices of the purchasing mission at 120 Boulevard Malesherbes. There they were given train tickets to Cherbourg and a final briefing. They would sit in twos or threes in the front or rear cars and speak no Hebrew.

When the train arrived in Cherbourg, the men were met by members of the Israeli naval mission and taken directly to the port. Most were lodged aboard the boats; some were put up with the Israeli families. To keep their presence from being noticed, they were ordered not to leave the boats and to minimize their presence topside. It was imperative that the local population not become aware of the sudden tripling of the Israeli contingent.

Supply Officer Shachak, avoiding the ship's chandlers who normally provisioned the boats, visited groceries and butcher shops all around town to purchase supplies in small quantities. When placing orders, he used his original name, Steinmetz, so as to obscure his Israeli connection.

Kimche, who had returned to Cherbourg a few weeks earlier, had chosen Boat Number Eight, the *Soufa*, as his flagship. Navigation Officer Geva, as soon as he settled in, began compiling a weather map of the Channel and the Bay of Biscay by recording meteorological reports on French radio and the BBC. This time there would be no peeking at the French navy's weather maps. A powerful storm was moving in toward Europe from the central Atlantic. If it turned northeast over England, the boats would be able to sail with the wind behind them. If it continued west to strike southern France, a barometric trough would be cutting across the planned escape route and creating headwinds impossible for the small vessels to sail into. If that happened, departure would have to be postponed to the next night or, more likely, to New Year's Eve.

It was impossible to conceal for long the presence of eighty men in a small town, or to camouflage the preparations being made. Every day's delay increased the risk of discovery. The danger was strongest at the shipyard, whose workers were in a position to note the odd goings-on. Most were friendly, but a few had displayed anti-Semitic sentiments in the past. A giveaway could come from a chance remark to the corner grocer by one of the Israeli wives, or from activities spotted by neighbors. Members of the permanent mission were told not to sell cars or make any other visible preparations for departure. The crew members had not been told of the planned departure date, but its imminence was plain. Those sailors still permitted to go to town were warned not to drop any hint of departure to girlfriends or others.

The head of the police Renseignements Généraux (RG) in Cherbourg, J. P. Havard, had learned in mid-December of the boats' planned departure, from his counterpart in the naval arsenal, the commander of naval security. The departure alluded to was apparently the Norwegian solution hinted at by Defense Minister Debré during his visit to the arsenal on December 14.

The RG is the intelligence arm of the police, dealing not with criminal matters but the broad scope of human affairs that might be termed political, including student unrest and labor problems. The Israeli boats had become a political matter. The commander of naval security told Havard that the boats would sail sometime after January 1, because the last boat had been launched December 16 and at least fifteen days were needed for testing. However, Havard had been informed of unusual activity on the boats, and he began making discreet inquiries. On the night of December 19, he learned from one of his sources that something unusual was indeed brewing, and not merely the sale alluded to by Debré. In a confidential memo sent the next day to his superiors under the title "Military Material Destined for Israel," he reported that "According to information we have received, the *vedettes* will shortly be leaving Cherbourg in a 'legal fashion.' They will be the object of a fictitious sale to a Northern European country and subsequently reach Israel."

It was on a Friday that the memo was drafted and dispatched. The fate of the boats could depend on how far upward in the bureaucracy that memo wended in the three working days officially left before Christmas. During this period, many key officials would be slipping away early for an extended holiday period.

Gadi Ben-Zeev had been asked by Limon to stay on in Paris to receive the reinforcements arriving from Israel and guide them on their way. The last group arrived on December 22. It was led by the flotilla's medical officer, Dr. Dory Horer. There were several hours to kill before the next Cherbourg train at 4:00 P.M., and Ben-Zeev acceded to Horer's request for his group to make a shopping expedition to the Galerie Lafayette. Ben-Zeev himself boarded the 4:00 P.M. train, but when he descended in Cherbourg he saw none of the other Israelis getting off, fore or aft. With departure due in two days, his report on the missing men caused deep concern at Kimche's headquarters. Every crewman was needed on the shorthanded boats, and it would be dangerous to undertake the long, arduous voyage without a doctor.

Horer was oblivious to the urgency of the situation. He knew they would be taking the boats from Cherbourg, but he believed it was a legal operation. The clandestine measures urged upon them seemed to Horer exaggerated. Ascertaining that there was another train at midnight, he decided that he and his group would spend a few extra hours in Paris. It was not every day one had such an opportunity, and the urbane, Rumanian-born doctor was determined to make the most of it. Checking their bags at the train station, he led his merry troupe toward the Champs-Elysées.

On the midnight train to Cherbourg, Horer did not bother splitting the men into different compartments. They sat together and chatted openly in Hebrew. A tight-lipped reception committee awaited them when they alighted. The men were hustled aboard the boats and Horer taken to the mission's headquarters. A furious Karish confronted him. Kimche was there, too, but he left the dressing-down to his deputy. "If it were any other officer," shouted Karish, "I would jail him." The doctor was ordered aboard the boats and told to stay there.

Ben-Zeev, meanwhile, was working round the clock to prepare Boat Number Eleven for sailing. Launched two months before, it was permeated with the smell of fresh paint and was far from ready. The aperture into which the deck gun would fit was still not watertight; the vessel lacked water, maps, and other essentials; and, except for his chief machinist, the officers and crew had no missile-boat experience and had to be intensively drilled.

Fueling of the vessels was nearing completion. The driver of the fuel truck, who brought a supply every other day, asked Supply Officer Shachak if he could absent himself for several days following Christmas and make up for it by bringing extra supplies in the two days before Christmas. Shachak was pleased to oblige.

On December 21, Kimche left the Cherbourg operation in the trustworthy hands of Karish and Tabak and caught the last flight out of Paris for London. He met that night with the Israeli naval attaché in a rendezvous kept secret even from the Israeli ambassador. Kimche informed the attaché of the pending escape and told him that he must inform no one, including the ambassador. On Christmas Eve, the attaché would remain on standby at his home. If the boats encountered difficulties after leaving Cherbourg, they might attempt to take shelter in British waters, probably in the lee of the Isle of Wight. If that happened, the attaché would be notified. He would then waken the ambassador and explain the situation to him, so that he could intervene if necessary with the British authorities. Until then the ambassador, like Ambassador Eytan in Paris, had best be kept uninformed, so as not to blemish his diplomatic integrity. Kimche caught the first plane back to Paris in the morning and returned by train to Cherbourg.

Micha Zand, a burly naval reservist, flew into Antwerp from Israel at the beginning of Christmas week and made his way directly to the Zim offices downtown, which served as the shipping agency's headquarters for Northern Europe. The manager had been informed of his coming and instructed by the home office in Haifa to comply with any request Zand would make.

"I want a list of all the ships you have in European ports at the moment," said Zand.

There were four ships—in England, Germany, Holland, and Antwerp itself. The last was the *Netanya*, a five-thousand-ton freighter that Zand knew to be a stable ship capable of speed.

"I'm going to be taking the *Netanya* to sea today," he told the astonished manager. "I can't tell you why. It'll be back in a few days." He then asked the manager to step out of his own office so that Zand could talk privately with Haifa on the phone.

A former naval officer and former Zim captain, Zand was now a shipping agent in Ashdod. He had been summoned to naval headquarters earlier in the month in his capacity as a reserve officer and briefed about the Cherbourg operation. Headquarters had decided to post a ship at the northern end of the Bay of Biscay to take in tow any Saars that might break down. This would reduce the risks during the critical first stage of the breakout, when the boats would be farthest from home. There was no naval ship capable of such a mission, but a suitable merchant vessel would be mobilized for the occasion. In addition, all Zim vessels sailing between Israel and Europe close to Christmas would be ordered to alter course as needed in order to provide a chain of potential mother ships for any of the small boats in trouble.

Stevedores were loading cargo into the *Netanya* when Zand arrived on the docks. He boarded the ship and knocked on the door of the captain's cabin. It was a former naval colleague who opened it.

"What are you doing here?" asked the captain.

"We're going to sea," said Zand. "Get your ship ready."

Zand explained that it was a security matter but did not go beyond that. The captain did not ask for written authorization. He contacted the harbor authorities to request a pilot and told the stevedore-crew chief that no more cargo would be loaded after the present shift ended. Zand checked on the towing cables and found them intact. Shortly after noon, the *Netanya* cast off and put out to sea.

The five Saar captains gathered in Moshe Tabak's apartment the night of December 23 for a final rundown. Kimche and Karish were there, too. Esther provided coffee and cake and discreetly withdrew.

The softspoken Kimche inspired total confidence among his officers. He projected thoughtfulness and self-assurance, and his every word carried weight. To his superiors, his restraint and lack of visible emotion could sometimes be unnerving. Karish was a flamboyant, hard-drinking seaman respected by his colleagues as a superlative sailor. During his initial stay in Cherbourg he had frequently played bridge with the French admiral commanding the arsenal, and adapted with gusto to the French life-style. When Boat Number One was undergoing its tests in Cherbourg, Karish had personally tested the galley by preparing a gourmet lunch for shipyard executives in the CIC. Tabak was the steady force who had been holding things together at Cherbourg in Kimche's absence for most of the past year. He had been responsible for the testing and acceptance of the Saars for the past two years. His warm home was an anchor for the young officers of the naval mission who would generally join the Tabaks for Sabbath dinner. They felt so at

home that they would sometimes invite foreign seamen and inform
Esther on Friday that there would be extra guests for dinner that night.

Kimche told the captains that departure would be at 8:00 P.M. the
next night. Careful inquiry into the town's Christmas Eve routine had
shown that Cherbourg's citizens would be sitting down to their holiday
dinner at that hour. Food supplies and spare parts would be brought
aboard the boats after dark. Kimche would sail aboard Number Eight,
the *Soufa*, Karish aboard Number Nine, and Tabak aboard Number
Twelve. They would provide experienced backup for the young captains during what promised to be a stormy passage. Kimche was especially worried about Number Twelve, which had endured only a few
hours of sea tests. If worse came to worst, it might be necessary to put
into some port along the way, even at the risk of being impounded. If
challenged, any boat forced into port would attempt to brazen it out by
claiming to be one of the first five Cherbourg boats, which had departed legally more than a year before. Each of the captains had been
provided with papers providing such an alternative identity. If they
adopted this guise, they would claim to be on a westward journey from
Haifa.

The ship's lockers also contained Panamanian and Norwegian flags,
to be used as circumstance dictated. Tabak had seen to it that the boats
bore wooden name plates identifying them as *Starboat One* to *Starboat
Five*. These had been fitted over the plaques bearing their respective
Hebrew names—*Soufa, Gaash, Herev, Hanit,* and *Hetz*. The boats
would take to sea flying no flags at all and with luck would have to fly
none till they reached Haifa. They carried no weapons, but they would
bluff their way home if they had to.

The fueling arrangements were the captains' main concern. Not yet
drilled in fueling a missile boat at sea, they listened intently as Karish
spelled out the system that had been developed during the trials in the
previous weeks with the *Lea* and the *Dan*.

Since only two of the vessels were equipped with radios, communication between the boats would be with the hand-held radios brought
from Israel. Their range of several kilometers should be sufficient. In
order to preserve their batteries, they would be activated only after the
boat wishing to communicate flashed its signal light.

Tabak asked the officers whether anything more was needed. Karish
and one of the captains asked if the galleys would be stocked with meat
or just canned goods.

"Really, fellows," said Tabak, "is that what's worrying you now?"

A more practical question was how to execute their very last act in Cherbourg—starting engines. Each boat had four engines, with a total of fourteen thousand horsepower. Starting up even one boat in the quiet of the night would make a holy racket. Igniting seventy thousand horsepower all at once would sound like the End of Days. The officers decided that it was better to start the engines simultaneously than to have a series of eruptions. They would hope that the good burghers of Cherbourg would be too filled with holiday spirit to take notice.

There was some speculation about whether the French Mediterranean fleet based in Toulon would attempt to intercept them after they had passed Gibraltar. Kimche did not think so. Civilized countries did not attack boats of other countries—particularly in international waters, because of debatable legal technicalities. Kimche did not take into consideration that civilized countries can act like furious schoolboys when their noses are tweaked, especially by countries that are much smaller than they are.

A nation with half the population of New York City had staked out a thirty-two-hundred-mile escape route from the Atlantic to the eastern Mediterranean with a marshaling of resources and an organizational proficiency that major powers could envy. It had done it with a piratical flair that only a small country with a powerful will and a small margin for failure could muster. Contrary to virtually all subsequent accounts, Israel's secret service, the Mossad, was not involved in the operation. It was Limon who conceived it and the navy that organized it. It had been a sophisticated effort involving imaginative planning, tight security, and superb staff work. All that remained now was its execution.

11

Breakout

The sky was heavy when Hadar Kimche looked out his window in the morning, and the wind was whistling in thinly from the west like an insolent messenger. The storm that had been moving in from the Atlantic was almost upon them. Townspeople were hurrying to make their final arrangements for Christmas celebrations that evening before the storm hit. Kimche drove down to the port to see to his own preparations for the evening.

There was nothing in the appearance of the five vessels lashed to the dock in two horizontal rows to indicate anything unusual: few sailors were in sight and there was no activity visible. Kimche boarded the boats for a final inspection. The fuel tanks were brimming, communication equipment and lighting systems checked out, and first-aid equipment was in place. Three hundred batteries had been brought by the arrivals from Israel to power the hand-held radios that would serve for interboat communication. The boats had not yet received their sophisticated navigation equipment, but they would make do with gyros and sextants. Kimche found the men in buoyant spirits. They sensed that departure was imminent, but some of the young officers had nevertheless ordered tickets for the New Year's Eve party in the Café de Paris, on the off chance that they would still be around in a week.

Limon arrived from Paris before noon in a car driven by one of his aides. He checked into the Hôtel Sofitel overlooking the harbor, the one

126

modern hotel in town, and drove to the Café de Paris, his favorite Cherbourg restaurant, overlooking the fishing-boat anchorage. He was joined there for a seafood lunch by Kimche, Tabak, and Karish, all of them in civilian clothes. The four men drank a toast to the success of the operation. Limon extracted a check from a billfold in his inside jacket pocket and held it up for viewing. "Has any of you ever seen this much money?" he asked, handing it around. Drawn on a Swiss bank, it was for close to $5 million. It was to be given to Amiot as final payment that night, after the boats had departed. Amiot himself entered the restaurant shortly afterward and joined the Israelis.

The elderly industrialist would also be making his own preparations for the evening's denouement. He telephoned after lunch to his manager for the Saar project, André Corbinais, one of the two shipyard executives he had informed about the escape, and told him that he would be leaving town the next day and would be inaccessible. Corbinais presumed that Amiot would be weathering the impending storm at his retreat on the Riviera. The two wished each other Bonne Noël. Amiot's apartment in Cherbourg was in the former Hôtel Atlantique, overlooking the harbor. The hotel had thrived during the days of the great ocean liners, when Cherbourg was a major port of entry to the Continent. Now part of Amiot's shipyard, the building served mainly as a mechanical workshop. His apartment on the top floor had a floor-to-ceiling window overlooking the port. It was to this apartment that Amiot invited Marc Justiniani, editor of *La Presse de la Manche*, on this last day before Christmas.

Justiniani's paper was the larger of the two local dailies. He was not an intimate of Amiot, but the local magnate had been a schoolmate of his father-in-law, which lent a school-tie ambience to their relation. Amiot expressed his appreciation of the fact that the local press had avoided mention of the Israeli *vedettes* to date. Construction of the boats was now completed. However, the shipyard would receive final payment only after they had been delivered to their purchaser. This, Amiot indicated, was imminent. Would Justiniani see to it that nothing of the transaction appeared in the press? The publicity could be damaging to the shipyard and therefore the town.

Justiniani felt extremely uncomfortable. He well understood the importance of Amiot's shipyard to the town's economy and appreciated that the deal involved matters of sensitivity. But he did not control the press, he explained to Amiot—he could not dictate either to the opposition paper, *Oest-France*, or to the reporters on both papers who served as part-time correspondents for major newspapers and radio stations in Paris and elsewhere. Amiot asked him to do what he could. Before Justiniani printed anything, said Amiot, would he please call him or Monsieur Corbinais?

In the late afternoon, the local customs officer boarded the Israeli boats to make the final on-site check, in accordance with the clearance papers issued by the customs authorities in Paris. He joined his Israeli hosts in a holiday toast. As he walked through the boats, the customs official noted that there were no markings in Hebrew and that the only identification was the wooden *Starboat* name plates on both sides of each bridge—this in conformity with the papers he had in hand showing the boat's sale to the Oslo firm.

Karish had been living in Tabak's apartment and staying out of sight since his arrival earlier in the week, because he was a familiar face to many of the locals from his long stay in 1967. On this last day he permitted himself to venture out to see the town again and do some shopping.

He was recognized in the first shop he entered. "Have you come for the holiday, Commandant?" asked the proprietor.

In a candy shop, he asked for a large quantity of chocolates in small bags. "Holiday gifts for orphans," he explained.

It was important for the men to have food in their stomachs if they were to keep from being sick when they hit the open sea, and the young Israeli sailors liked chocolate. Karish carried a transistor radio to hear the weather reports, but the rain that had begun to lash the town boded ill. The gaily decorated streets were filled with people carrying shopping bags and gift-wrapped packages, hurrying head-down against the wind-driven rain.

With the departure of the shipyard workers for the day and the early onset of darkness, sailors swarmed up from below decks, to stow provisions brought down to the pier by the supply officer and his assistants, to tighten lines, lash down barrels, and complete final preparations for sailing. A few of the junior officers who had been stationed in Cherbourg for some time obtained permission to take some of their recently arrived colleagues to an early dinner at a seafood restaurant. Their intention was to demonstrate their newly acquired savoir-faire and introduce the newcomers to crusty, crawly things that usually appall Israelis brought up on kosher food. Some of the newcomers gamely picked at mixed seafood platters under the raucous prodding of the Cherbourg veterans, while others stuck to the bread. The newcomers got theirs back when the proprietor emerged from the kitchen to indicate gently to the "veteran" who had ordered the wine that he had chosen the wrong kind.

On their way back to the port, some of the officers piled into the salvaged wreck owned by Chief Engineer Avraham Nave. They had to push it first to get it started. The car was well known in town because of its muffler roar and its black door, which fitted oddly into an otherwise gray car. The car had no first gear or reverse and, as Nave discovered when he neared the quay, no gas, either. With departure from Cherbourg close, he had not filled the tank. The car stalled on a railroad track a few hundred yards from the dock, and they had to push it. Senior officers were impatiently waiting for them when they sprinted to the boats through the gusts lashing the waterfront. "Where have you been?" snapped Karish. "We're sailing at eight."

For Cherbourg residents the rain rattling their windows made home seem even snugger. Whatever wanderings of the heart Frenchmen may indulge during the year give way Christmas Eve to the embrace of the family. Dinner tables are graced with turkeys, and trimmed Christmas trees transform the living rooms. Most families have their main meal before going to church, but some make do with a light meal until after returning from church, when they sit down to oysters, foie gras, and similar delicacies. The loneliest man in Cherbourg on Christmas Eve is the naval lookout manning the observation post on the breakwater at the main entrance to the harbor.

Kimche's plan to make his getaway when the townspeople would be gathered around dinner tables deep in the bosoms of their families had been dashed by the early-evening weather forecast. The storm had become a Force Nine gale, in which even the captains of ten-thousand-ton freighters—forty times larger than the Saars—would be reluctant to put to sea. The barometric low was still heading west across their intended path. The next forecast, at 10:00 P.M., was just as discouraging. Unless the low turned north toward Scotland, there could be little hope of departure this night. The five captains had joined Kimche for this weather report; he told them to return for the midnight forecast.

Kimche still hoped the three-day-old storm might veer in the next few hours. Limon had joined him in the captain's cabin. Periodically radiomen entered with transcriptions of weather reports from a variety of sources. Additional radiomen and equipment had been brought over from other boats to reinforce the Soufa's radioman. They used an international handbook giving times and wavelengths of weather reports around the world. They monitored French radio and the British navy's weather service, but the main source was the BBC. Even the Cherbourg fishing fleet relied on the BBC, because the British tracking stations were farther west.

Late in the evening, Corbinais came down to the quay to see the boats off. The shipyard guard posted at the head of the pier flagged the executive down.

"I don't know what's happening," said the guard, "but there seems to be lots of activity on the boats."

Corbinais assured him that everything was in order. For Corbinais, a former French naval engineer, the Saar project had been an exceptional professional and personal experience, and this night of parting was laden with emotion. He admired the Israeli naval personnel and had learned much from them, particularly from Naval Architect Shahal, with whom he had worked closely. Shortly before eleven, Corbinais excused himself to drive to Trinity Church, elsewhere on the harborfront, for Mass. As the choir's voices soared at midnight in the fourteenth-century church, Corbinais added a prayer of his own: "May they reach safe harbor."

The message Kimche was getting from the heavens at that precise moment was not optimistic: the midnight forecast portended no change in the weather. The moment of decision was close at hand. To miss sailing this night might be a mere annoyance and a brief delay, or it might mean the loss of the boats, with all that that meant for the navy's future. Despite their caution, Kimche knew, it was not possible to cover completely the tracks of eighty additional men and the extensive preparations that had been made for departure. The likeliest alternative departure date was New Year's Eve, which meant keeping the men hidden for another week. It also meant more time for some suspicious French official to put together the loose ends the Israelis had inevitably left lying about, or for leaks to emanate from Frenchmen who knew or suspected that the boats would not be going to Oslo. The navy could lose half its missile flotilla to a single persistent gendarme. If the escape plot was uncovered, the miffed French would be unlikely to raise the embargo for a very long time.

On the other hand, the dangers of departure were real. The waves out there were twelve to fourteen meters high and the wind was over seventy kilometers an hour. To leave and then be forced back into harbor by the storm would most likely torpedo the entire operation—the French authorities would hardly regard the departure of the boats at midnight in the middle of a severe storm as a routine training exercise or an attempt to deliver them to Oslo. If the boats pressed on into the Bay of Biscay in the face of headwinds and towering waves, it was questionable whether all would make it across. Twenty-five years before, a storm in these same waters had faced General Eisenhower with the same kind of agonizing calculation about the launching of D-Day. He had in fact postponed the invasion by a day and then daringly decided to aim for a predicted clear-weather "window" on June 6. The scale of that decision had of course been immensely grander, but the poignancy of the dilemma for Kimche was not much less. He recalled the remarks attributed to a French general facing a critical decision. "I want you to be strong," the general told his men, "because fears and hesitations I have of my own."

There was no hesitation evident among Kimche's officers, who made it clear they were eager to sail if there was even a marginal chance. They pointed out that the first Saar, which had arrived in Israel shortly before the *Dakar* was reported missing a year before, had participated in the search for the submarine in a Force Seven gale, the severest the eastern Mediterranean normally sees, and had ridden out the storm well. But, for all their enthusiasm, Kimche knew they were awaiting his judgment. A military organization is not a democracy, and although Kimche might solicit his officers' opinions, the final decision was his alone. He would put it off, he concluded, until 2:00 A.M., but no later. If they waited for subsequent forecasts, there was no certainty they would be clear of French territorial waters before first light; he wanted to be well away in case of pursuit. Mulling over the midnight forecast, which had referred to severe gale-force winds, Kimche called for an English dictionary to see if "severe" was something less than serious. The dictionary offered no consolation.

The captain of the flagship, Lieutenant Commander Arye, who had been busy with the boat's preparations all day, suddenly remembered that he had forgotten to remove his own belongings from the hotel. Dashing down to the pier, where his car was still parked, he drove the few hundred meters to the hotel and ran up the stairs. He gathered up two huge dolls he had bought for his daughters—the main object of his concern—and whatever else he could grab, leaving a good part of his possessions behind as he flew out the door.

The captains did not return to their vessels after the midnight forecast but remained with Kimche in the crowded cabin, conversing quietly and drinking coffee. There were about ten people in the room; since only six could sit on the two benches straddling the table that jutted out from one end wall, the others stood. On the table lay the weather map, updated regularly by Lieutenant Geva. Periodically there would be a knock on the door and a radioman would enter and hand the navigation officer a sheet of paper with the latest weather bulletin. Nothing in Kimche's demeanor betrayed his tension. Limon, puffing on his pipe, said little, but his strong presence seemed to be willing the boats to sea. As the clock on the wall showed them slipping into the next day, Limon briefly abandoned his taciturnity and urged Kimche to leave this night. "If we who have such an interest in leaving are hesitating because of the weather," one of the officers present would later recall his saying, "then we can be sure no one will pursue."

The decision, however, was Kimche's alone. The lives of the crew and the fate of the boats were his responsibility, and neither Limon nor naval headquarters could order him to sail against his judgment. It was clear to him that he could not risk sailing unless the weather forecasters offered some hope of the storm's turning.

A loud "hello" from the dock momentarily broke the tension. The shipyard guard, who seemed to be slightly tipsy, had come down from the pier entrance to wish them a Merry Christmas. Returning from church a few minutes later, Corbinais told the guard he could go home: he did not want the man there when the boats sailed. Corbinais himself joined the officers in Kimche's cabin. At 1:00 A.M. a police car halted briefly at the head of the pier and then moved on. This was one of the routine checks made several times each night to guard against a Palestinian attack upon the boats.

A few moments after one-thirty a radioman entered with a weather bulletin just announced by the BBC for ships at sea. Sitting at the table, Kimche took the paper and read from it aloud. The wind was shifting from west to northwest, said the bulletin, and its speed was diminishing. The atmosphere in the small cabin instantly became electric. The storm was turning. Kimche calmed his captains: he wanted confirmation. It came on the 2:00 A.M. forecast given by both the BBC and the French radio. The wind was shifting toward the north.

Kimche looked up at his captains.

"We're sailing," he said.

Glancing up at the round brass clock on the wall, he set departure for two-thirty. The officers synchronized watches and dispersed to their vessels.

Limon clasped Kimche's hand. "Good luck," he said. Limon descended from the boat along with Corbinais and Supply Officer Shachak, who would be staying behind in Cherbourg to pick up the pieces.

As they waited in the rain on the pier, the supply officer said to Limon, "How lucky it was that they expelled us from the arsenal."

"From there, Haim, we wouldn't have gotten out."

The captains made a final survey of their boats to make sure that everything movable was lashed down. They rechecked navigation maps and spare parts as they went down the items on their presailing check lists.

On Boat Number Twelve, Tabak assembled his crew in the CIC. He could read on their faces both eagerness to get under way and concern at what awaited them outside the harbor.

"We're sailing at two-thirty," he announced. "We're going out into a stormy sea, and you may feel sick at the beginning. You all know what we came here for. Our success depends on you. To your stations."

His was the inboard boat in the rear row of Saars and would be the last to pull away. From the vessel's bridge he could see his own apartment two hundred yards behind him. Several figures were silhouetted in the windows of the living room. With his wife, Esther, were the Israeli fiancés of two of the officers and the wife of a third, all of whom had apartments in the same building.

Esther had come down to the quay early in the evening to bring him a pillow, something he could not sleep without. Her concern about the storm was apparent on her face, and Tabak's deputy, a strapping young officer, tried to jolly her: "As long as *we're* on the boat, there's nothing to worry about."

Tabak blinked a flashlight toward the apartment window in farewell. The lights in the apartment went on and off in reply.

At two-thirty Kimche's engines exploded into life. Tabak pressed the engine-room buzzer twice and his own engines thundered. The roar as the other boats joined in was so awesome that Esther Tabak was certain it could be heard all over Cherbourg. The acrid smoke pouring out of twenty exhausts smarted the eyes of the men on deck.

As Kimche's boat, inboard in the first row, slipped its lines, Shachak and Corbinais leaned into the wind and shouted *"Bon voyage"* over the noise. Someone on the bridge waved back. In the dim light from the streetlamp at the end of the pier Shachak could see tears on Corbinais's face. "There go four years of my life," said the Frenchman. Nearby, Limon stood silently.

Kimche's boat was the first to pull away. The others followed at evenly spaced intervals. Lieutenant Arye lit the mast lights so that those captains unfamiliar with the harbor could follow. Each vessel lit stern lights, embedded deep in their sockets so that the boat following had to be directly behind in order to keep the lights in view. Looking at the town falling astern, Kimche could see the familiar pattern of lights growing dimmer. An illuminated Christmas tree decorated a freighter they passed, but no movement could be seen on the deck.

The order to start engines had been greeted with applause by the crewmen below. Their long wait was over at last. Despite the security precautions that had marked the voyage of the eighty most recent crewmen to Cherbourg and kept them hidden aboard ship, the men had not been led to believe that anything illegal was involved.

Dr. Horer, who had gone to sleep early, was wakened by the blast of the engines. He made his way up to the deck to see the boat pulling away from the pier. It struck him as odd that they were going out on a training exercise without having been briefed beforehand.

"We're going home," an officer told him with a broad smile.

"You mean they've released us?" said Horer.

"We're escaping," said the officer.

The word quickly spread through the boats: They were not just sailing home. They were on the run.

From the pier, the boats' navigation lights were lost to view within a few minutes. Shachak and Corbinais walked to their vehicles, but Limon remained standing on the pier alone, the collar of his blue trench coat turned up against the rain. He wanted to be sure that the storm out in the Channel did not force one or more of the boats back to port. He waited half an hour before walking back to his car at the head of the pier.

There was still one more task to perform. At the nearby Hôtel Atlantique, he had to wait a few moments before hearing Amiot's sleepy voice respond to his knock. "*C'est moi, Félix, Mocca.*" Amiot was in a robe when he opened the door and ushered his visitor inside.

"I want to inform you," said Limon, "that the Starboat boats have sailed."

Amiot bowed his head and began weeping. Limon sensed the old man's relief that his contract had been honored. The Frenchman poured cognac into glasses and the two men toasted each other and the operation's success. Before turning to leave, Limon took his billfold out of his jacket pocket and handed Amiot the check for $5 million.

12

Running Free

The sea and wind rushed at them in the darkness as they emerged from the shelter of the Cherbourg breakwater, but the land mass of England to the west shielded them from the worst of the storm. The boats maintained the formation Kimche had spelled out before departure as they moved through the Channel—a column of three boats with the *Soufa* in the lead, and a parallel column of two. They attempted to stay a kilometer apart—far enough to avoid collisions but close enough to keep track of the next boat's mast lights. The wind was at their back, and long swells carried them down the Channel. It was not until they emerged into the Bay of Biscay that the sea's fury caught them. Mountainous seas thundered out of the west, where the storm had been raging for the past three days—waves as high as a three-story building foaming out of the blackness. From the northwest, to which the wind had shifted, came smaller waves moving very fast. The boats tossed dizzyingly in this cross-turbulence and were soon scattered over the sea's surface. Kimche ordered that no one venture out on deck unless secured by a line around his body and under the surveillance of an officer. Even for the most veteran sailors aboard, this was the worst ride of their lives.

On the bridge of the *Soufa*, Lieutenant Geva was serving the first watch as duty officer. Half an hour after departing from Cherbourg, he flashed the command vessel's signal light toward the other boats to alert them to a communications check. "This is number one," he said into his walkie-talkie. "Count off." The other four boats responded by predesignated number. When Geva checked again an hour later, there was no response from the *Herev*, at the rear of the two-boat column parallel to his. Geva asked the officers aboard the boats closer to the *Herev*'s position to attempt to raise it on their walkie-talkies, but the efforts were fruitless. Projector flashes likewise drew no response. Geva called down by telephone to the *Soufa*'s commander, Lieutenant Commander Arye.

"They can't be missing," said Arye when he reached the bridge. "Try them again." When all attempts failed, Kimche was summoned. Sleep was still heavy in the flotilla commander's eyes as he reached the bridge. "This is all we need," he said when he heard Geva's report. He ordered speed reduced and continuous attempts made to raise the *Herev* on the radio.

Aboard the *Herev*, Skipper Haim Shaked, soaked from exposure on the bridge, had gone below to change clothing. The storm had battered his vessel badly, knocking out its radar. As he pulled on dry clothing in his cabin, he sensed a change in the boat's motion: instead of pitching up and down, it was rocking from side to side. Either the waves had shifted direction or the boat had.

Shaked pulled on his oil slicker and raced up to the bridge, where he had left his deputy in charge. "What's happening?" asked Shaked.

The deputy was taken by surprise at his worried tone. He pointed at the stern light of the vessel some distance ahead of them, bobbing up and disappearing in the stormy waters as it had since they left Cherbourg. As soon as Shaked could focus on it, he knew they were in trouble. The Saars had two stern lights; the boat ahead had only one. Questioning his deputy, Shaked quickly grasped what must have happened. Another vessel, running for the French port of Brest, had cut through the scattered Israeli formation. His deputy, mistaking it for the lead Saar, had turned east to follow it.

Shaked altered course to the southwest and increased speed in an attempt to catch up. He tried to raise the other boats on his hand-held radio and flashed his signal light, but there was no reply. Only as dawn forced itself through the storm clouds did he see the other four boats moving slowly to the northwest. He had outrun them in the darkness, and hastened now to rejoin the formation.

Micha Zand had positioned the *Netanya* at the northern end of the Bay of Biscay on Christmas Eve. He spoke by radio telephone to Binny Telem in Haifa, who ordered him to cruise near the Ile d'Ouessant, west of Brest. The deputy navy commander, who was monitoring the operation from his home, informed Zand that there was a problem with the weather: the boats might not put out from Cherbourg this night. The officers and crew of Zand's commandeered freighter were still at a loss about their sudden departure and their seemingly aimless circling. Before he went to sleep, Zand informed the duty officer of the emergency wavelength to which the ship's radio had been turned. If there was any call, he was to be immediately wakened. Zand wakened on his own in the darkness and glanced at his watch. It was 4:00 A.M. The ship was pitching badly. On the bridge, the duty officer greeted him drowsily and said the radio had remained silent.

"A lot of small boats passed us in the night," said the officer offhandedly. "They were moving fast and heading south."

Zand permitted himself a trace of a smile and prayed that the radio would continue to transmit its silent message that all was well.

The mad roller coaster continued for the Saars as day lit the raging sea. Some bridge officers lashed themselves to their chairs. As the boats rose higher and higher toward the crest of a wave, a huge green wave would lunge from behind and crash just astern. Then the descent began, a stomach-turning downward rush in which the helmsman would begin to feel the wheel reluctant to respond as speed increased. When the boat plunged into the bottom of the trough, the surging sea brimmed the deck and seemed about to submerge it. Then the vessel somehow pulled itself loose and began its agonizing climb again. For the men on the bridge, it was an extraordinary and frightening sight. Below decks the crew would feel the boat shudder from the strain and wonder whether it would rise up out of the trough.

Except for an occasional terse order and the noise of the storm, there was almost total silence; most of the men were too sick to talk. Anyone venturing topside wore an oilskin over a heavy sweater and dungarees. The strain on the helmsmen fighting the wheel to keep on course required their frequent rotation. Instead of one crewman handling the throttles on the bridge, two men were assigned on the flagship by Lieutenant Commander Arye, because of the strain and the constant alterations of speed.

Each wave had to be played correctly if the boats were to avoid damage. Kimche stood on his bridge for hours with a stopwatch adjusting the boat's speed. If the propeller was turning too swiftly when the boat was descending a wave, the prow could be thrust into the water and control lost. If the boat was too slow in climbing out of the trough, tons of water would crash upon its stern. Kimche had hoped to sail at twenty-five to thirty knots, but this proved impossible. An average speed of eighteen knots was finally arrived at.

The constant changes of speed ordered by the bridge required quick and precise response from the engine room. Although most of the crew members were sick, they worked steadily, keeping buckets close to hand. Dr. Horer, who was himself never seasick, prayed that there would be no injuries that would require him or his medic to transfer to another boat in this sea. Chief Engineer Nave, on the command boat, periodically ascended to the bridge to see what was happening topside and to stare at the tumultuous sea. Kimche's face and voice were calm, but Nave could see the tension in the commander's clenched fists.

As navigation officer, it fell upon Lieutenant Geva to work out a course that would compensate for the winds buffeting them from the starboard quarter. The strongest such wind he had ever made a calculation for in his officers' course was thirty knots. The winds now were seventy knots. As the boats neared Cape Finisterre, jutting out from the Portuguese coast, he saw on the radar that his calculations had been several degrees off—the land mass loomed dead ahead. The boats turned into the wind in order to work their way around the cape.

The wind subsided somewhat on the second night, but the sea was still a fury. Kimche was too busy leading his storm-tossed flock to communicate with Haifa, and the tension in naval headquarters mounted. Messages began to pour in when the boats were off Portugal: "Where are you? Please report position. What is condition of boats and crews? What is fuel situation? Why have you not reported? Please reply." The radioman rapidly decoded the Morse signals, removed his earphones, and trotted up to the bridge with the written message. It was not just the navy command that was expressing concern but the General Staff and Defense Minister Dayan as well. The queries were coming in so fast that Kimche could not reply. He finally raised Telem at home on the radio telephone. "If you'll stop sending messages for a minute, I'll answer them," he said.

Periodically, as his vessel topped a wave, Kimche scanned the sea to check on the presence of the other boats. Unless they, too, were cresting a wave at that moment, he could not see their lights. It would sometimes take him more than ten minutes to account for all his charges.

In the sheltered bay on Portugal's southern coast where he had dropped anchor, Captain Amnon Tadmor had been following the progress of the storm on the radio since the early hours of Christmas Eve.

"Do you think they'll sail in this?" his chief mate had asked.

"I don't know," said Tadmor. "I wouldn't take the *Lea* out in this weather. And if I were out, I'd seek shelter." His ship was twenty times the size of the Saars. As he waited, he could pick up messages being sent from Haifa to other Zim ships along the boats' route. He himself made radio contact with his brother, who was serving as chief mate aboard one of the backup ships.

"What are you doing in the area?" asked the brother.

"I can't say," said Tadmor.

"Well, I think we're on the same business."

When Haifa informed him Thursday morning of the boats' departure, Tadmor ordered his radioman to raise Kimche on the naval frequencies assigned them by headquarters. Contact was made close to dusk on Friday, the 26th, a Morse message from the *Soufa* informing him that they had just rounded Cape Vincent, at the tip of Portugal. Tadmor informed Kimche of his precise location. It was 10:00 P.M. when he saw them rounding the corner of the bay five miles away—five small boats showing only navigation lights and moving fast.

The empty pier in Cherbourg had been noted on Christmas morning by residents of the adjacent apartment buildings but awakened no suspicions. The Israelis were taking boats out for testing all the time, and Christmas, after all, was not a Jewish holiday. Even their failure to return by the next morning—Friday, the 26th—failed to ruffle the pleasant postholiday torpor enveloping the town. Journalist René Moirand, who covered marine affairs for *La Presse de la Manche*, had still not heard about the boats' absence at six on Friday evening, when

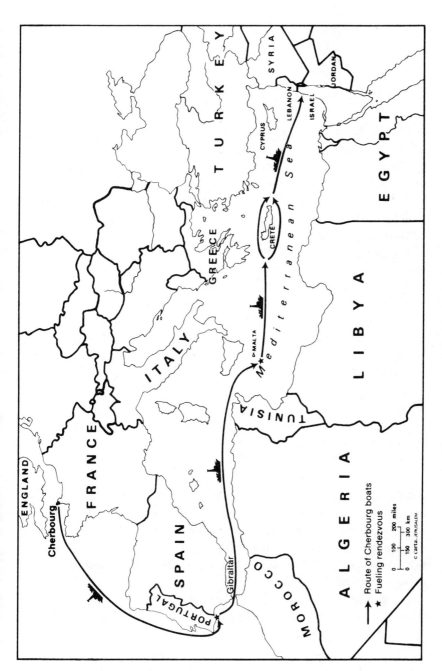

The escape route of the Cherbourg boats. *Carta*

he took his daughter to the family dentist for treatment of a toothache. The dentist was the distinguished looking Dr. Michel, president of the small Jewish community in Cherbourg. He seemed to Moirand unaccountably excited. As Moirand took off his coat, the dentist looked at him as if expecting the journalist to remark on something.

"You've seen?" Michel finally burst out. "They've gone."

When the elderly dentist saw the uncomprehending look on Moirand's face, he hastily turned to his young patient.

The dentist's agitated state puzzled the journalist. As he drove home with his daughter, he suddenly thought of the Israeli boats. Could that have been what Dr. Michel was referring to? After dropping off his daughter, Moirand drove down to the port. The pier was empty. It was not unusual for the boats to be out, even at night, but Moirand recalled Debré's remark to Mayor Hébert at the launching of the *Terrible* two weeks before—a solution for the five *vedettes* was in the offing, one that would be acceptable to both sides. Moirand did not think the boats had gone for good, but if they had, then it was plainly some arrangement to which the government was party. A former naval officer himself, Moirand thought the most likely solution was for the boats to be dispersed "for testing" to other ports—Dieppe, Le Havre, Brest— and after a few months be permitted to slip quietly away to Israel.

Dropping in to his office, he found an unusual amount of activity for what should have been a quiet news night. The Israeli boats, he quickly discovered, were the cause of the buzzing. They had been gone, it seemed, for almost two days, and there were rumors that they would not be coming back. There had been unusual goings and comings all day between the maritime prefecture and the arsenal, which had apparently inspired the rumors. Unknown to the journalists, Amiot himself had telephoned the duty officer at the prefecture at ten on Christmas morning to inform the authorities, as he was legally obliged to do, of the departure of vessels built in his yards. He left his seemingly routine notification to percolate upward through the chain of command and departed for his holiday retreat.

For a year now, Moirand had been sitting on the story of the embargo. If the boats had indeed gone, there was no longer any need for restraint. The reporter knocked on the editor's door.

"Is it true, Monsieur Justiniani, that the boats have gone for good?"

"I don't know, Monsieur Moirand," said the editor, "but in any case we're not going to write about it."

He had promised Amiot not to do so without first consulting him, explained Justiniani, and he had been unable to locate the industrialist.

Frustrated, Moirand returned home. He could only hope that the story would not break anywhere else during the weekend. The journalist was relaxing with his family when the doorbell rang at eight-thirty. It was highly unusual to have unexpected callers at such an hour, and when he opened the door he was astonished to see Dr. Michel, plainly agitated.

"I'm very sorry to be troubling you at home," apologized the dentist. "May I speak to you privately?"

In Moirand's study, a conscience-stricken Michel began: "About what I told you . . ."

"I already know," said Moirand.

Michel explained that he had been asked to help look after the Israeli families who had remained in Cherbourg after their menfolk had sailed. He begged Moirand not to make use of the information that he, Dr. Michel, had so injudiciously let slip. Moirand assured Michel that the departure of the Israeli boats was already well known in Cherbourg. In fact, Michel had offered Moirand the first confirmation that the boats were not coming back. But with Justiniani refusing to run the story, there was nothing Moirand could do with the information. He was also a correspondent for Radio Europe and for Paris newspapers, but his primary loyalty was to *La Presse de la Manche*. As marine reporter he was supposed to write the story for the local paper, and he did not regard it as ethical to file for another outlet. Half an hour before the midnight deadline, he telephoned the news room to ask if Justiniani had changed his mind. The reply was negative.

Not all Cherbourg's journalists, however, were bound by Amiot. *Oest-France* was preparing a story on the boats for Saturday's edition with a front-page headline reading "Where Have They Gone?" More important, journalists employed at both provincial papers had already begun feeding the story to the major newspapers and agencies on Friday night. Anthony Mann, back in London, was alerted early that evening by his Cherbourg stringer, whom he had asked to keep an eye on the boats. Mann was able to get the story into the early edition of the *Daily Telegraph* of Saturday, December 27, which hit the streets of London between 9:00 and 10:00 P.M. Friday. The headline read "Israeli Gunboats Vanish." He then succeeded in reaching Limon by telephone in Paris, to get his reaction in time for the second edition.

"We got our money back from the shipyard some time ago," said the Israeli official. "The gunboats were sold to a civilian concern, I think."

In that case, said Mann, it was odd that Limon had attended the launching of the last boat only two weeks before.

The discretion of Cherbourg's journalists, who had kept the story of the embargo under wraps for a year, would give way within hours to worldwide headlines and news broadcasts as the awesome power of the modern media was unleashed. Mann's story in London was picked up by the Associated Press and was on the wires shortly before midnight. So were bulletins put out by the other news agencies in Paris. Moirand was called at home ten minutes to midnight by an editor at Radio Europe in Paris.

"What's happening with your Israeli gunboats?" asked the editor.

"It's on the wires," said Moirand, with a wrenching recognition that he had been scooped.

The editor read aloud the one-sentence dispatch: "Five embargoed Israeli gunboats have disappeared from Cherbourg."

"All right," said Moirand. "I'm going to work."

Between midnight and 3:00 A.M., the journalist wakened by telephone the admiral of the arsenal, the head of naval security, the chief of police, the head of police intelligence, the chief of customs, and others—a dozen persons in all. Generally it was the official's wife who answered, with a mixture of alarm and annoyance. The duty officer at the arsenal reported that the lookout at the harbor entrance on Christmas Eve had seen no boats leaving port in the storm. Moirand speculated that the champagne his newspaper had sent as a Christmas Eve present—in appreciation for the help the navy gave it in reporting on sinkings and other nautical events—had probably not sharpened the lookout's alertness. Moirand wanted to know whether they had sailed through the main exit on the western side of the harbor, or whether they had slipped out the smaller, dangerous eastern exit. He also wanted to know whether they had turned north or south upon leaving harbor.

The reaction of those officials who chose to respond to Moirand's questions was that the boats had left Cherbourg in a perfectly legal fashion for a destination that was not Israel. The customs agent who had handled the paperwork for the shipyards, Georges Leveque, was unhappy about being wakened in the middle of the night. When

Moirand told him that newspapers all over France would be running the story on their front pages in the morning, Leveque's tone of sleepy annoyance changed to wide-awake alarm. "I'll call you back in half an hour."

When he called, he read from a document from the Bureau for Export of Armaments in Paris. It described the sale of "warships without military armament" to the Starboat Company for "supply missions between the Canadian coast and oil rigs off the Alaskan coast." The boats, said Leveque, were to be refitted in Norway for the Alaskan operation.

This Alaskan diversion had been thrown into the pot to compound the confusion over the destination of the boats when Starboat's Norwegian and Panamanian identities emerged. Suspicious minds began to speculate that all these exotic venues were merely a cover for an Israeli destination. Like many other journalists around the world this night, Moirand spread a map of Europe on his desk. On the phone to the radio editor in Paris, who was scanning his own map, he tried to estimate how far the boats could travel with fully loaded fuel tanks. Their rulers swiveled north toward Scandinavia and south toward the Mediterranean.

At that very hour, the objects of their concern were bobbing with almost empty tanks around their mother ship eight hundred miles to the south. A pronounced swell caused Kimche to change the original plan to fuel all five boats simultaneously, for fear that the boats alongside the *Lea* might be holed if they were swept against the freighter. Instead, two boats at a time would take on fuel from lines extended over the *Lea*'s stern. Implementing the techniques they had been practicing off Ashdod, the *Lea*'s crew tossed thin heaving lines onto the decks of the boats. Attached to these light lines were heavier lines, which the navy men hauled onto their decks. These lines, in turn, were tied to flexible steel pipes, which the men aboard the *Lea* slowly played out into the water as the sailors aboard the Saars pulled. Although the pipes had to be lifted only about two meters from the water to the decks of the boats, the exhausted and undermanned crews had difficulty manhandling them aboard.

The fueling began about midnight and proved a slow and tedious business. The first pair of boats were still nursing from the *Lea* when dawn lit the beautiful bay around them. From a nearby fishing village, boats began putting out to sea. The *Lea,* during the days it had been waiting, had drawn no attention, because ships frequently anchored in the sheltered bay. But its sudden mothering of five small vessels with the cut of warships did not go unnoticed. The first fishing boats paused as they caught sight of the vessels and then continued out to sea. Finally one boat turned back, and the Israelis knew they would soon have visitors. Close to 8:00 A.M. a boat put out from the village and headed straight toward the Israeli vessels lying two hundred meters offshore. It halted near the *Lea,* and a uniformed man with a white cap and three stripes on his sleeve, apparently a police sergeant, attempted to talk to the men on the deck. The Israelis did not respond, except by signaling him not to draw too close. The sergeant looked up at the *Lea's* name and Haifa registry painted on the merchantman and marked them down on a pad. He could be seen studying the *Starboat* sign on one of the Saars and writing again. The rest of the boats were ordered to unhook their signs before he reached them.

Kimche raised Tadmor on the radio. "Let's get out of here."

Tadmor raised anchor and towed the two vessels linked to his ship out of territorial waters, continuing to fuel them on the way, as he had practiced off Ashdod. While the vessels were regrouping, a helicopter with official-looking markings took up position off the *Lea's* bridge. Two men were aboard, and they appeared to be reporting by radio and photographing, but they made no attempt to contact the Israelis.

It was not the sound of the helicopter but the sputter of his own engines and the white smoke pouring from the exhausts after the re-fueling of his boat that alarmed Kimche. A look at the color of the liquid in the fuel-tank gauge confirmed his fears: water had somehow gotten into the fuel.

Chief Engineer Officer Nave was aghast. "We'll have to get rid of the fuel," he said. Kimche vetoed the idea. The *Lea* did not have enough fuel to refill the boats a second time, and if they entered Gibraltar for refueling they would risk seizure.

Kimche proposed another solution. Since water sinks in oil, it might be possible to drain it from the bottom of the fuel tanks.

"Can we do it?" asked Kimche.

"We'd be risking engine failure," said Nave.

"I want a clear answer, yes or no," said Kimche. "Knowing the importance of our getting these boats to Haifa and what will probably happen if we go into Gibraltar, do you think we can make it?"

Nave looked at Arye and Geva as if for help. "That's not a fair question to ask me," he said. Kimche, however, persisted, and Nave finally nodded. "We'll have to work hard at the draining."

Most of the crew pitched in for the next few hours in draining water from the tanks until the color of the liquid in the valves turned yellowish. Under Nave's direction, they would drain off water, wait for more to settle, and then drain again. Periodically Nave would judge how water-free was the fluid emerging from the tanks by tasting it with the tip of his tongue. The fueling of the five boats and the slow draining of the two whose fuel had been mixed with water took the better part of the day, but it at least gave an opportunity for brief napping to officers who had not slept for two days.

Weariness probably accounted for the tangling of fuel lines in the propeller of the last boat being fueled. Captain Tadmor turned to the navy diver who had been dispatched by Karish aboard the *Lea,* and who had been complaining for the past ten days at having been given a no-work assignment. "Now you know why you're here," said the *Lea's* skipper. "Put on your suit and earn your keep."

The diver extricated the lines without damage to the propeller. The Saar crewmen aboard the *Lea* were transferred to the boats as welcome reinforcements, along with a supply of food and spare parts. It was not until Saturday afternoon, December 27, that the fueling was completed. The fuel on two of the boats might still be tainted, but Kimche had decided that if they had to refuel earlier than planned the *Nili,* in the central Mediterranean, would be asked to sail westward to meet them.

The parting from the *Lea* was quick and without ceremony: an exchange of *Shaloms* between Kimche and Tadmor. The latter sent across a letter to his family to be mailed when the *Soufa* reached Israel. Eager to make up for the delay in fueling, Kimche led his formation southeast, toward the Straits of Gibraltar.

Zand had kept his ship circling in the Bay of Biscay until the boats reached the orbit of the *Lea.* Now, as the *Netanya* headed back toward Antwerp, Haifa signaled him that the boats' escape was being reported by the BBC. For the first time, Zand informed the *Netanya's* captain what their mission had been. "You can tell the crew," Zand said.

Many of the Israelis involved in the operation had believed that the boats' departure would pass unnoticed, or at least without publicity. Not a word had been written, after all, about Boats Six and Seven—virtually no one had known about their irregular leavetaking a year before, not even the Cherbourg journalists—and no French official had chosen to make of it a public issue. Even the resultant eviction from the arsenal had been handled discreetly, so that the Cherbourg public was unaware that the Israelis were being punished for having run off with two boats. The paperwork legitimizing the departure of the last five boats was entirely in order, and it seemed possible that they, too, would be able to slip anchor and quietly sail away. Even if the French government became aware of the ploy and took umbrage, it would be against their own interests to make a public issue of the matter.

This time, however, the eye of the press was fixed upon the boats, and there could be no discreet closing of accounts. The discovery that an embargo existed made the boats a story. It was not a very important story—five unarmed gunboats were not impressive men-of-war—but one that nevertheless required an accounting of how the embargo would be resolved. It was the dramatic nature of the boats' disappearance and the mystery enveloping it that turned this political story of limited interest into an international cliffhanger. *Oest-France*'s question "Where are they?" would within a few hours be repeated around the world. If the Christmas Eve timing had been aimed at catching the French authorities off guard, it also coincided with the slack news season that usually prevails during the holiday, when politicians and other newsmakers are resting from their labors. A Christmas Eve departure of embargoed Israeli gunboats for an unknown destination was a holiday gift of exceptional generosity for news-hungry editors. In displaying it in banner headlines, they would unwittingly become a key part of the story themselves.

Amiot's brief call to the maritime authorities on Christmas morning had been making its way through the defense establishment like acid through a copper wire in a time bomb. When a senior official routinely called the Maritime Prefecture from home to ask if there was anything special to report, the unsuspecting duty officer passed on the message received from Amiot shortly before. The sale of the boats to Norway and their pending departure were known to some officials, but even to them the Christmas Eve sailing into a gale seemed highly irregular.

The supervising officer asked if the departure had been reported by the lookout on the breakwater. "No, sir," said the duty officer.

Puzzled, the supervising officer telephoned the shipyard but got no reply. He promptly wired a report of the boats' departure to the Defense Ministry in Paris.

Because of the political sensitivity of the embargo, officials on duty at the Elysée Palace decided to interrupt President Pompidou's holiday vacation at his country home and inform him of the unusual development by telephone. A year later Pompidou would tell General Cazelles, who had chaired the critical meeting of the Interministerial Committee on Arms Exports which approved the Starboat sale, that when he was first notified of the incident he had an intuitive feeling that the boats were sailing toward Israel, not Norway. Nevertheless, on this Christmas afternoon he gave no operative order other than to confirm whether the boats had departed legally. If the boats were in the legal possession of Norwegians who chose bizarre hours of departure, it was not a matter for official concern.

The protocol of Cazelles's committee meeting was duly checked the following morning by Defense Ministry officials, along with customs records and other relevant documents. All appeared to be in order. When a ministry spokesman was wakened that night by journalists seeking a reaction to the midnight bulletins on the boats' departure, he was able to issue a statement at 2:00 A.M. affirming that the vessels were civilian craft that had been sold to a Norwegian firm in a routine commercial transaction.

This did not still the troubled waters for long. The Norwegians had been reading the news dispatches out of Cherbourg and Paris with interest, and the possible political implications had not been lost upon them. If Israel was involved in some hanky-panky, the reports could implicate Norway as an accomplice in the eyes of the Arab world. Early Saturday afternoon, while the boats were still being fueled off Portugal, the Norwegian ambassador in Paris issued a statement that the Starboat Company did not appear in standard registries of Norwegian firms. An hour later officials in Oslo declared that the Starboat boats were not registered in Norway and therefore were not entitled to fly the Norwegian flag.

Instantly the story took on new proportions. It was not just a mystery anymore but an extraordinary international caper. The Israelis were apparently running off with the boats, with or without French complicity. For the French authorities, either of these possibilities was as distasteful as the other. If there was complicity, France's position in the Arab world—and its credibility—would be seriously compromised. If the Israelis had made off with the boats by tricking Paris, the government would be a laughingstock. Few public bodies are more conscious of their dignity than governments of France. Even staunchly pro-Israeli officials like Premier Jacques Chaban-Delmas felt a sting of anger at becoming a subject for ridicule.

The official who vented his sense of outrage most forcefully was Defense Minister Debré, whose ministry was most directly involved. Debré was a staunch supporter of the embargo. Limon had found him the most difficult of all French ministers to deal with. Some Israeli diplomats, not all, attributed his unfriendliness to Debré's distancing himself from his family's Jewish origins—his grandfather, in fact, had been a rabbi, although Debré himself was a Christian. In outlining alternative courses of action, Debré included an option that air-force planes intercept the fleeing boats. An attack on foreign nationals in international waters was a grave matter, but so was France's honor. The Israelis had not been operating according to the niceties of international law, either. According to the premier's own account later, he rejected the idea forcefully. "I don't want the air force to move," Chaban-Delmas told Debré.

In Israel, the extraordinary reports from France slowly penetrated the Sabbath detachment from worldly news that the population normally permits itself. Orthodox Jews who do not listen to the radio on Saturdays learned of the episode from secular acquaintances in the street. The Israeli public had not known of the Cherbourg boats or the embargo until now. No Israeli source had ever leaked the story, and the only public mention had been in two brief and little-noticed wire-service stories from Paris in recent weeks, inspired by the Mann article and the article in *Combat Fleets,* reporting that the French embargo included not only fifty Mirages but also five patrol craft. Haifa residents on balconies and rooftops began peering out to sea in premature vigil.

The Israeli public's chortle at the reports was not shared by the government, most of whose members had been in total ignorance of the plan to escape from Cherbourg. Golda Meir, who had confided the matter only to her Kitchen Cabinet intimates, had been assured that the boats would probably be well into the Mediterranean before any public explosion in France over the issue, if indeed there was to be any. But the delay in fueling and the enthusiasm with which the press was pursuing the story had brought on an uproar even before the boats were past Gibraltar. If the French Mediterranean fleet attempted to intercept, the most likely place would be the narrow straits. What Mrs. Meir did not want was any physical confrontation that would endanger the boats and exacerbate relations with France, relations that would in any case be stretched taut by the escape.

Growing increasingly concerned as the reports from abroad built up through the evening, she told aides, "The matter is getting too serious. I want a meeting of the Cabinet tonight."

It was 1:00 A.M. Sunday when the Cabinet gathered. A factual presentation was given by Zvi Tsur, the senior aide to Dayan who had been the liaison between Limon and the defense establishment on the Cherbourg arrangements. Various scenarios were explored by the Cabinet, including a possible attempt by the French fleet to intercept, along with response options. Admiral Avraham Botser, the navy commander, said he regarded a French attack as unlikely, though the Egyptian navy might attempt to intercept as the boats approached the eastern Mediterranean. The Saars in Israel, already armed with missiles, would be deployed to meet this contingency if necessary.

Several of the ministers expressed anger at not having been consulted beforehand. Some were upset at the operation itself. Justice Minister Yaacov Shimshon Shapiro asked why the boats had not been sent to Norway and only later transferred to Israel. Tsur explained the fear of the boats' being impounded in Oslo. Defense Minister Dayan said little and left it to his deputy to handle the ministers' questions. Despite the assurances from the military, the meeting broke up with a foreboding that an adventure had been launched whose outcome was far from certain.

The boats approached the Straits of Gibraltar late Saturday afternoon in rough seas, which caused speed to be reduced to twenty knots. As the familiar profile of Gibraltar loomed to port, a signal light flashed a routine query from atop the rock: "What ship?" The boats made no reply. A Lloyd's helicopter monitoring traffic through the straits circled briefly overhead in an attempt to identify the boats but could detect no identity numbers or flags. Fifteen minutes later the light atop Gibraltar flashed again: "*Bon voyage.*" The men on the bridge of the *Soufa* laughed at this evident signal of recognition.

"When the British admiral was informed that five boats were passing without offering identification," speculated Kimche to his officers, "he must have known it was us. It took him a quarter of an hour to get his staff together to raise a toast to us for screwing the French."

Shortly afterward, the BBC reported that a Greek vessel entering Gibraltar had reported five unidentified boats entering the straits. It seemed to the Israelis an elegant British way of notifying the French of the boats' passage without becoming directly involved in the affair themselves. Not to report the passage would have been an unfriendly act. The report meant that the French could now have no doubt about which direction they were heading.

The original route drawn up by Geva would take the boats through the central Mediterranean on a direct route to Haifa. Kimche decided now to distance himself from the French coast by taking a more southerly route that would place his vessels in a well-traveled shipping lane about forty miles off the coast of North Africa. Although Kimche felt it unlikely that the French navy would attempt interception, many of his officers disagreed with him. As they passed through the straits, Geva calculated that French warships from Toulon could easily intercept. Granting the possibility, Kimche wanted other ships around so that he could alert the world if it happened. His only weapons were his speed and his radio.

13

Eye of the Storm

The fading storm was still at their backs as they entered the Mediterranean, but the Israeli sailors now had the feeling of being on home ground. One of Nave's men kept polishing every piece of brass in the engine room, out of sheer joy. Nave himself was busy changing injectors and fuel filters every hour, to prevent the recurrence of the blockages due to the tainted fuel. Listening to the radio, the men began to realize that they and their five small boats were at the focus of world interest. Journalists were reported flying out over the North Sea and the Mediterranean in rented planes to search for them. One report had them headed for Alaska. Late on Saturday, Europe Number One Radio reported the Lloyd's agent in Gibraltar sighting five small vessels headed eastward. The vessels, said the agent, flew no flags.

The Saars passed many ships, including American and Russian freighters, but no one seemed to pay them special note. Off Algeria, the French fleet finally made contact. A twin-engined Atlantique observation plane from the fleet's air arm based in Nîmes in southern France circled overhead for three hours and took photographs. Whenever it made a low run from the side, in an apparent search for identifying numbers, the boats turned their bows toward it.

The sailors who appeared in the photographs developed a few hours later were in civilian clothing, but French intelligence officers had no trouble identifying the vessels. If French warships from Toulon attempted to intercept, the Saars might attempt to outrun them. However, they would be dead in the water for more than twelve hours during their second refueling. The French navy knew the boats' range and should easily be able to calculate when they would have to stop for refueling.

Toward evening, a small plane with civilian markings appeared overhead. Radiomen aboard the boats heard the excited voice of a radio reporter saying he had just spotted the five Israeli boats from a plane he had rented on Malta. With darkness, Kimche changed course to the northeast. The rendezvous he headed for was a tiny island remote from any shipping lane. As they drew near the next day, the men on the bridge could see a single ship drifting on the horizon. Kimche had no difficulty in making out the familiar profile of the *Dan*.

The French pilot boarding the *Lea* outside Dunkerque was an old acquaintance and he greeted Tadmor boisterously. "You clever bastards really did it to us," he shouted. Tadmor was startled for a moment before he realized that the Frenchman was referring to the escape of the boats as reported on the radio, not to the *Lea*'s role.

As the pilot oriented himself on the bridge, however, his expression suddenly froze. He stared at the pumping equipment on the rear deck and the extensive oil stains on the wooden planks. The crew's efforts to clean them had been only partly successful. "You didn't have anything to do with it, did you?" asked the pilot in astonishment.

"Are you crazy? We've got a cargo of phosphates to deliver."

The pilot kept staring at the pumps and the oil stains and then, with a widening grin, turned to Tadmor and winked.

Avi Primor, the press secretary at the Israeli embassy, could hear his footsteps ringing as he and the embassy's chargé d'affaires, Eytan Ron, followed their escort through the empty corridors of the Quai d'Orsay. They had received a highly unusual Sunday summons to the Foreign Ministry to meet with the minister himself, Maurice Schumann. The Israelis could read the anger on Schumann's face the instant they were ushered into his office, although it was not clear whether this was feigned or real.

The minister wasted little time on formalities. The French government, he said, did not want to believe that the stories being broadcast about the five Israeli boats were true. "It is clear to the French government that the boats sold by Israel will not be going to Israel." If, however, it became clear to the French government that it had erred, then *"les plus graves conséquences"* would follow. These consequences would be particularly felt, said Schumann, by Limon, who had signed a document waiving Israel's rights to the boats, and by Primor, who had been issuing statements to the same effect. "The French government of course does not want to believe these stories," reiterated Schumann. The Israelis understood that he was telling them to keep the boats from entering Haifa.

Even before the summons to the Foreign Ministry, Primor had felt the tempo of events building up over the weekend. He had been wakened early Saturday morning by a reporter from Agence France Presse checking out the story from Cherbourg about five embargoed Israeli patrol boats that had disappeared Christmas Eve. Yes, said Primor, Israel had ordered the boats in Cherbourg, but it had since renounced its interest in them. They had been sold, he understood, to a Panamanian company, but whether they had taken delivery he didn't know. The reporter sounded highly skeptical and rang off.

A few moments later the phone rang again. The caller identified himself as the AFP duty editor who had asked the reporter to call. "Excuse me, please, but I just want to check. You are Avraham Primor, the spokesman for the Israeli embassy?" The editor gave a telephone number and asked whether this was Primor's office number. Primor confirmed.

"Now, about these boats," said the editor. "You say they were sold to a Panamanian company?" Primor went through the story again. The French press had not picked up the Mann story and had been ignorant of the boats' existence. From the editor's questions, pauses, and intonation, Primor could sense him slowly ingesting the meaning of this odd tale—that there had been warships built in Cherbourg for Israel that virtually no one knew about, that these boats had been embargoed and no one knew about that, either, and that they had now disappeared into a storm on Christmas Eve, ostensibly bound for Panama. "This is an unbelievable story," said the editor, using the phrase that encompassed both the bizarre nature of the facts being offered and an inkling of the tremendous tale that must lie behind it.

Revelation of the boats' departure by the press had sent the three governments implicated—France, Israel, and Norway—scurrying for legal cover. A French Defense Ministry spokesman, asked by reporters on Saturday afternoon about Oslo's denial of the boats' Norwegian identity, said, "According to the documents presented by the firm, it *is* Norwegian." He suggested that the Norwegian authorities may have checked out the wrong company name. "The affair is confused," he said wearily, "and we're trying to shed light on it." At the Foreign Ministry, a spokesman denied reporters' suggestions that the French government might have been party to the breaching of its own embargo. "It's just not true," he said plaintively.

The Norwegian ambassador in Cairo, summoned to the Egyptian Foreign Ministry for an explanation, issued a statement denying his country's connection to the matter. The French ambassador, likewise summoned, said he was waiting to hear from his government. In Oslo, where officials had spent a busy Saturday opening up locked offices and pulling files, a Foreign Ministry spokesman announced that the Starboat Company, which was registered in Panama, did have a post-office box in Oslo but had no other connection with Norway. Investigation had established that the boats were not flying Norwegian flags when they left Cherbourg, said the spokesman, nor were there any Norwegian nationals aboard. Although an import license was required for the purchase of boats abroad, no application had been made in Norway for the five boats built in Cherbourg. If the boats arrived in Norway, the spokesman said, they would be detained.

In the face of these strong denials, Paris could not maintain its previous position, which had dumped the matter in Norway's lap. On Saturday night, the office of Premier Chaban-Delmas issued a new statement. "Upon learning that the Norwegian government contests the nationality of the company to which the gunboats were sold, the French government has opened an inquiry." The statement said that the French government had consented on November 18 to the sale of the vessels—unarmed vessels, it emphasized—to "a commercial firm claiming to come under Norwegian law." It had done so after Israel had agreed in writing to waive its claims to the vessels in return for the refund of its money.

With Ambassador Eytan on a holiday in the Swiss Alps, and Jerusalem maintaining silence on the matter, Primor was the sole official spokesman for the Israeli side. A word he kept hearing from the journalists to whom he repeated his official story deadpan was *rocombolique*, comical. It was not the Israelis they were laughing at. Enterprising journalists in Cherbourg who had tracked down four Israeli naval personnel left behind were told that the Israeli crews had been asked by the Norwegians to sail the boats to their new port—a provision indeed covered by the formal request from Siemm. The journalists quoted them as saying that the Israelis had been joined on the voyage by Norwegian officers and noncoms. This statement, if actually made, was virtually the only outright untruth passed on to the press by any of the parties. But the half-truths were providing fog enough.

In Panama, an official of a local law firm—Arias, Fabrega and Fabrega—told Reuters that his firm had formed and registered the Starboat Company on behalf of a London law firm he refused to identify. Although Arias was resident agent for Starboat, the official said, the Panamanian law firm was not its head office. He declined to give further information.

The Lebanese government, in whose interests de Gaulle had supposedly imposed the embargo in the first place, following Israel's raid on Beirut Airport, did not reciprocate France's gesture in this strained hour. In announcing the government's plans to put the boat affair on its agenda, a government source said, "The question uppermost in Lebanese minds is what effect this affair will have on French-Arab relations."

The British press, reveling in the embarrassment of their neighbors across the Channel, gave the sale of the boats "to a non-existent Norwegian company" top play in their weekend editions. "It looks as though the Israelis have pulled off a cheeky coup," wrote the *Sunday Telegraph*. With the failure of any port to note the arrival of the five boats for refueling, said the paper, it seemed increasingly likely that they were heading for a rendezvous with a tanker at sea.

Greek merchant-marine authorities issued a routine alert to all coastal boats and harbors to report any sighting of the missing gunboats. Maritime officials in Athens said that if the boats were flying an internationally recognized flag, Greece could not by international law deny them refueling facilities—a clarification intended to head off anticipated Arab protests. A deputy premier of the army-backed government in Greece voiced admiration for the Israeli exploit. "When a country wants to survive, it shall survive," he declared. "A small nation under duress can bring forth unsuspected latent strength. The same goes for Greece."

In Cairo, foreign military attachés noted apparent preparations for an Egyptian naval force to put to sea.

In Israel, reports were received that the Soviet Mediterranean fleet near Crete had weighed anchor.

14

Homecoming

Fueling from the *Dan* was well under way when a mastful of antennas appeared on the horizon. As it drew closer, Kimche could make out through binoculars the shape of a Russian spy trawler. The ship had plainly been tracking the Israeli craft for some time. It made no pretense of just happening by. Sailing straight toward them, it dropped anchor three hundred meters away and calmly took them under observation. Only three men could be seen above decks, one of them holding a camera with a long lens. The other two were presumably the captain and the officer of the watch.

Despite the uninvited guest, the fueling operation went perfectly. Floodlights were turned on as darkness set in. The car-ferry-turned-tanker sent a rubber boat across to the Saars with a supply of food and cigarettes. One of the engines in Boat Number Twelve, Tabak's vessel, had developed a crack in a cylinder head on the second leg of the journey, and the vessel was traveling on only three engines. Kimche decided to fuel Tabak's boat first and to send it on ahead because of its reduced speed. Accompanying it would be Boat Number Nine, with Karish in command. It seemed highly unlikely to Kimche that the Egyptians could hope to ambush high-speed PT boats, but he decided that he would split his force. Tabak's troubled boat with Karish's as escort would take the northern route past Crete, because it was the shortest. The rest of the boats would sail south of Crete. At 10:30 P.M. Monday, the last three boats completed their fueling. The Soviet trawler was still in place when they moved off at thirty knots.

Haifa businessman Mila Brenner was wakened by the phone at 2:00 A.M. The pause and faint rustle he heard when he lifted the receiver signaled an overseas call. A distant voice with a Scandinavian lilt asked for Mr. Brenner.

"This is Christian Siemm," the caller said. Despite its agitation, Brenner recognized the voice of the son of his old friend and business associate Martin Siemm.

"We've got problems," said the younger Siemm. The boat affair, he explained, had created a major political storm in Norway. At its center, alone, was his father. Could Brenner come to offer support? Could he come on the next available flight?

Brenner was a partner in the Maritime Fruit Carrier Company, the Israeli shipping company that had ordered more than a score of ships from the firm headed by Siemm. Although Brenner himself had played no part in the Cherbourg episode, he could not ignore the plight of his friend and long-time business associate.

It was not easy to get a plane ticket during the Christmas season, but Brenner managed to book a 7:00 A.M. flight on a plane to Zurich, from where he had a connection to Oslo.

Brenner wakened a contact in the defense establishment to inform him of his intention to fly to Oslo. The message was passed on to Zvi Tsur, who was appalled at the notion. Israel's intention was to maintain a low profile to the point of invisibility, at least as long as the boats were at sea. For the expansive Brenner, who knew virtually nothing of the elaborate cover operation, to fly to Europe and implicate Israel publicly could be disastrous.

At 5:00 A.M. Tsur telephoned a close aide and Motti Friedman and told them to head Brenner off at Ben-Gurion Airport. The two men, flashing special passes, went through passport control and found their quarry in the departure lounge. They pressed him to abort the trip, stressing the extreme delicacy of the affair. When he said he could not, they hinted that he would be exposing himself to charges of violation of national security. As they spoke, loading for the Zurich-bound flight was announced over the public-address system. Brenner said goodbye and passed through the gate.

When he landed at Oslo at 9:00 P.M., Christian Siemm was waiting for him at the airport.

"How's Father?" asked Brenner.

"All right, all right," said Christian, "but we've got problems with the government."

As they drove toward town, Christian Siemm gave Brenner a quick fill-in. There were legal problems—apparently Starboat had not been properly registered—and there were questions about its foreign-currency arrangements. But the basic problem—the reason the authorities were making such a fuss—was the political problem. The largely conservative coalition government was under attack by newspapers and leftist opposition for its alleged part in the boats' escape. The critics said that the episode violated Norway's neutrality. Shipping interests were particularly upset, for fear of an Arab boycott against Norway's large tanker fleet. The Liberal Party was threatening to bring down the coalition unless the government disassociated itself from the episode by taking legal action against Siemm, for violating the country's neutrality and for being a party to acts harmful to Norway politically and economically. A measure of the seriousness of events was that no one in the Cabinet had gone home for the holiday. Brenner was told that the collapse of the government appeared imminent.

After checking in at his hotel, he was driven to the elder Siemm's house. It was surrounded by floodlights and huge guard dogs. On the street were police cars with flashing lights.

"His life has been threatened by the Fatah," someone said.

Inside, Brenner found his old friend very troubled and grateful for his appearance. Like most of the Israelis involved in the episode, Siemm had hoped that the departure of the five boats with legal cover would pass quietly. The only Norwegian involvement was a few sheets of stationery with the Starboat letterhead, a rented postal box in Oslo, and a small Starboat medallion Siemm had displayed on the gateway to the Akers property. The scandal that had suddenly intruded on his orderly life had shaken him, particularly the charges that the former underground leader had harmed Norway's national interest.

The day before, under intense public pressure for clarifications, he had issued a statement affirming that Starboat was registered in Panama and that he was its Norwegian representative. "It was only a short time ago that the company I represent acquired the five boats in Cherbourg," the statement said. "As far as I know, they did not fly the Norwegian flag. I regret that the company's international obligations forbid me from releasing more complete details."

The statement had only whetted the demand for more information. Brenner was told that meetings with several political figures had been arranged for him this very evening, as well as a television appearance. Brenner had not slept since the 2:00 A.M. phone call, but the pace of events was keeping him wide awake. He put in a call to Limon in Paris to inform him that he was going public to defend Siemm. Limon, aghast at the notion, spoke cautiously, as if fearing a phone tap, and said he would call back. When the call came (Brenner believed it was from a public phone), Limon cautioned him not to make any public statements.

The television interview came first—live on the 11:00 P.M. news broadcast. An outgoing, avuncular personality, Brenner was not intimidated by the warning against his unauthorized plunge into muddy waters. His shipping firm, the biggest foreign client of the Norwegian shipbuilding industry, he told the interviewer, was the major shareholder of Starboat. Basing himself on what he had learned of Israel's fallback cover story, he said the Cherbourg vessels would be used for servicing oil-drilling rigs off Israel's Mediterranean coast. This was the first public statement by an Israeli that Israeli interests were involved in Starboat or that the boats were heading toward Israel. Brenner's revelation would infuriate Limon and other Israelis involved in the affair, but the statement in distant Oslo by a little-known Israeli businessman that conflicted with previous reports involving Panama, Alaska, and Norway added to the general confusion.

Asked why his company had bought gunboats when other vessels would better serve their purpose, Brenner replied that it was difficult to obtain suitable craft because of the oil boom in Indonesia and other places. As for the apparent intrigue surrounding the sale, it was nothing unusual: "It is not customary in the oil business to advertise one's next moves and the transaction was therefore carried out with some discretion."

The boats, he stressed, were not warships but unarmed vessels. He acknowledged that in times of war they could be armed, as could any vessel. If Norwegian law had been inadvertently broken in this affair, he, Brenner, assumed full responsibility, because it was done at his request. His friendship for Norway was well known, he said. As an officer in the British merchant fleet in World War II, he had navigated the first supply ship through a mined fjord to Trondheim in the wake of the retreating Germans. The tie was renewed and strengthened by his shipping activities.

Referring to the Starboat episode, he said, "If things were the other way around, if Norway were in the same position as Israel, I would have done the same for Norway." Siemm, who was also interviewed, said he had founded the Starboat Company on behalf of several financial groups, "some of them Israeli."

From the television studio Brenner was taken to two different locales in Oslo. At each place he was introduced to several important-looking political figures. It wasn't entirely clear to him who they were, but one was apparently a Liberal minister. Brenner touched the same points he had made in the television interview and found the atmosphere receptive. At one point one of the politicians said something to Siemm in Norwegian.

"He said to tell you that Norway is a friend of Israel," said Siemm.

When they parted for the evening, Siemm told Brenner, "I think the political crisis is over."

Detectives were guarding the corridor outside Brenner's hotel room when he returned. Dead weary, he glanced at his watch before getting into bed. It was 2:00 A.M.

General Cazelles heard the news of the boats' departure with considerable bemusement. He was at his sister's home in the south of France, where he had gone for the holiday. Just six weeks before, his committee had approved the boats' sale to Norway; the radio was now reporting them off Gibraltar. Cazelles immediately thought of the published reports that France was negotiating the sale of fifty Mirage fighters and other armaments to Libya despite its embargo on arms sales to the Middle East.

"The government is clever," he told his sister. "It's letting the boats go to Israel and the planes to Libya."

When he returned to his office after the weekend, a summons from Debré awaited him. It was clear to Cazelles from the moment he was ushered into the defense minister's office that Debré was not amused. The minister rebuked Cazelles for his committee's approval of the boats' sale without having sufficiently established the bona fides of the purchaser. Cazelles was appalled by the rebuke, since he was convinced that Debré himself had to be involved in the boats' departure. The general did not yet realize it, but he was about to pay the penultimate price for his country—his career.

Newsmen tracked Amiot down to his retreat in Cannes. The shipyard owner insisted that the Norwegian firm he had sold the boats to was real, not a dummy corporation, as many were beginning to allege. He had correspondence from the firm and had met with its officials in Paris and Cherbourg.

The senior civil servants who gathered Monday in the Matignon, the offices of the premier, could sense the bureaucratic mine field they were being drawn into by the boat affair. They were informed by Chaban-Delmas's aide that each of their ministries was to provide documents and explanations regarding the affair in time for the Cabinet meeting in two days. Even before the facts were gathered, it was clear that there were enough officials guilty of negligence and, most probably, conspiracy to provide the political guillotine an awesome feast.

Coastal listening stations in Sicily picked up an unusually large number of Hebrew messages in the clear and in Morse during the night. Italian maritime sources reported Israeli ships of an unidentified nature moving through the southern Tyrrhenian Sea, between Sicily and Sardinia, and in the waters between Sicily and Tunisia. Unidentified experts in Naples were quoted as saying that NATO tracking stations had been following the boats' movements since they entered the Mediterranean but were keeping silent so as not to disclose their whereabouts to a potential enemy. An Italian trawler reported seeing the gunboats off eastern Sicily on Tuesday morning, escorted by "numerous other Israeli ships," including an oil tanker and two submarines. The Norwegian press carried reports that a former Norwegian whaling factory ship may have refueled the fleeing boats.

For the Israelis, sailing without escort, the sense of danger grew the closer they got to home. If an interception was attempted by Egypt, it would likely be in the eastern Mediterranean. The Israeli navy command did not anticipate Soviet intervention, but the government was less certain.

Once again the boats had to plow through stormy seas, but there was a west wind at their back. Passing through the Aegean at night, they skirted two unidentified ships. The two Saars north of Crete ran into thick fog. Tabak and his chief engineer checked the cracked cylinder head again and decided that the fault was small enough to permit the engine to be run without danger. The fourth engine allowed them to increase speed from twenty-two knots to thirty.

Aboard the *Soufa*, a sailor named Haim had been too sick to get out of his bunk since entering the English Channel. He was the best cook in the flotilla and had been brought from Israel by Shaked as a gift to the flagship for the voyage. The problem with Haim was that he became wretchedly seasick even in a gentle swell; the storm had rendered him totally immobile. Lieutenant Geva found his sympathy for Haim's condition steadily diminishing as the half-strength crew, many of its members also sick, labored round-the-clock to keep the vessel moving.

"This can't go on," Geva finally told him. "You've got to get up and relieve someone. You can be a lookout on the bridge. You wouldn't have to do anything but stand there."

"But I can't stand," groaned Haim.

Geva pulled the covers off the cook, helped him to his feet, and handed him his rough-weather gear. After escorting Haim up to the bridge, Geva propped him against the mast and lashed him to it with heavy line. Haim groaned as the boat danced dizzyingly in the waves.

"I'll have someone bring you down when the watch is over," said Geva. "Keep your eyes open."

Several hours later, Geva was talking to Kimche in the captain's cabin when he suddenly leaped to his feet. "My God, I've forgotten Haim," said the navigation officer. The watch had long since ended. When Geva told Kimche what had happened, the commander told him to go up personally and cut Haim loose. "And don't ever do it again." Geva found him ashen faced and too weak to protest. The officer cut him loose and helped him down to his bunk.

Fifteen hours after splitting up, Kimche's formation linked up with Tabak and Karish east of Crete. As they pushed through the rough waters, the lookout on the *Soufa* suddenly bellowed, "Planes dead ahead." Two warplanes were fast approaching the formation at a low altitude from the east. One of them peeled off and dived toward the boats. It leveled out and roared over the masts with its wings wagging before pirouetting up into the sky. In that brief pass, the sailors could make out the Star of David on the Phantom's wings.

Despite the crisis, President Pompidou had not cut short his Christmas vacation at Cajarc, five hundred kilometers south of Paris. By telephone he made it clear to his Cabinet colleagues and subordinates in Paris that he wanted a low-decibel reaction. Paris would plainly have to show its displeasure over the affair some way, if only as a sop to the Arab world, but Pompidou did not want thunder.

"Remember, I'm not General de Gaulle," he told a caller.

His was a statesmanlike approach that recognized that angry roars and flailing about would only augment the embarrassment. The situation was an extraordinary mixture of farce and political humiliation and required extremely judicious handling. Polls showed that three-quarters of the French population applauded the Israeli getaway. On the other hand, the boats' escape exposed the government as either criminally inept or Byzantinely devious.

Although government officials were insisting that the boats had been legally cleared for departure by customs and the Defense Ministry, the harbormaster of Cherbourg insisted that the captains of the boats had broken a century-old law obliging them to inform his office of their sailing and destination twenty-four hours ahead of departure. However, visiting journalists found the residents of Cherbourg clearly not sharing the embarrassment of the central government. They expressed delight at the escapade and saluted the Israelis with a "Well done."

Pompidou returned to Paris Tuesday night and met the next day, December 31, at a working lunch with Premier Chaban-Delmas, Defense Minister Debré, and Foreign Minister Schumann before the regularly scheduled Cabinet meeting. Despite their fury at the Israeli government, the four agreed that it was not in France's interests to sever relations with Jerusalem. Pompidou also opposed a showy witchhunt for conspirators within France itself. What had to be determined was who *would* pay the price. The biblical practice of sending a goat off into the desert on the Day of Atonement burdened by the high priest with the sins of the nation may not have been fair to the goat but it was healthy for the nation—a piece of folk wisdom instinctively understood by the high priests of politics through the ages.

Schumann demanded the suspension of General Bonte, the official most directly connected with the "Norwegian option." He also proposed the banishment of the Israeli purchasing mission headed by Limon. However, Pompidou said a distinction should be made between the mission as such, which had placed more than $1 billion worth of orders with French industry over the years, and Limon personally.

Debré was particularly adamant about Limon. The Israeli official had violated the most basic standards of diplomatic behavior, asserted Debré, by signing a false declaration—namely, that Israel was ceding its claim to the boats. Debré also demanded the dismissal of General Cazelles. The general was probably innocent of conspiracy, but he should have made it his business, argued Debré, to have the identity of the purchaser checked out. Although Cazelles was a protégé of Pompidou's, the president reluctantly agreed to offer up his head.

The ground was laid for the Cabinet meeting, which got under way in the afternoon. Participants were handed detailed reports on the Cherbourg affair that had been drawn up by the officials summoned to the Matignon two days before. The reports traced developments from the start of the boats' construction four years earlier. A report from the Renseignements Généraux cited the contract signed the week before between Limon and Amiot rescinding the earlier contract between them and the contract between Siemm and Amiot. One report also mentioned the *Starboat* name plates observed on the boats by the customs officer on the afternoon of December 24. A paper submitted by the prime minister's office noted that the contracts between Amiot, Siemm, and Limon had not been approved by any government representative and apparently did not include a non-re-exportation clause. An RG report stated that an eyewitness had seen the boats leave "fully illuminated." The RG even noted remarks made the previous day to Italian television by some of Cherbourg's leading citizens, including Mayor Hébert, "who treated the incident in his usual ironic manner."

Among the officials summoned to the Cabinet meeting was Jacques Marti, who had signed the customs clearance for the boats. A veteran of bureaucratic battles, the Corsican had prepared for the occasion by bringing copies of the relevant documents he needed to protect himself. Missing from the documents presented to the participants was the permission given by the Defense Ministry to Customs to issue final customs clearance. When a ministry official denied that such approval had been given, Marti distributed copies of the missing document.

Pompidou rejected a proposal that relations with Israel be severed. Nor, if France wished to retain a middleman position in the Middle East, would it recall its ambassador to Israel. He outlined instead the steps agreed upon at the luncheon with his senior ministers. Glancing frostily at the ministers and senior civil servants around the long table, he said, "We have been made to appear ridiculous because of the incredible lightheadedness and intellectual complicity of our officials."

Before the meeting ended, an aide entered the room and handed Pompidou a note. The five Cherbourg boats, it said, were entering Haifa harbor.

They had arrived off Haifa close to noon but were ordered to stay out of sight of the coast until dark. A daylight arrival filmed by television cameras would, the Israeli government feared, be flaunting their escape in the face of Paris. The sea was the worst it had been since the Bay of Biscay, and for six hours the captains struggled to keep position. Instructions from navy headquarters for the debarkation were pouring through the radiomen's earphones. Journalists and television crews from all over the world were waiting for them ashore, but the boats' entrance would be as low-key as possible. They would not enter the main harbor but the adjacent port of Kishon, where they would dock at the Israel Shipyards. Officially the boats were civilian, and the men would remain dressed in civilian clothing; overalls would be ferried out to the boats for the men to don before disembarking. Officials of the Netivai Neft Oil Company would be on hand to "take possession" of the vessels. No one would speak to the press except for Karish, who would field questions at a press conference but say as little as possible. Kimche's identity as commander of the operation would remain secret.

Light planes carrying cameramen circled overhead periodically. With darkness, the boats headed toward the Bay of Haifa. In the anchorage outside the port, a score of freighters waited to load oranges. As the Saars passed among them, one of the merchant ships sounded its whistle in recognition. Within seconds all the freighters were sounding a raucous salute.

As the Saars turned into the tricky approaches to Kishon harbor Kimche asked all captains to place their walkie-talkies next to the ship's public-address system so that he could address all hands. "This is a historic day for the navy," he said. "These boats that we have brought will double the navy's strength. It's been a difficult passage but you've performed splendidly. Well done."

The Saars came into dock at five-minute intervals, their own sirens sounding warning. Television projector lights glaring directly into their faces blinded the helmsmen and captains feeling their way into the docks, and more than one feared that the voyage would be marred at the very last moment by collision with the dock. Sailors onshore had to force their way through the press of newsmen to take the docking lines. The foreign journalists were astonished at the youth of the crewmen— teen-agers in civilian clothing—and noticed that their pallor contrasted sharply with the weatherbeaten faces of the bridge officers. Some suspected that the crews had been changed during the hours in which the boats had unaccountably stayed out of port. The pallor was due to their having been kept hidden below decks in the days before departure from Cherbourg and having remained below for much of the sailing because of the bad weather.

When Lieutenant Commander Ben-Zeev shut down the motors of Number Eleven, he had fuel left for only ten minutes' sailing. In the week since they had left Cherbourg, he had had no more than three hours of sleep and had lost thirteen pounds. Tabak, on Number Twelve, glanced at the boats neatly aligned again at a dock, as they had been a week before in Cherbourg, and thought of all that had transpired since his first arrival in Cherbourg to oversee the testing of the Saars. "This hasn't been a week's voyage," he thought. "It's been a two years' voyage."

In the engine room of Number Eight, Nave listened for a moment to the deep silence of the engines after their shutdown. They had endured more in the past week than any test could inflict upon them, and they had proved faithful. Mounting the steps to the deck, he emerged into the blinding glare of the floodlights.

The press conference, attended by more than a hundred journalists and television crewmen, was held in the shipyard canteen. Karish, an accomplished raconteur, curbed his expansiveness for the occasion. For close to an hour he told about the weather they had experienced en route and provided deliberately inane answers in English to the questions hurled at him.

"How did you leave Cherbourg?"

"How? Well, normally."

"Who gave you permission to leave?"

"We got notice from the company to go, so we went."

"How is it that you, a naval officer, take orders from a commercial company?"

"No problem. I was told to sail, and sailed. Is that a customary practice? I don't know."

"Who gave you permission to sail?"

"I didn't deal with the formalities. The company's agent took care of that. I only know that I had permission to sail."

An official of the Netivai Neft Company was introduced to the press and said he was taking possession of the boats for his firm. The boats, he said, would be used for general purposes in connection with off-shore drilling.

The crews were bused across Haifa to the naval base in the main port, where they were joined for an emotional reception by their families and a jubilant Moshe Dayan. In a brief ceremony, the defense minister handed each of the captains a large Bible for his boat. Exhaustion prompted most of the men to make their farewells early and drift off with their families to their first deep sleep in a week.

As the party wound down, others were starting up all over the country. It was New Year's Eve.

The hour of the diplomats had arrived. It was for both sides now to firmly assert their national dignity while simultaneously easing back from confrontation. On New Year's Day, the Israeli ambassador in Paris was summoned to the Quai d'Orsay to be informed by Foreign Minister Schumann of the government's decision the day before to request Limon's recall. From there, Ambassador Eytan hurried back to his embassy to change into tails and make his way to the president's New Year's reception at the Elysée. It would be Pompidou's first meeting with an Israeli representative since the boat affair.

The ambassadors filling the reception hall awaited the confrontation with delicious anticipation. There would, however, be no diplomatic spectacle. Pompidou shook Eytan's hand firmly and moved on without comment. The year before, de Gaulle had utilized his formal address to the assembled diplomats to chastise Israel for its raid on distant Beirut Airport. Pompidou, in his remarks, avoided any allusions to Cherbourg and confined himself to calling for universal peace. When the diplomats mingled at the subsequent reception, Eytan showed Deputy Foreign Minister Jean de Lipkowski the car-check stub that had been given him by the doorman upon his arrival. It was numbered 007. De Lipkowski burst into laughter and passed on the doorman's joke to other diplomats.

The Israelis had been braced for far worse than Limon's recall. Foreign Ministry officials had been contemplating which embassy would represent their interests in Paris if relations were severed. Even the move against Limon was relatively mild. It had been anticipated that he would be declared *persona non grata*—a status that would have barred his subsequent re-entry to the country even as a tourist. Israeli officials had indicated to the French that if they took strong action, Israel would release the texts of the relevant contracts, including the contract that Paris had not previously seen by which Siemm had leased the boats to Netivai Neft. What these contracts added up to was that Israel had done nothing illegal and that the French government had been made a fool of.

Jerusalem termed the French demand for Limon's recall "unjustified," but the official statement lacked the bite of indignation, and there was no reciprocal expulsion of a French diplomat, as is usual in such cases. In a Tel Aviv speech, Foreign Minister Abba Eban declared that Israel did not stand as the accused in its dialogue with France, "since there had been no breach of law," but as the injured party. Israel demanded redress, he said, from an unfair embargo policy that withheld arms from Israel despite signed agreements while channeling arms to Israel's enemies. He was pleased to note, said Eban hopefully, that the French had put the boat affair "in proper perspective" as a minor episode. Eban informed the French ambassador that the boats were to be used to service and "protect" offshore oil rigs, the latter addendum neatly opening the way to providing the boats with armaments.

There remained only the wrapping up. In Cherbourg, Supply Officer Shachak had begun, the morning after Christmas, to make the rounds of shops the Israelis had patronized to pay off any outstanding debts. At the hotel where the crewmen had been staying, he called the proprietor and said, "Monsieur Grenier, let's make the bill." When Grenier noted that he had purchased ten chickens for the absent men's Christmas lunch, the supply officer readily agreed to pay for them.

Three days after the boats' departure, Shachak was asked to report to Cherbourg police headquarters. The police commissioner, Monsieur Foch, happened to live in the apartment beneath Shachak's. Foch had suffered an unhappy relationship with the Israeli officer who had earlier occupied the upstairs apartment, and who had viewed Foch's complaints about noise as expressions of anti-Semitism. Shachak had made a point of calling on his downstairs neighbor upon moving in and asking him not to hesitate to tell him when he was being disturbed.

Before going to the commissioner's office, Shachak phoned Limon in Paris to inform him of the summons. Limon told him to be prepared for an expulsion order.

Also present in Foch's office when Shachak was ushered in was a stranger, evidently from one of the security services, who remained silent. Foch greeted the Israeli courteously and asked, "What are your plans?"

Shachak said that he wanted to oversee the return to Israel of the equipment and papers of the naval mission and see to the repatriation of the ten Israeli families left in Cherbourg without their menfolk. "We're not going to leave them to the Cherbourg Welfare Department," he said amiably.

Foch gave Shachak no deadline for leaving; the Israeli would stay on for two more months.

One week after New Year's Day, Ambassador Eytan held a farewell party at the embassy for Limon, who was to depart the next day after seven years in Paris. He was to have left in August in any case, but to friends who expected to find him jubilant over the success of the operation he seemed saddened, even depressed, by the circumstances of his forced departure. Limon, however, had no pangs of conscience over having misled the French government. France had violated a contractual commitment. Paramount in his thinking was the awareness that the boats were the backbone of the new navy, and that there had been no practical alternative to the escape he had engineered.

"All of you know," he told the Israelis at the party, "that we are fighting for Israel's survival."

Before leaving, he telephoned his farewells to French friends, including General Bonte, and detected no trace of anger toward him among any of them.

For Bonte and Cazelles, the Cherbourg affair would mark a tragic end to illustrious careers. Bonte refused to accept his suspension passively and appealed to France's highest judicial body, the Council of State. He also awaited the verdict of the inquiry committee appointed by the government to investigate the affair. Meanwhile, he retired to a small town on the French Riviera. He was still awaiting exoneration eighteen months after the flight of the boats when he was struck by a motorbike while crossing a street. He died of a fractured skull in a Nice hospital.

Cazelles had been summoned, immediately after the New Year's Eve Cabinet meeting, to the office of Chaban-Delmas. The manner in which the premier's aides turned away in embarrassment when Cazelles arrived was a clear portent of bad news. Chaban-Delmas informed the general that the government had decided on his suspension. He was being suspended, the premier emphasized, not sacked. When Cazelles asked what the difference was, the premier gave no direct response.

The suspension of the generals was hailed by Arab states as a voucher of the French government's noncomplicity in the affair. The government could see no way of reinstating the generals, innocent or not, without calling into question its own credibility. After a year, Cazelles requested an interview with Pompidou. When his former patron made it clear that his status could not be changed, Cazelles retired from the army.

Limon, shortly after returning home, began a new career as the Israeli representative of Baron Edmond de Rothschild. The baron, whom he had come to know during his Paris sojourn, had extensive business interests in Israel. Limon's connection to the House of Rothschild would become more intimate when his daughter married the scion of another branch of the Rothschild family. Although Limon's new duties required frequent visits to Paris, he put off returning for half a year after his forced departure.

It was with some apprehension that he finally flew to France to attend a business meeting. Although he had not been declared *non grata*, the border police could turn him back without explanation. The officer to whom he handed his passport at the airport studied it for some time, turned the pages, looked at it sideways, and then looked up at the tall traveler. "You are Admiral Limon?" he asked. Limon acknowledged his identity. The officer rose and reached over the glass partition to shake his hand.

"Congratulations," said the Frenchman.

While the fate of the Cherbourg boats had been visible to all—much too visible for the parties concerned—knowledge about the fifty embargoed Mirage planes at remote military airfields and aircraft factories was limited to what the parties chose to reveal. The planes would remain a subject of bitter public controversy until Israel finally announced in 1972 that it was waiving its claims and accepting a refund of its money, leaving the planes to be turned over to the French air force.

However, fifty Mirages had already made their way to Israel in packing cases marked "spare parts"—some of them having been disassembled, some shipped in parts straight from the factories. At the Israel Aircraft Industries plant they had been put together on a special assembly line, with minor structural changes and an American engine. The reborn aircraft, later to be named the Kfir, was more powerful than the original Mirage. Among the ports through which the "spare parts" were shipped was Cherbourg.

It had begun with the wisp of an idea hesitantly floated at a staff meeting in navy headquarters on Mount Carmel in 1960. The force mobilized by that idea had proved powerful enough to overcome resistance within the navy, opposition by rival services, the deepest instincts of the Israeli General Staff, the technological state-of-the-art, the indifference of Western navies, and now the French embargo. This force was distilled through a small group of men charged with responsibility for Israel's sea defenses. They had perceived a threat, devised a solution, and moved to implement it, letting nothing stand in their way. Ahead of them still lay the ultimate test—the performance of their homegrown concept in combat against the technology of a superpower.

WAR

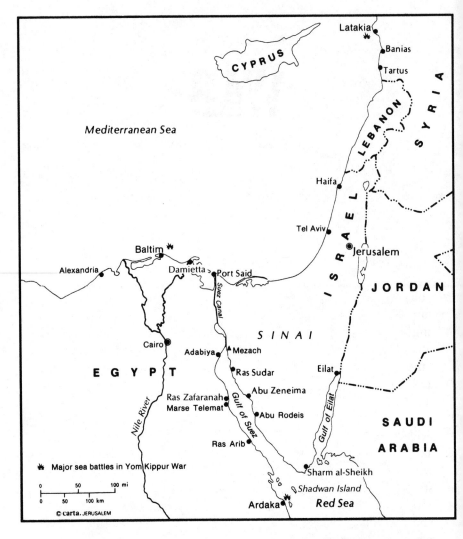

Israel and sites of the major sea battles fought in the Yom Kippur War. *Carta*

15
Warship

The sight of the small boats scurrying out to sea in the morning and returning late at night would become as familiar to residents of Haifa as it had been in Cherbourg. The only change in the boats' appearance initially was the small guns installed on deck. For several months five "Starboat" vessels had no weaponry at all, their role as leased civilian equipment continuing to be played out. The twelve "Cherbourg boats," as Israelis came to call them, would require a major transformation before becoming missile boats. Given the absence of Israeli experience, the Defense Ministry turned to Italy, which agreed to install and integrate the complex weapon and electronic systems at La Spezia. However, the Italians subsequently backed down for political reasons, and the Israeli navy and Israel Aircraft Industries decided to undertake the task themselves. Technicians worked round-the-clock from rafts alongside the boats, in order not to clutter the narrow quays at the navy base. Once again Israel was being pushed into new areas of technological achievement by lack of alternatives.

There was an enthusiastic turnout of volunteers for the flotilla all through the navy. A new kind of warfare was involved, one in which brawn and even seamanship mattered less than an ability to control electronic systems without faltering in the stress of battle. Outstanding officers from the torpedo and destroyer flotillas, all of them with engineering degrees, were chosen to organize the training program. First they had to master the intricate systems themselves, and then devise standard operating procedures that ordinary seamen could cope with.

The systems' complexity was increased by the planners' decision "to leave a man in the loop"—that is, not to automate the missile firing system fully, on the grounds that a trained man could distinguish between real and false targets better than any electronic sensor. The crewmen, many of them not out of their teens, would be operating near the extreme of their capacity. In battle situations they would be called on to make life-or-death decisions in split seconds. There was concern in the navy hierarchy about whether Israeli crews, with their limited experience, would be capable of meeting these demands. The same concern had been voiced by the heads of the German rocket development program in World War II when the V-2s were to be turned over by the scientists at Peenemünde to army crews who were to fire them against England. The missile-boat crews, unlike the V-2 crews, would be operating under fire against fast-moving targets.

Discipline among the Israeli crewmen differed strikingly from that in other navies. Men and officers addressed one another by first name, only the captain being addressed formally as "Hamefakaid" ("Commander"). There was no saluting except by the gangplank sentry when the captain boarded the vessel. If an officer told a passing sailor to mop up a spill, the rating might easily argue the point, noting that it was not his compartment or that he was just coming off watch.

This lack of conventional discipline was balanced by a sense of involvement by the ordinary sailor in the general running of the boat, and by personal initiative. Sailors learned not only their assigned duties but those of others as well. They would not settle for being told that the boat would sail in twenty-four hours—they wanted to know where it was sailing to and why and, if it was a battle exercise, what the tactical situation was supposed to be. Officers took a close interest in the men's affairs and would visit their homes in the event of family problems or illness, something rare in other navies. The officers themselves were highly trained and motivated personnel, on whom the success or failure of the program would depend.

Within the flotilla, confidence in the direction they were taking grew daily. The crews worked with mockups, and then with the boats themselves, as the Saars began to arrive from Cherbourg. Because of the intense concentration involved in monitoring the electronic instrumentation, it was decided that the crews would stand watch three hours, even though the standard four-on/four-off routine would have permitted longer stretches of sleep.

No navy in the West had yet developed a comprehensive battle doctrine for missile warfare, and a completely new way of thinking was required. In combat, captains would not be on the bridge, observing the enemy through binoculars, but below decks, watching dots moving on screens in the Combat Information Center. Electronic impulses flitting across the spaces between opposing fleets would now determine the course of battles.

Unlike conventional shells, missiles were not in the lap of the gods once fired but could be manipulated by one or both sides while in the air. The small radar in the Gabriel missile itself would lock on a target "illuminated" by the large radar on the launch vessel—the fire-control radar. The missile would "ride the beam" provided by the fire-control radar until about halfway to target, at which point its own radar would take over the homing and free the radar on the boat to guide another missile. The side being attacked, if it had an EW system, could attempt to baffle the incoming missiles with false signals. However, should the enemy attempt to do this to the Gabriel, the operator on the launch vessel could resume command of the missile, override the jamming, and steer the missile to the true target via a small rearward-facing receiver on the missile.

Unlike the Gabriel's system—called "semiactive homing" because of the missile's partial dependence on a beam from the launch vessel—the Styx employed an active homing system, in which the missile itself transmitted the only radar signals and followed them to the target without the mother ship's having to light the way. This mode would be employed by virtually all missile systems to be developed in the West, including the French Exocet and American Harpoon and even the later versions of the Gabriel, because missile ranges extended well beyond radar range and they could therefore not be beamed onto target by the mother ship.

Even-Tov had chosen the semiactive approach partly because the Soviets were expert at jamming and he believed beam-riding could overcome any jamming systems that the Osas and Komars might carry. The main reason, however, was his uncertainty over whether his theoretical calculations concerning the Gabriel's ability to home in on a target were correct. The missile's small radar would have to distinguish the target through the background electronic "static" that radar soundings elicit. Even-Tov decided that the missile had best be helped at least halfway on its course by a beam-ride from the mother ship to ensure that it was close enough to the target to discern its signal clearly. If worse came to worst, and the missile's unconventional "stiff-necked" radar homing failed altogether, the missile could ride the radar beam projected by the launch vessel all the way to target.

In the eternal game of invention and counterinvention, each side tried to anticipate the enemy's reaction and provide suitable counter-measures. A major factor was the characteristics of the search radar—distinct from the fire-control radar—which sought to detect targets at long range. The search radar could betray the sender, because its electronic beams were detectable by a target ship with proper instrumentation at two or three times the distance at which the sender itself could see the target on its screen.

In World War II this phenomenon had caused the German battleship *Bismarck* to betray itself to its British pursuers in the Atlantic, after its sensors detected British radar. The German captain did not realize that while he could pick up radar emissions he was actually too far away for any radar echo to be picked up by the British. Believing himself exposed, he broke his radio silence in order to signal to his headquarters. Although the British radar had not detected the *Bismarck*, the premature radio message was picked up, enabling the British to intercept and destroy the German raider. The Israelis fitted their missile boats with passive detection systems that could reveal an enemy's radar without betraying their own presence as long as the Israeli boats maintained radar silence.

The Israelis were for long totally ignorant of the characteristics of the missile they would have to face. If Western intelligence sources knew more about the Styx, they were not telling. Not even a picture of it was available. Many experts believed the Russians incapable of developing sophisticated homing radar. They were convinced that the Styx was merely a ballistic missile—in effect, a shell with a longer-than-normal range and a larger-than-normal payload but without an electronic brain that could chase its prey. The Russians, Western authorities noted, had gone through World War II without developing radar. Even the names of the Soviet missile boats, Komar ("Mosquito") and Osa ("Wasp"), were cited as evidence that the Soviets themselves did not attribute killing powers to their weapon system. Another school of thought believed it unlikely that such an expensive weapon would have been developed without a homing capacity, but few followers of this school believed the Styx capable of hitting a small target.

Commander Herut Tsemach, a brilliant electronics officer, had been summoned to Erell's office in 1964, two years after the Soviet missile boats had been delivered to Egypt. The deputy navy commander asked Tsemach to look into the question of the Styx: "Do we have a problem? If so, what do we do about it?"

It would take Tsemach six months to think the problem through. He had worked on a homing system for the Gabriel after being seconded to the IAI by the navy. He had provided important input but clashed with Ori Even-Tov over different engineering approaches and was forced off the project. Trying now to imagine how his counterpart in Soviet naval headquarters in Leningrad thought, and examining what was known about Soviet missile technology, he concluded that there was indeed a problem. In a paper submitted to Erell, he sketched out possible solutions for jamming or deceiving the enemy radar. For the moment these solutions remained on paper.

Commander Shoshan, head of the navy's electronic division and future commander of the *Eilat*, had also been asked by Erell to examine the problem. Shoshan had read in a foreign maritime magazine about the commercial availability of chaff dispensers. Chaff, strips of aluminum, had been dropped in large quantities by air forces in World War II to confuse enemy radars by reflecting their beams in the same manner as did airplanes. They were being offered now as rescue devices for lifeboats. Fired from hand-held dispensers, they could be picked up by the radar of search vessels from far greater distances than flares could be seen. After obtaining Erell's approval of a budget allocation of 20 pounds sterling, Shoshan ordered twenty of the chaff rockets from abroad.

In an experiment carried out near Haifa, Tsemach manned a radar on the shore, as Shoshan sailed past on a torpedo boat and fired a single chaff rocket. By radio, Tsemach reported to Shoshan that he could still clearly see the boat on the screen. Shoshan and two assistants then fired three rockets simultaneously. A moment later Tsemach reported that he could no longer distinguish the ship because of the confusion of images. The men were jubilant—the radar lock could be broken. But a more sophisticated answer would have to be found than hand-held dispensers. They would also need EW instruments that could blind the Styx's radar by jamming or tricking it with false signals.

The first order of business was to construct an instrument that would identify enemy radar emissions by their electronic fingerprints, including the distinctive radar used in the guidance of missiles. This electronic intelligence is the basis of ESM (Electronic Support Measures), whose task is to signal the presence of an enemy and warn of incoming missiles. Such instruments existed in some advanced navies, but none was available to Israel. Developing them from scratch could be expected to take years. Tsemach decided to try improvising a detection device from available materials. Scouring the navy's warehouses in Haifa, he came upon World War II American radar equipment that could provide the basis for the system. With the assistance of one of the electronic plants beginning to be established in Israel, he devised a prototype detection instrument. It was declared operational just six months after Tsemach undertook the project, an effort for which he would receive the coveted Israel Prize for technology in 1966. The instrument was placed aboard the *Eilat*, as were mountings for chaff dispensers.

The chaff system was not yet operational when the destroyer set out on its doomed voyage in October 1967. The detection device was functioning but its operators were unable to identify the characteristics of the radar they could detect locking on the ship. When divers retrieved the instrument from the sunken destroyer, it was found to have faithfully recorded the distinctive emission of a Komar's fire-control radar in Port Said homing in on the *Eilat*. It had been Egypt's President Gamel Abdel Nasser who had personally given the order to launch the missiles.

Tsemach heard about the *Eilat*'s sinking on his car radio as he returned from a Sabbath outing with his family. He drove to naval headquarters and found everyone in shock.

"Well, their missiles do hit, don't they?" Erell said to him mordantly.

Tsemach phoned the senior engineering officer who had been the principal advocate of the Styx-can't-hit school. When Tsemach reported that Styx had not only hit but sunk the *Eilat*, he heard the officer gasp, "*Mama mia.*"

In the next few days, Tsemach visited survivors in hospitals and at home to obtain a description of the missile attack. It quickly became apparent that the Styx had not only muscle but a formidable brain as well. Tsemach came down with the flu during this survey and was visited in his home atop Mount Carmel by Commander Rami Lunz, slated to become the navy's next chief intelligence officer. The two men talked of the need for an active EW system that would not only monitor incoming missiles but also deceive them. Known as ECM (Electronic Countermeasures), this system included jamming and deception. If ESM could provide technical details such as the enemy radar's wavelength and pulse rate, then similar emissions could be sent by ECM at the enemy radar to drown out its emissions with brute electronic force or to divert it into pursuit of electronic ghosts.

Tsemach spelled out the outlines of what had already taken shape in his mind. Despite the sophistication of some of its elements, it was a relatively simple system whose great advantage was that it was achievable within a reasonable time and at reasonable cost. Lunz recognized Tsemach's genius in being able to provide quick and practical answers to complex problems without becoming bogged down in the search for ever more clever solutions. Russia's Admiral Groshkov, who built up his country's postwar fleet, expressed his preference for such rough-and-ready solutions over the brilliant-but-prolonged approach when he asserted, "Good enough is the best." What Tsemach proposed appeared to be good enough.

The wooden-hulled fishing vessel *Orit* set out from Ashdod in mid-May 1970 to work the waters off northern Sinai. The Six Day War had opened new fishing grounds for Israel's small trawler fleet, particularly during the warmer months, when there is scant fishing farther north. Off El Arish, the four-man crew cast two nets. After hauling in their catch, they continued westward. By the light of deck lamps, two crewmen, aged seventeen and twenty-one, began sorting out the fish and storing them below. They were concentrating on their work, and so did not see the light lifting over the western horizon and speeding silently in their direction through the night sky. A violent explosion in the water nearby knocked them off their feet as the missile struck. The boat's lights went out and the vessel shuddered. Another missile, following close behind, exploded alongside the small vessel, shattering the wooden hull.

The two young crewmen lifted themselves off the deck and found themselves uninjured, the wooden timbers of the vessel having absorbed much of the blast. Feeling their way in the darkness, they stumbled on the engineer, lying mortally wounded near the bridge. Below decks they found the captain dead. The two crewmen strapped lifebelts on the wounded engineer and on themselves. As they prepared to leap into the water, they saw two more missiles diving at them out of the western sky. Fortunately for them, they remained on board as the missiles exploded in the water. Discovering that the engineer had died, they strapped his body to a large plank in the hope that it would be washed ashore.

The pair slipped into the water and began swimming toward the Sinai shore eleven miles to the south. Almost twenty-four hours later they reached it, staggering ashore at Bardiwill Lagoon. The exhausted pair dug themselves into the sand as protection against the cold desert night. At dawn they began walking, and soon met a Bedouin fisherman. He gave them food and hot tea and took them across the lagoon in his small boat to an Israeli settlement, the farthest west in Sinai. A few hours later the two young crewmen had been helicoptered back to Israel and were telling their story to naval intelligence officers.

The Egyptians had demonstrated that the Styx could home not only on a twenty-five-hundred-ton destroyer but also on a seventy-ton wooden boat. Most officers in Israeli naval headquarters had believed the Saar boats too small to be hit by a Styx, but the *Orit* was one-third the size. For the moment there was nothing the navy could do about it except avoid surface encounters.

Even before becoming the first victim of the new technology, Israel was already far ahead of anyone else in the West in coming up with a system designed to counter it. The platform for the new system was being launched in Cherbourg, and the EW outlines were being fixed by Tsemach. Following the sinking of the *Eilat*, Tsemach had no problem getting all the funding and engineering personnel he needed; the problem was obtaining the necessary electronic equipment. He toured NATO countries but found that they had no serious answer to the problem. Although the United States had begun developmental work on anti-Styx jammers in the early 1960s, it was not yet sharing this equipment even with its NATO allies. Tsemach had been able to put together his initial detection system with found items and some local developmental work, but the Israeli electronic base was not yet at a level to produce the sophisticated equipment he had conceived to ward off missiles by jamming their radars or sending them false signals. He turned instead to a major electronics firm in Italy that could meet his specifications and provide the project with its own considerable electronics input.

Colleagues would say that it was the Jewish people's fear of having no grave to mark the burial of kin lost at sea that motivated Tsemach to build such a high survivability factor into his program. Such a motivation had led Israel to request that the British destroyers acquired in the 1950s be provided with refrigerated morgues during refitting, so that men killed at sea could be brought home for interment rather than committed to the deep. Tsemach, however, was conscious only of the need to build as effective a system as possible to stand against the Soviet missile.

In addition to the electronics, Tsemach and his team developed a chaff system that had no parallel elsewhere. It included the use of both long-range and short-range rockets—the former to create a diversion in the early stage of battle and make the enemy waste missiles on electronic shadows, the latter to divert missiles that managed to home in on the Israeli vessels by creating a large decoy target at the last moment that left the real target somewhere off center. The chaff had to be fired according to a precise sequence, and failure of nerve by the men responsible for it could lead to disaster.

The critical importance of EW to the entire program became even more apparent in the mid-1960s, when the Israelis learned that the Styx had a forty-five-kilometer range. The range of the Gabriel, still in the developmental stage, was less than half that, only twenty kilometers. This meant that for a lengthy period at the beginning of a battle—perhaps half an hour—the Saars would be exposed to missiles and could not hit back. Without the EW cover, there would be no way of crossing the twenty-five-kilometer-wide "missile belt" in order to get within Gabriel range of the enemy ships. No navy in the world had antimissile EW on small boats, but for the Israeli navy these were ships of the line.

The Gabriel's range had been fixed to permit the missile—initially intended to be mounted on destroyers—to outreach the Egyptian

Skory destroyers. Discovering that the Gabriel was outranged by the Styx, the naval command debated the possibility of asking Ori Even-Tov to change the characteristics of his missile by developing a new motor for long-range propulsion. The idea was dropped, because the change could drag out the development process for an extended period and it was considered preferable to have an operative missile in hand as soon as possible, even if its range was limited. This would prove one of the most important executive decisions in the entire program.

The deadliness of the Styx was proved again during the Indo-Pakistani war in 1971, when the Indian navy used the missile to sink a destroyer and a minesweeper on the open seas, as well as several vessels in a Pakistani port.

To some Israeli naval officers, the concept of EW seemed a flight of fancy, a conceit of the electronics spooks that had little relevance to real combat. When Tsemach briefed missile-boat commanders for the first time on his EW approach, he was challenged by Lieutenant Commander Eli Rahav, the officer who had led the torpedo boats in the action off Romani in July 1967 in which two Egyptian vessels were sunk.

"I don't believe in all this hocus-pocus," said Rahav. "What we need are boats that move fast." Stung by the phrase "hocus-pocus," Tsemach said, "All right, your boat will get the equipment last."

Which it would.

The sinking of the *Eilat* reverberated in naval circles throughout the world. Even before the Amiot shipyard in Cherbourg had completed the last of the Saars in 1969, it received orders for similar missile boats from Greece. Within the next few years it would receive orders for more than fifty more from Asia, South America, Europe, and Arab countries. Other shipyards around the world also entered into production. A few months after the sinking of the *Eilat*, France, whose experts had been briefed on the development of the Gabriel by the Israelis, began developing its own sea-to-sea missile, the Exocet, and other European countries launched similar development programs.

The United States navy, reacting strongly, after the *Eilat*'s sinking, to the belatedly recognized danger of the Soviet missiles, began to pour large sums into the development of EW systems to protect its ships— overextravagant sums, according to some American experts. In 1970, under the command of Admiral Elmo Zumwalt, it would also begin to develop its first effective sea-to-sea missile, the Harpoon. Zumwalt was the first "black-shoe" admiral from the surface fleet to become chief of naval operations after a string of admirals from the air arm. He was determined to restore offensive capability to other naval elements, rather than relying so heavily on its vulnerable carriers. Israel's diminutive navy, meanwhile, was moving steadily along its own course.

The Gabriels had initially been intended to be used against the Egyptian Skory destroyers, it being presumed that the missile boats on both sides were too small a target for missiles. Erell had therefore envisioned the second series of six Cherbourg boats which had the larger 76mm guns doing double duty by engaging the enemy missile boats with shellfire. The sinking of the *Orit* demonstrated that the small boats were themselves vulnerable to missiles. The Gabriel proved equally able to hit pinpoint targets. The missile boats then would be using their missiles against each other.

It fell to Hadar Kimche, as the first commander of the missile boat flotilla, to turn the Saar from a bare platform into a warship. Building on concepts originally advanced by Binny Telem and others, he took the boats out almost every day to test tactics as they were formulated. In the battle doctrine being developed, the primary objective was to cross the missile belt while evading the Styx's long reach with EW, speed, maneuver, and, if all else failed, gunfire. The enemy could theoretically keep out of Gabriel range by launching his Styx at maximum range and then beating a retreat to nearby harbors before the Saars' superior speed could close the gap. The answer was somehow to use EW to draw the enemy near, to confuse him about the Israeli boats' whereabouts, and then to pounce on him from out of an electronic cloud somewhere near effective Gabriel range.

The flotilla received a major boost in efficiency in 1970, when four years of work on a tactical trainer was completed. Every day officers trained individually or in groups in endless permutations of combat situations—confronting various combinations of enemy craft, by night and day, in stormy weather and calm, with gunfire or missiles. Computer readings informed them whether they had sunk the enemy or gone down with all hands. In group debriefings, the officers were encouraged to evaluate one another's performance frankly, and the youngest ensigns were free to question even their squadron commander's judgment.

The trainer permitted effective development of the revolutionary tactics that would be needed—numerous alternatives being assessed on the machine before selected options were tried out at sea. In hundreds of war games the missile-boat officers skirmished with make-believe fleets, using tactics known to be employed by the Egyptian and Syrian navies. The "Arab" commanders in these games were naval intelligence officers who created a worst-case situation for the Israeli commanders facing them, by using their knowledge of the Israeli missile-boat capabilities.

Confidence steadily grew among the missile-boat men as the pieces of the system began to come together. Confidence and constant drilling were essential for men who would have to charge an enemy with a reach twice as long as their own—a reach whose lethalness in the sinking of the *Eilat* was still fresh in everyone's mind. One officer whose confidence in the EW defenses was less than total was the man who had devised them, Herut Tsemach. He could only make an educated guess as to the way the system's electronics worked. He had guessed correctly in 1964 that his opposite number in Leningrad would install a homing device in the Styx, but determining what kind of device was another matter. If he had guessed wrongly, he knew, the electronic umbrella he had devised for the Israeli fleet could prove a shroud.

16

Red Sea Command

Four small patrol boats were moored in the bay at Sharm al-Sheikh, near the southern tip of the Sinai Peninsula, when Captain Zeev Almog flew down in August 1972 to assume command of Israel's Red Sea fleet. Aside from five vintage landing craft, the lightly armed patrol boats made up virtually the entire naval force responsible for preventing infiltration along some 350 kilometers of Sinai's coastline opposite the Egyptians.

Almog, who had established his reputation as leader of the naval commandos, received a strong hint immediately after the change-of-command ceremony from the chief of the General Staff, General David Elazar, that the size of his fleet might not be his major problem.

In a tone only half joshing, Elazar said, "Any boat that breaks down at sea, Zeev, I'm going to hold you personally responsible for."

Elazar related that he had recently gone to sea with Almog's predecessor in a patrol boat whose engines stopped dead after ten miles. "Never mind that the problem turned out to be that they simply hadn't checked the gauges before sailing and had run out of fuel. We'll put that aside for the moment. What I will never forgive is that I was stuck on that damn boat vomiting my guts out for five hours before they could get another boat to us."

The story was still reverberating in Almog's mind the next morning as he began to study documents in his new office. At 9:00 A.M. he laid

189

the papers aside and said to the officer he had brought down as his deputy, "Let's take a look."

The base seemed deserted when they stepped out into the hot sunlight. The sound of neither human voices nor machinery interrupted the howl of the wind. Entering the barracks, the two men found virtually all base personnel, including officers, sound asleep. Almog was astounded at seeing a navy unit succumbing so completely to the phenomenon of Bedouinism, which sometimes afflicts military units stationed for long in the desert—a lassitude deriving from the heat, the remoteness, and a surrender to the enormity of the surroundings.

The acquisition of the Sinai Peninsula in 1967 had quintupled the shoreline in Israel's hands and bestowed an operational importance on the navy it had never had before. Upon it fell much of the responsibility for preventing Egyptian infiltrators from landing on Sinai's desert shores, and for providing protection for the offshore oil wells Israel had begun exploiting at Abu Rodeis on the Gulf of Suez.

This was a task that brought the naval commandos into their own. Hitherto a highly trained but little-used elite, the commandos, under the leadership of Almog, staged eighty sorties across the Suez Canal and the Gulf of Suez during the War of Attrition in the Suez Canal area in 1969–70. The most daring was the raid on Green Island, a fortress built on a coral outcropping three kilometers south of the entrance to the Suez Canal. In a night attack, a small force of commandos swimming underwater against a strong current came silently out of the sea to eliminate the sentries and penetrate the fortress's heavy defenses. With the assistance of the boat-borne paratroopers who followed, they overcame the Egyptian commandos posted on the island in a sharp battle and blew up defense positions. The operation took just fifty minutes, and the raiders got away moments before artillery on the adjacent Egyptian mainland opened up in an attempt to interdict their retreat.

In September 1969 a large armored force transported by naval landing craft crossed the Gulf of Suez in the largest amphibious operation Israel had ever staged. The force rolled up Egyptian defenses along an eighty-kilometer stretch of coast before being retrieved by the landing craft and ferried back to Sinai.

Thus, while half the navy was building the missile force of the future in pristine R&D conditions in electronics laboratories and in Mediterranean waters, the other half was waging old-fashioned cut-and-thrust warfare in the south, with commando knives and light patrol boats commanded by young ensigns.

Little Israel-bound traffic passed through the Red Sea besides oil tankers from Iran. Sinai itself became a major oil source following the capture of the Abu Rodeis wells on the Sinai coast in the Six Day War.

The wells, extending for fifty kilometers along the Sinai shore, had been seized virtually intact by a reserve army unit commanded by Mordecai Friedman, the director of the government oil exploration company who would two years later put Limon in touch with Martin Siemm. Friedman was charged by the government with restoring the oilfield to operation, which he did within two weeks.

His major concern was whether the Egyptians would permit oil to be pumped from the captured wells without interference. The Gulf of Suez was just twenty-five kilometers wide, and the Egyptians could easily hit the offshore rigs with artillery or launch air or naval strikes. The Egyptians, however, had oilfields on their side of the gulf, which were no less vulnerable.

Even during the height of the War of Attrition, when both sides were raiding across the canal, Israeli tankers making the fourteen-hour run to Eilat after loading at Abu Rodeis would peacefully pass down the center of the gulf, within two kilometers of the offshore rigs of the Egyptian-controlled Morgan Fields.

It seemed likely that both sides would continue to exclude the Gulf of Suez oilfields from their conflict zone, short of all-out war—and perhaps even then. By 1973, production from the Abu Rodeis fields had doubled to 45 million barrels a year, Israel's total fuel needs. Abu Rodeis's production was shipped to Eilat, where a newly built pipeline carried it across Israel's southern Negev to Ashkelon, on the Mediterranean. The Abu Rodeis fields had become one of Israel's major economic assets.

Despite its remoteness from the Israeli heartland and from the minds of most Israelis, the Red Sea was a major strategic zone and a tripwire. Its closing to Israeli traffic in May 1967 had been the *causus belli* for the Six Day War.

Before this, history had taken little note of the Red Sea beyond the biblical account of the Israelites' crossing, and the opening of the Suez Canal in 1869. The sea stretched for eleven hundred miles, between Bab al-Mandeb, the narrow straits between the Horn of Africa and the

Arabian Peninsula, and the tip of the Sinai Peninsula, Ras ("Cape") Mohammed. From there it split into two narrow waterways.

The eastern one, called the Gulf of Eilat or Gulf of Aqaba, extended for a hundred miles, to the Israeli and Jordanian towns of those names coexisting amiably at the head of the gulf. Like the Red Sea itself, the gulf lay along a geologic fault extending for two thousand miles, between Turkey and East Africa, and its waters were as much as eighteen hundred meters deep. The coral reefs along its shores and its colorful fish were among the most spectacular in the world.

The western waterway, extending for two hundred miles, from Ras Mohammed to the Suez Canal, was the Gulf of Suez. Its waters were shallow—forty meters was the average depth. The shallowness created long stretches of dangerous reefs barely covered at high tide and small islands the Egyptians had fortified. Although it could not compete with the Gulf of Eilat in underwater beauty, it was compensated by oil deposits beneath its waters and along its shores. With the closure of the Suez Canal in the Six Day War and the Israelis' occupation of its eastern shore, the waterway had become a battle zone instead of a major international passageway. Nevertheless, both sides continued to honor the tacit agreement not to attack each other's oilfields. Within clear view of the Israeli oil rigs of Abu Rodeis was the main oil area under Egyptian control, the Italian-owned Morgan Fields, which were closer to the Israeli-held shores of Sinai than to the Egyptian mainland.

Although the largely landlocked waterways enjoyed almost perpetual sunlight, their waters were far rougher than the Mediterranean, an almost constant north wind building up waves that made sailing in small boats extremely uncomfortable, as General Elazar had discovered.

The defense establishment had decided to bring the Red Sea region into the missile age. It had been Moshe Dayan who had suggested, shortly after the Six Day War, the deployment of missile boats in the Red Sea, in order to alter its strategic balance. The Egyptian blockade in 1967 had been imposed at the Strait of Tiran, off Sharm al-Sheikh, at the southern end of the Sinai Peninsula. This was now in Israeli hands, but there was another pinch point a thousand miles south where the Egyptians could impose a blockade in the future, the Strait of Bab al-Mandeb. Dayan ordered the navy to develop vessels with range enough to show the flag at Bab al-Mandeb and prevent its being sealed off. Naval architect Haim Shahal was still in Cherbourg, overseeing construction of the early Saars, when the request was passed on to him. His first thought was that the Saars might serve the purpose if two of their four engines were replaced with fuel tanks. When his calculations showed that this would not suffice, he turned again to Lurssen in Bremen, designers of the Saar. Basing themselves on one of their existing vessels, the German shipbuilders came up with a design of a 415-ton boat—80 percent larger than the Saar—with a three-thousand-mile range. This was enough to reach Bab al-Mandeb, linger to patrol or fight, and return without refueling.

This time the Defense Ministry did not seek a foreign shipyard to carry out construction: if it could be avoided the ministry would not run the risk of embargo again. The technological know-how that had fast been accumulating in Israel since the Saar project was launched enabled Israel Shipyards in Haifa to undertake construction of the new Reshef ("Flash") class boats itself. Israel's burgeoning defense industries were now able to design and construct electronic systems for the Reshef class that were far more sophisticated than the Saar-class equipment for which European engineering help had been needed just a few years before. The first two Reshef-class boats were scheduled to be launched early in 1973, and to sail around Africa for the Red Sea toward the end of the year. Four more were to follow when completed.

Since leaving the commandos eight months before, Almog had been trained on missile boats in order to prepare him for his new task. When he surveyed the tactical situation as Red Sea commander, however, Dayan's proposal made little sense. To reach Bab al-Mandeb from Sharm and return would involve close to four days' sailing in a seventy-mile-wide waterway lined all the way by hostile shores. Along most of the route, the boats would be outside Israeli air cover while subject to Arab air and sea attacks. The main arm of the Egyptian Red Sea fleet lay at Ras Banas, 250 miles from Sharm al-Sheikh, out of easy reach of the Israeli air force and protected by SAM missiles. Based there were two destroyers, two submarines, a frigate, and four torpedo boats. To go up against enemy vessels that had air support was a disquieting scenario to contemplate. Others in the naval command thought it possible, but Almog saw no feasible means of controlling Bab al-Mandeb from Sinai, even if he had thirty missile boats.

He did see an urgent need for them in the Gulf of Suez. Here Egypt had four Komar missile boats, which were a constant threat not only to the Israeli patrol craft but also to any Israeli invasion fleet that might attempt a landing on Egypt's Gulf of Suez coast. The arrival of the first two Reshef-class boats would permit Israel for the first time to challenge Egyptian naval supremacy in these waters.

Until then, Almog would have to make do with what he had. Although the prospect of war seemed unlikely, he determined to give his existing fleet an offensive capacity in the event war did break out before the arrival of the missile boats. His four patrol boats, called Daburs ("Hornets"), were American craft designed for river duty in Vietnam. They were armed with one light 20mm gun and two machine guns. The boats could deal with infiltrators in rubber boats or other lightly armed craft, but they had not been conceived for serious naval combat. Almog decided they would have to behave as if they had been, until something better came along to replace them. A 20mm gun could not sink enemy warships, but at close range there was a chance of hitting a fuel tank or an ammunition locker. Intensive drills were begun in closing to "zero range."

Almog ordered that the three-day patrols of the Gulf of Suez the Daburs had been going out on once a month be expanded to ten to fourteen days. In addition to the operational information thus gained, familiarity with the gulf would increase confidence when the time came for doing battle in these waters.

With the Daburs pretending to be destroyers, Almog directed that the LSTs, for all their garbage-scow appearance, be made to simulate patrol boats. If they were fitted with machine guns and 20mm guns, there was no reason why they could not sail along the Sinai coast to protect against infiltrators in small boats. The main task of the LSTs remained the strategic one of transporting an invasion force across the Gulf of Suez, thereby outflanking the strong Egyptian defenses along the Suez Canal. The General Staff had rejected on budgetary grounds a navy request to build a fleet of new landing craft, but the five retread LSTs that had been provided—one of them a converted African ore-carrier—could handle the job. One of Almog's first priorities was to draw up detailed plans for the LSTs to transport hundreds of tanks across the ten-mile-wide gulf in forty-eight hours by ferry runs. By offering access to the vulnerable flank of the Egyptian defenses, the LSTs constituted an important strategic element.

The Egyptian Komars remained a worrisome problem for Almog,

particularly because of the danger they posed to the large, slow-moving tank-landing ships, which had no EW defenses against Styx missiles. If any of the troop-filled vessels was sunk, it would be a far worse disaster than the *Eilat*.

Meanwhile, at Sharm al-Sheikh, jetties were built out into the anchorage for the expected missile boats, barracks were constructed for the additional personnel, and a cave was blasted out of a cliffside to serve as a storage hangar for missiles and an electronics laboratory.

The changes instituted by Almog were greeted initially by murmurings among the men. "He thinks he's still with the commandos," was one remark that reached Almog's ears. But desert lethargy rapidly fell away before the spirit of innovation. The decision to extend the Dabur patrols in the Gulf of Suez meant that a new infrastructure had to be built up along the western coast of Sinai to service the vessels, instead of having them sail back to Sharm al-Sheikh for servicing. Jetties were repaired or built from scratch at a number of points, fueling equipment and water-storage tanks were installed, and a communications network was established.

"I don't know if there's going to be a war," Almog told his men, "but if there is we won't be caught with our pants down."

In May 1973 an Egyptian de Castro patrol boat crossing the Gulf of Suez fired on Ras Sudar, the northernmost Israeli naval base in the gulf. Ensign Zvika Shachak, commanding a small Bertram patrol boat about to be phased out of service, returned fire from five thousand yards, but neither side's firing was effective. When the young officer reported on the incident to Almog, he was forcefully rebuked.

"Why were you firing at that range?" demanded Almog. "You weren't the *Graf Spee*."

Despite the incident, the ensign was shortly afterward given command of a larger Dabur. Before leading a two-boat patrol into the Gulf of Suez in mid-August, he was briefed by Almog. "If the Egyptians try it again, you are to close on them without awaiting orders as soon as they open fire. You can begin squeezing off shots at fifteen hundred yards, but hold off until six hundred yards before you open sustained fire. Then keep closing to zero range."

A chance to put these directives into practice was not long in coming. Shortly after arriving at Ras Sudar, Shachak was warned by radar of a vessel approaching from the Egyptian side of the gulf. A burst of fire directed at the naval base indicated that it was the de Castro trying the same maneuver. This time it was not an old Bertram that emerged from the Israeli anchorage in pursuit, but two far more powerful Daburs. The Egyptian patrol boat turned and fled toward home at top speed.

With Almog's rebuke still fresh in his ears, Shachak began squeezing off shots at about a thousand yards and held off sustained fire from both Daburs until six hundred yards. The fire was effective, and the Egyptian vessel began to zigzag in an attempt to avoid hits, thereby permitting the Israeli vessels to close the gap. As they drew almost alongside the damaged vessel, however, both Daburs found their ammunition exhausted. At this point the boats were ordered by General Staff headquarters, which had been monitoring the skirmish, to break off contact and return to base.

Shachak was expecting his commander to have warm words for him at the debriefing for his hard pursuit, but once again he was given a cold shower by Almog. "You should have used less ammunition until you closed on him. And if you were out of ammunition, so what? You still had Uzis [submachine guns], you still had grenades, you still had your bows. You could have rammed him."

A humbled ensign returned to his boat, wondering whether he would ever get another chance to close to zero range.

17

Dress Rehearsal

Commander Yaacov Nitzan gripped the gun in the darkness as he sat in the high-backed commander's chair on the open bridge of the missile boat cutting through a velvet sea. The voices of the watch officer and helmsman drifted out occasionally from the adjacent wheelhouse. Below decks half of the crewmen were trying to catch up on their sleep in the brief interval between watches. Nitzan raised the gun and fired. At three thousand feet a parachute opened and a flare hung in the sky.

"*Til*," shouted Nitzan into the intercom. "*Til, til*."

As the Hebrew word for "missile" echoed through the vessel, boots could be heard pounding across the deck. Within seconds all battle stations reported ready and guns were clattering.

Nitzan had acquired a supply of distress rockets from the merchant fleet and distributed them to the captains of the four boats in his squadron. They would be fired at odd hours of the day or night to simulate a missile attack. The drills were an essential part, psychologically as well as operationally, of the antimissile training in the early 1970s. With the memories of the *Eilat* and the *Orit* never far away, it was essential to inculcate confidence that the Styx could be dealt with. The men were forbidden to take their boots off even when sleeping, so that they could get to their stations no more than seven seconds after the alarm was sounded.

Commander Peleg Lapid, the electronics engineer who would inherit Tsemach's post, was responsible for refining the EW tactics and helping make the system operational. Although the Soviets had made tremendous advancements in rocket engineering since World War II, they were not believed by Western experts to have moved in their radar development much beyond the state-of-the-art at the end of the war. To be safe, however, Lapid adjusted the EW defenses as if he were up against the current state-of-the-art.

Binny Telem had succeeded Botser as O/C Navy in 1972 and gave top priority to completion of the missile-boat program, with which he had been intimately involved since its inception. The myriad pieces were falling into place, but the system was not yet fully operational. Although the Gabriel had proved that it could hit its target, each firing was still being prepared by technicians from the IAI, not by sailors. The EW system had not yet been completely installed, nor the EW tactics fully developed, and there were numerous bugs to be worked out of the engines, the 76mm gun, and other elements. The awful memory of the navy's impotence in the Six Day War instilled a breathless pace into the work of Telem and his officers, even though there was no sense of imminent conflict.

Things began to gel early in 1973. Missiles were now being launched by regular crews and hitting targets as small as torpedo boats. The pinpoint accuracy was a happy mistake stemming from Even-Tov's poor command of French. The objective he had been given at the beginning of the program was to develop a missile capable of hitting the Skory destroyers then constituting the backbone of the Egyptian fleet. When he had conferred, shortly thereafter, with naval officials in France to ascertain the radar cross-section of a destroyer, the figure given him was forty thousand square meters, but he had misunderstood *quarante* to mean fourteen thousand. To hit so small a target the radar had to be far more sensitive. The mistake was discovered by Shalif and Lapid some time afterward on the basis of their own calculations, but Shalif urged his fellow officer to keep quiet about it, in order not to cause a delay in the program. Only when it became apparent that their principal opponent was no longer destroyers but the far smaller Komar and Osa missile boats did the Israeli team appreciate their luck.

In May, Lapid was given a four-boat squadron to hold the first extensive exercise in the EW tactics that had been developed. In the debriefings that followed, the lessons learned were spelled out for the entire flotilla. The new tactics were driven home with repeated exercises at sea and in the tactical simulator ashore.

In July, Commander Michael Barkai was appointed flotilla commander. Known to his colleagues as Yomi, the Rumanian-born officer was a short, combative figure whose aggressive style of command set him apart in the navy. He thrived on pressure himself and maintained pressure on all around him. His men feared his tongue-lashings, which were laced with vulgarisms in Hebrew and Yiddish, and he did not hesitate to chew out officers in front of their men. The officers came to refer to these dressings-down as Yomization.

Anecdotes about him were legion. On a training exercise as a squadron commander, one of the two staff officers running the exercise with him in the CIC failed to heed an order quickly enough, and Barkai sent him up to the bridge in punishment. When the other officer attempted to say something in defense of his colleague, Barkai sent him down to the engine room and ran the rest of the exercise himself. During his term as commander of the Ashdod naval base, the diminutive officer used to take on hulking stevedores in fistfights when they tried to bar the entry of his car into the strikebound port area he had to pass through in order to reach the base.

His aggressiveness was offset by other traits which made him respected by all who dealt with him. On a personal level, he was regarded as a *mensh* who did not stand on ceremony. Any sailor could approach him with his problems and be assured of a sympathetic hearing. Operationally, the tension he introduced into his command translated into a high state of readiness. His grasp of the complicated elements involved in this new kind of warfare, and his capacity for command, inspired confidence. Although he had been with the flotilla just two years and was junior squadron commander, it had been his squadron that Lapid had chosen to carry out the EW exercise, because of the electronic engineer's admiration for Barkai's quick grasp. Like Kimche, Barkai had come to the missile boats from the submarine flotilla, where he had spent ten years. He brought with him the submariner's analytical approach, exactitude, and operational discipline.

At the flotilla ceremony in which he assumed command, Barkai opened his address with a salutation that drew laughter from the ranks: "Fighters of the Missile Flotilla."

The navy's combat history had been modest at best, and the only unit whose men were ever referred to as "fighters" was the commandos. But the laughter died quickly before Barkai's sober mien. He made it clear to the men in the olive-drab ranks before him that he regarded them as fighters, not just sailors. If the testing came, he affirmed, they would prove it to the world.

Barkai undertook the study of his new command methodically. Leading the flotilla out on exercises, he found, to his dismay, that he could not wield control over more than two or three boats at a time. With larger formations the radio net produced a confusing babble of voices. He could not follow what was happening, let alone direct it effectively. The flotilla commander did not have his own staff or his own vessel but made use of the CIC of the boat in which he happened to raise his flag. Both he and the boat's captain used the same plotting table, on which the battle picture was displayed in the form of dots representing the shifting position of the boats of both sides. Barkai had to rely on the boat's officers for his staff needs and for communication. The quality of these officers varied with each vessel.

After a few brief exercises, Barkai decided that it was impossible to continue operating this way. Missile-boat formations moving into combat at forty knots in intricate maneuvers aimed at evading incoming missiles were more difficult to control than conventional task forces in the best of circumstances. Close coordination was essential, because the EW efforts had to be carefully orchestrated if they were to induce nervous breakdowns in the incoming Styx missiles. Coordination was also necessary in order to maneuver the enemy fleet into effective range of the Gabriel.

Barkai decided to create his own hand-picked staff, which would operate with him, independently of the staff of the boat they happened to sail on. He would choose for this the best of the young officers available to him. From his former flotilla Barkai obtained one of the vertical plastic panels used in submarines as plotting boards, which would be hung in the missile-boat CIC to free the flotilla commander from the need to share the boat's plotting table. It was primarily to test this new command system that Barkai called for three days of maneuvers by the entire missile boat flotilla to be held the first week in October. Checking his calendar, he saw that the maneuvers would be ending on Thursday night, less than twenty-four hours before the onset of Yom Kippur.

The two new Israeli-manufactured missile boats would participate in the maneuvers. The *Reshef* had come off the ways of the Israel Shipyards in February in the presence of Prime Minister Golda Meir; the *Keshet* had been launched at the end of August. The boats hit the water virtually combat-ready, unlike the Cherbourg boats, some of which had required years to be converted from boat platforms to missile boats. The two boats were to depart in mid-October for their month-long foray around Africa to the Red Sea—merchant ships would fuel them en route, as with the Cherbourg boats—and they had to be ready to meet the possibility of a military challenge when they penetrated the Strait of Bab al-Mandeb from Egypt or from one of the Arab states bordering the narrow waterway.

Although Dayan had ordered construction of the large boats for the Red Sea area, the navy believed their primary usefulness would eventually be in the Mediterranean. The Saars did not have the range or the stability in bad weather for long-range operations, and the navy command, increasingly confident of the fleet's combat potential, was now thinking in broad operational terms, not merely of coastal defense. The Reshefs' larger size permitted the mounting of a second 76mm gun along with seven missiles, and there were fifty crewmen compared with forty on the Saars.

Commander Eli Rahav, the torpedo-boat officer who had been appointed commander of the Reshef-class squadron, took the *Keshet* out on a three-week shakedown cruise to Italy in mid-September. The *Reshef* was waiting off Crete to meet it on its way back. The two boats, approaching from the west, would play the role of the enemy in the maneuvers Barkai had organized.

To Admiral Telem the Saars made a grand sight as they swept past the breakwater in column and headed out into the Mediterranean Tuesday morning, October 2. It had taken all of the three years and nine months since the last of the Cherbourg boats had arrived in the Bay of Haifa to create an operational missile-boat flotilla. From a "fourteen-knot navy"—the cruising speed of the destroyers—they had become a thirty-knot navy. Shaping the original concept into a steel-and-electronic reality had been an excruciating task, and two of the boats were still not fitted with missiles. The pair were still useful as gunboats, however, and were favored as command vessels by squadron commanders and by the flotilla commander because of the additional space in the CIC afforded by the absence of the missile-control consoles. Boat Number Six was now in dry dock for overhaul, so that eleven Cherbourg boats and the two Reshef-class boats would be participating in the exercise, the largest and most extensive yet held. It would be the first time that all systems would be tested simultaneously in what amounted to a full dress rehearsal for war.

War still seemed well beyond the horizon to Telem, even though his senior intelligence officer, Captain Rami Lunz, had for the past few days been reporting unusual movements of the Egyptian fleet, which had gone on alert status September 25. As the signs accumulated, it became increasingly apparent to Lunz that this was not just a routine exercise. On Sunday, September 30, Telem summoned a staff conference to hear Lunz's report.

"The signs are clear," said the intelligence officer. "I say this is war."

Telem remained dubious, but he ordered Lunz's warning passed on by telephone to every navy unit by a senior staff officer, rather than by telegram, to ensure that the message was taken seriously. He also requested a meeting for Lunz with the chief of military intelligence on the General Staff, General Eli Zeira. To lend support to his intelligence chief's presentation, Telem accompanied him to Zeira's office. After patiently hearing Lunz detail the Egyptian naval preparations, Zeira discounted the idea of war.

"Why do you maintain there will be no war when my G-2 insists there will be?" asked Telem.

"Because I have better information," said Zeira.

Even though similar signs were coming from other arms of the Egyptian military, Zeira remained convinced that Cairo was not ready for war against Israel and that all these movements were part of a large-scale military exercise. The Syrians had also strengthened the deployment of their army opposite Israel, but Zeira and his staff believed Damascus was bracing for possible Israeli action. Zeira was convinced that Syria would not attack without Egypt and that Egypt would not attack before it had bombers capable of striking at Israeli air bases. Zeira was a brilliant personality and his arguments persuaded Telem as they had the rest of the military establishment. Just a few months before, there had been similar indications of Egyptian war preparations. Zeira, standing fast against the prevailing opinion of the General Staff, had said there would be no war and had been proved right. The Egyptians, he argued, simply were not ready to meet Israel in an all-out war, and knew it.

Telem left Zeira's office feeling somewhat chastened at having challenged the intelligence chief's judgment, but Lunz remained convinced that the Egyptians were about to embark on war. This feeling was reinforced on Monday, October 1, the day before the Israeli missile boats put to sea for their exercise, when the Egyptian navy went to the highest state of alert.

Naval headquarters had been shifted the year before from Haifa to General Staff headquarters in Tel Aviv. Chief of Staff Haim Bar-Lev, who ordered the move, believed that the naval command on its "Olympus" atop Mount Carmel, as he referred to it, was too detached from the rest of the armed forces for proper strategic integration. Bar-Lev blamed that lack of integration for the attack on the *Liberty* in the Six Day War. It was from "the pit," the underground command bunker assigned to the navy in its new Tel Aviv premises, that Telem exercised overall command of the flotilla during the early part of the maneuvers.

He was ferried out to the fleet to join Barkai for the last stages and could see the new command system functioning efficiently. The flotilla commander's own staff marked positions on the vertical plotting board with grease pencils and transmitted Barkai's orders smoothly to the other boats, without interfering with the crew of the host vessel. As they sailed back toward Haifa Thursday evening, Telem looked at the thirteen boats in formation with a feeling of profound satisfaction. The exercise had gone brilliantly. The missile-boat flotilla was now as ready as it could be. The one unknown—a factor on which all else hinged—was the efficacy of the EW system. This could be proved only in the ultimate test of combat.

Debriefing of the senior officers who participated in the exercise got under way early Friday morning. Telem had wanted the men released by 1:00 P.M. so they could reach their homes in time for a last meal before the Yom Kippur fast began at sundown. However, Lunz had woken him at 4:00 A.M. to present new evidence of Egyptian preparations, and Telem decided to cancel all leaves. If the men were needed, it would not be easy to recall them on Yom Kippur, when most would be in synagogue and the radio stations—on which emergency mobilization orders would ordinarily be broadcast—would be shut down.

At the General Staff meeting Friday morning, attended by Dayan, it was decided to place the standing army on the highest state of alert. Russian advisers had inexplicably begun flying out of Egypt with their families the day before, and Israeli intelligence officers along the Suez

Canal this Friday morning had seen in the first light an ominous Egyptian deployment on the opposite bank that they had not previously witnessed. In Syria, Soviet advisers and their families had been hurriedly placed aboard buses and driven toward the port of Latakia, where a Soviet ship was waiting to evacuate them. Israeli intelligence learned that the buses had been turned around halfway to Latakia and driven back to Damascus Airport, where the passengers were transferred to Soviet transport planes for an even speedier getaway. The possibility that the Egyptian military exercise and the Syrian defensive alert were only covers for a planned attack could no longer be dismissed. The chance of this happening, however, was still considered small.

The review of the flotilla's maneuvers had just gotten under way at the Haifa naval base when Barkai strode in. "The debriefing is off," he announced. "We're on alert. Get back to your boats and prepare them for action."

18
War

In the final hours before Yom Kippur, the pace of everyday life around the country was slowing to a halt as the nation prepared for the most solemn day in the liturgical calendar—the Day of Atonement. Stores and offices closed by 1:00 P.M., radio stations went off at two, buses stopped running, and the streets emptied as the population ate its prefast meal and prepared for synagogue. The Haifa naval base, however, had never seen more activity than on this day, as hundreds of men swarmed over the missile boats to prepare them for war.

The Cherbourg boats had been used for patrols against terrorist incursions by sea. One of the missile pods had been detached from each vessel for 20mm guns more suitable against the small terrorist craft attempting to infiltrate than the missile boats' larger guns. The missing launchers now had to be replaced, the missiles themselves brought from the armories to be checked and installed, ammunition lockers stocked, fuel tanks filled, and a myriad of other details attended to. Work would continue until midnight. The base kitchens had been closed in anticipation of Yom Kippur, and canned battle rations were broken out.

With darkness, Telem dispatched the *Herev* ("*Sword*") southward to serve as a forward radar picket. As cantors in synagogues around the country chanted the Kol Nidre prayer, the boat commanded by Lieutenant Shmuel Peres eased out of Haifa harbor, where nothing else stirred except another Saar, starting north on a similar mission. Peres headed south at top speed and took up position off the Sinai coast. Visibility was excellent in the moonlight, but nothing could be seen or heard. A few dozen miles away, two armies faced each other along the Suez Canal, but on this holy night the desert seemed to be sleeping the sleep of the ages.

In the Israeli bunkers spaced widely along the canal, unease felt by forward intelligence observers at the preparations visible in the Egyptian lines across the canal for several days was not assuaged by assurances from higher command that there was little danger of imminent war. In the northernmost bunker, code-named Budapest, which lay on the Mediterranean, the small naval unit attached to the army garrison had been reinforced during the week by an officer who had been apprised of Lunz's warning. "There's going to be a war," the ensign had told the startled reservist army captain commanding Budapest.

At the other end of Sinai, Zeev Almog ordered his men assembled in a small amphitheater at the naval base at Sharm al-Sheikh, after the conclusion of Yom Kippur services conducted in the base synagogue by a chaplain. The cold and silence of the desert night enveloped them as they sat. Almost all the men were fasting.

According to intelligence reports, said Almog, war might break out tomorrow. "Because of this and because of the holiness of the day, no one will go down to the beach tomorrow. From dawn, all anti-aircraft positions on the boats and onshore will be manned."

Night shrouded the movement of the Arab armies as they made their final preparations for war, but the intentions of the Arab leaders would be revealed to Israel before dawn. General Zeira was wakened by the telephone shortly before 4:00 A.M. The message passed on to the director of military intelligence from a source he could not ignore shattered the concept he had been gripping stubbornly for more than a week in the face of a rising tide of evidence. War would come before sundown this day, on both the Egyptian and Syrian fronts.

Zeira immediately telephoned the prime minister, the defense minister, and the chief of staff, and within moments the message was being passed on to the service chiefs. Telem could report that his boats were armed and his men at their stations. The frantic pace at which the navy had driven itself since Erell began propelling the missile-boat concept a decade before had managed by a hair to bring it to a state of readiness at the time of testing.

The *Reshef* and *Keshet* were to have set out in ten days for their voyage around Africa to the Red Sea. The war had now caught up with the two large missile boats in the Mediterranean, where their advanced electronic systems and ability to stay at sea for extended periods would be put to good use.

Against the eleven operational Israeli missile boats and two Saars without missiles the Egyptian Mediterranean fleet had twelve Osas and two Komars, the Syrians three Osas and six Komars. The Osas and Komars of the Arab fleets carried four and two missiles respectively, while the Israeli boats were armed with six or eight Gabriels as well as guns.

The decisive combat factor, however, would not be the number of boats or missiles but the five-to-two disparity in range between the Styx and the Gabriel, and the ability or inability of the Israeli EW system to overcome that handicap.

The Egyptian and Syrian coasts were roughly equidistant from Haifa—about 150 kilometers. Telem had the advantage of working on interior lines that enabled him to switch his boats between the two fronts as the need arose. Although the Syrian fleet was weaker than the Egyptian, it posed the more immediate danger. Its missile boats could slip down the Lebanese coast unseen by Israeli radar and suddenly dash out to sea to lob missiles at Haifa's oil refineries, or at the city itself, less than thirty kilometers from Lebanese waters and thus well within Styx range.

Barkai obtained Telem's permission to dispatch two boats northward at 10:00 Saturday morning, to serve as a blocking force in case the Syrians tried to come south. The boats would take position off the northern Lebanese coast, out of sight of land, and await further orders. One of the boats was the *Mivtach*, the first Saar to be launched—six years before—at Cherbourg, and the other was the *Reshef*, first of the new class of boats launched in Israel just seven months before. The *Mivtach* was still not armed with missiles, but its guns were operational. In synagogues on Haifa's slopes, worshippers glancing out the windows noted with surprise the holiday stillness being broken by two missile boats moving out of the harbor. The boats cleared the breakwater and turned north.

Despite the shutdown of newspapers, radio, and television on this day, it would soon become apparent to Israelis all over the country that something unusual was happening. The burr of tires cutting through the Yom Kippur silence, normally indicative only of an ambulance delivering a pregnant woman or a cardiac case to the hospital, began to be heard with increasing frequency as the morning wore on. At 8:00 A.M. the government had decided on large-scale mobilization, and army vehicles began making their way into residential neighborhoods. Following a well-drilled mobilization procedure, military couriers with lists of names and addresses emerged from the vehicles and scanned house numbers. Each courier represented a military unit. If the reservist he was seeking was at home, the soldier handed him a call-up order to report to his unit's pre-fixed assembly point. More often than not, the courier was directed by a wife or a neighbor to one of the nearby synagogues.

In a Jerusalem synagogue the sexton mounted the podium to read names handed him by a courier. At each name a man in prayer shawls detached himself from the congregation and headed for the doorway. As the sexton went down the list, he paused for an instant, then called out the name of his son. "A war has begun," said a rabbi in another synagogue. "Let us pray for our soldiers. May God give them courage and protect them." A young man rose when his name was called, but his father, weeping, held him and refused to let him go. "His place is not with us today," said the rabbi gently. The father released his son, and the rabbi placed his hand on the young man's head to bless him. Rising upon hearing their names, men in prayer shawls accepted the embraces of their synagogue neighbors and hurried home to don their boots. Many drove their wives and children to relatives before setting out for their unit assembly points. If mobilization was being conducted on Yom Kippur, it was virtually certain not to be an exercise.

Herut Tsemach was in his Haifa home Yom Kippur morning when he was startled by the ringing phone. Like most Israelis, he had never heard the phone ring on the holy day, and had certainly never used it. Against all his instincts, he picked up the receiver. It was his sister calling. "What's happening?" she asked.

"I don't know what's happening," he said in annoyance. "Why are you calling on Yom Kippur?"

"There's traffic on the streets," she said. "Something seems to be happening."

Tsemach hung up and looked out the window. Cars were indeed moving. Their headlights were lit, to indicate that they were on official business and thus not offend those observing the sanctity of the day. Tsemach was on terminal leave from the navy before retirement, but he telephoned his former superior at headquarters to ask what was afoot.

"I can't tell you on the phone," said the officer.

"Can I come down?" asked Tsemach.

"I'll be happy to see you."

Tsemach made the hour's drive to navy headquarters where he was informed of the war footing. The man who had replaced him as head of the electronics division was in Europe, and Tsemach's offer to resume his post temporarily was warmly welcomed. He drove back to Haifa to put on the uniform he thought he had put away for good. Around him on the road, the cars carried sober-faced reservists heading for their units.

At the Haifa base, Barkai was periodically dispatching boats as the hours passed. He sent a pair to join the first two, which had gone north, and ordered three pairs to the south to take up nighttime ambush positions rehearsed many times on the simulator. Watching the activity with a deep sense of frustration was Barkai's twenty-five-year-old operations officer, Ehud (Udi) Erell. The son of Admiral (ret.) Shlomo Erell, the driving force behind the missile-boat program, Udi had successfully completed an examination for promotion a few weeks before, and it was clear that he and two other young officers would be divided among three positions—command of two of the Cherbourg boats still unarmed with missiles, and flotilla operations officer. Erell had craved command of one of the boats, but Barkai, with whom he had served before, prevailed upon him to take up the staff position. After six months, Barkai promised, Erell would go directly to command of a fully armed missile boat.

Watching the boats move out on the morning of October 6, Erell bitterly regretted his choice. A war command was a war command, even of a gunboat without missiles. Shortly before 2:00 P.M. he pointed out to Barkai that the vessels at the dockside were fast disappearing. "If we don't get on one soon, we're going to miss the war." Carrying his plotting board, Barkai boarded the *Miznak* (Boat Number Three) with his staff and ordered its captain to cast off and head north. As the boat was leaving harbor, the sailors heard the sirens going off in the city,

Independence Public Library

signaling the onset of war. The Egyptians and the Syrians had begun their attack four hours earlier than expected.

Zeev Almog saw them before he heard them. Glancing up at the sky as he was about to enter his office at 2:00 P.M., he spotted the formation of MIGs coming out of the southwest. The dark planes began to peel off and dive toward the air-force base at Sharm al-Sheikh.

"The show's begun," said Almog to the officer alongside him.

"Should I sound the siren, sir?" asked the officer.

"What are you waiting for?"

There were twenty-six MIGs in all, and two Israeli Phantoms had risen to meet them. One of the MIGs scored a direct hit on the radio-telephone antenna on a hilltop, which served as the main communication link with military headquarters in Tel Aviv.

A MIG circled overhead and Almog said to his deputy, "This one's coming for us."

The plane dived at the Daburs in the harbor, but the guns that had been patiently manned since dawn sent up a curtain of fire that sent the plane spinning into the water. Seven other planes were brought down by the Phantoms.

Within moments, reports were streaming into Red Sea headquarters from naval outposts all along the western coast of Sinai. Egyptian helicopters, apparently laden with troops, were crossing the Gulf of Suez along its length and landing behind Israeli lines. Some had been shot down by Israeli Mirages, but most had gotten through. In the afternoon an Eilat-bound tanker flying a foreign flag reported being attacked in the Red Sea by an Egyptian submarine that fired four torpedoes. All missed, and the sub did not attempt a surface attack.

With communications garbled, it was not clear what was happening along the Suez Canal and on the Golan Heights. One thing, however, was already apparent—this was not a local action but a general war.

19
Latakia

The other four boats in the northern task force were waiting for Barkai off northern Lebanon when he arrived on the *Miznak* in the darkness. On the way up, headquarters had informed him that a state of war existed and authorized him to sink any enemy ship encountered. Barkai felt personally affronted by the news that the Egyptians and the Syrians had launched a surprise attack; that it had come on Yom Kippur increased his anger. Before moving into Syrian waters, he detached one of the telephonelike handsets dangling from an overhead hook in the CIC.

"This is number one. Captains, to your communications stations."

From one of the loudspeakers in the CIC ceiling came the first response.

"Number two here, sir."

The other captains responded in predesignated numerical order.

Although there was a Russian spy ship in the area, Barkai spoke in the clear in order not to waste precious time in the coding and decoding of messages. If the Russians did pick up his words, by the time they were passed on to Leningrad and back to Damascus the action would be over.

The task force's objective, Barkai told his captains, was to draw Syrian warships out of Latakia, Syria's main harbor, and to sink them.

"If they don't come out, I mean to sail into the harbor and destroy

211

them with guns. We're going to go in close enough to heave our docking lines if we have to."

In his combative mood, that was precisely what Barkai intended to do, despite the danger of the Syrian coastal guns. This would be the first testing of the missile-boat system on which the navy had expended its energies and hopes for the past decade. He was determined that the night would not end without drawing enemy blood.

Deploying the boats in battle formation, Barkai swung his force wide to the west, toward Cyprus, in order to avoid Syrian coastal radar. The approach to Latakia would be made from the north, so as to come from the direction least expected. The boats sailed in two parallel columns—the *Miznak*, *Gaash*, and *Hanit* to port and the *Mivtach* and *Reshef* several miles closer to the shore and slightly astern. Circumstance had teamed these two prototypes in the eastern column for this first missile-boat battle foray.

Thirty-five miles southwest of Latakia, the *Miznak* in the lead of the western column picked up a sighting on its radar. At the plotting table in the center of the CIC, a seaman receiving the targets' position from the radarman placed a dot on the translucent map spread across the tabletop. Although the two were just a few feet from each other, they conversed via communications headsets in order to keep down the noise in the confined space. The *Miznak*'s own position was indicated by a slowly moving point of light projected upward from a lamp beneath the table's translucent top linked to the vessel's gyroscope. A second seaman, using colored pencils to indicate friend and nonfriend, linked the dots placed by the first seaman, giving the officers scanning the table a clear picture of the course and relative speed of all boats in radar range.

Watching the plotting of the radar reports on his own vertical board, Barkai could follow a vessel four miles to the northwest moving across their course at rapid speed as it headed toward Latakia in an apparent bid to escape the Israeli formation. The bridge reported her sailing without lights and bearing a low silhouette. It was almost certain to be a Syrian warship, perhaps a torpedo boat on picket duty, but Barkai thought it odd that such a small vessel would be alone so far from port. He could not rule out the possibility that it was a civilian vessel, perhaps from Cyprus, caught in the war zone.

To test its reaction, Barkai ordered the *Miznak* captain to fire several shells in the boat's direction, but not to hit. Doubts about the unknown vessel's identity ended when it responded to the 40mm rounds with several desultory bursts of machine-gun fire. A projector on one of the Saars briefly illuminated the target and showed it to be a Syrian torpedo boat. The vessels in Barkai's column opened fire, but the small Syrian craft, in full flight, passed unharmed through the plumes.

In the CIC of the *Reshef* on the right flank of the Israeli formation, Commander Micha ordered full power as he moved to head off the torpedo boat running for Latakia. Sitting on a high stool from which he could see all the instruments around the room, he called out the code designation assigned to the target moving eastward on the plotting table and ordered the weapons officer to fire upon it with the vessel's guns. The torpedo boat was too small to warrant the expenditure of a missile.

Firing would be directed entirely from the CIC. The gun was even loaded from below decks, where a carousel automatically fed shells upward. The radar and fire-control system on the *Reshef*, unlike those on the Saars, were Israeli-produced. The weapons officer checked a scope to ensure that the gun's fire-control radar was locked on the designated target and then pushed a console button. The men in the CIC could hear the 76mm gun begin to bark overhead.

Micha had ordered firing to commence at ten kilometers—an extreme range. The results were too far away for the men on the bridge to observe in the darkness, but after several dozen shells they were clearly visible to the radar operator. "Target dead in the water," he reported.

However, the young Syrian commander of the torpedo boat, Lieutenant Ali Yehiya, had already fulfilled his mission as an outer picket. A few seconds before his radio went dead, he had alerted his headquarters that he was being attacked by three enemy warships. Syrian navy headquarters ordered a minesweeper that had been on picket duty ten miles from shore to head for the cover of the coastal guns at full speed. Three Syrian missile boats that had just headed south from Latakia were notified of an enemy force approaching from the west.

At this critical juncture, on the verge of the first hazardous crossing of the missile belt, Barkai decided to abandon major elements of the plan the Israeli fleet had been preparing so arduously for years. He had considered requesting air assistance, because if the enemy boats were kept busy dodging planes, the Israeli vessels would stand a better chance of crossing the twenty-five-kilometer belt in which they would be in range of the Styx while unable to reach the enemy vessels with the Gabriel.

With battle about to be joined, however, Barkai decided to go it alone. It was questionable, on this first night of the war, whether planes could be made available on short notice, and time was now the critical factor. If the Arab missile boats were out and the torpedo boat had alerted them, they were probably already scurrying back to port. Wisdom sometimes lay in recognizing when to disregard the rules, and this, Barkai sensed, was one of those times.

Addressing his captains on the radio, Barkai ordered the *Hanit* to stay behind to finish off the wooden torpedo boat, which continued to float. The flotilla commander was determined that the battle results be clear and decisive and that every enemy vessel hit be sunk. The other four boats would move directly toward the coast. They would forsake not only air cover but also some of the intricate EW maneuvers they had rehearsed so painstakingly. These were aimed at detecting enemy vessels at long distances and placing the Israeli boats in optimal attack position. The bantam-sized officer who had not hesitated to take on the burly longshoremen of Ashdod was determined to close to striking distance of the Syrian fleet and would not risk precious time by being overly artful. "If the enemy's out there he's between us and the coast," Barkai told his commanders. "It's not important to know exactly where. We're going full speed for Latakia."

The *Reshef*, in the lead as the boats swung east, picked up a radar sighting twenty-five kilometers to the east. The vessel, the Syrian minesweeper that had been serving on picket duty, was still out of Gabriel range as it ran for the shore. With the *Hanit* left behind to deal with the torpedo boat, the two remaining Saars in Barkai's wing, his own *Miznak* and the *Gaash*, were pursuing on a parallel track to the north, their forty-knot speed permitting them to draw abreast of the slower *Reshef* escorted by the *Mivtach*.

The *Gaash* fired first, launching a Gabriel at the maximum, twenty-kilometer range. Barkai winced and felt like swatting the captain of the *Gaash* on the head for firing. "Too long," groaned the flotilla commander as he watched the track of the missile disappear from the radar screen short of the target. Since the minesweeper was fleeing at top speed, it had pulled out of Gabriel range in the two minutes during which the missile was in the air.

Aboard the *Reshef*, Commander Micha watched the plotting table intently as the range closed. When the *Reshef* was eighteen kilometers from the target, he addressed the weapons officer: "Prepare missile for firing."

At the missile-selection console, the operator designated one of the boat's missiles for firing and pushed buttons to confirm that its electrical connections were functioning. "Missile ready," he said.

The weapons officer locked the fire-control radar onto the minesweeper. "System on target," he announced.

Commander Micha descended from his high stool to check the radar in one corner of the room, the plotting table in the center, and the three consoles against the opposite wall. Satisfied that the radar was locked onto the correct target and that the target was in range, he leaned over the operator at the central console and pressed a white button labeled "Permission to Fire." In missile firings, only the captain was permitted to push this button. Instantly all the buttons on the panel turned red, and a grating alarm sounded throughout the vessel, below decks and above. The bridge officer looked down at the deck to check that no sailor was standing near the launchers.

The center of activity now shifted to a rotating cubicle on the open bridge, the optical director. Atop the cubicle was the fire-control radar with its large dish antenna. The cubicle was a "slave" to the radar, turning as it turned. It had now been locked on the Syrian ship, invisible in the darkness, by a console operator in the CIC below. Inside the cubicle, wearing a helmet, was the "aimer," who would actually launch the missile and start it on its course. With the alarm raucous in his ears, he kicked aside with his left foot a metal safety shield and pressed down on the firing pedal beneath. Instantly the alarm ceased throughout the boat, and the top of one of the white fiberglass missile canisters on deck swung open, revealing the pointed snout of a Gabriel. The engine of the missile ignited for a fifth of a second and the Gabriel shot into the sky.

The small flame from its exhaust traced its trajectory as it arced upward for three hundred meters, then dived toward the sea. It leveled off at twenty meters. Looking through fixed binoculars, the aimer used a joy stick, reminiscent of the Luz control, to guide the missile, which had been launched only roughly in the direction of the target, into the center of the circles etched on the binocular lenses. In doing so he was placing the missile in the path of the radar beam with which the binoculars were aligned.

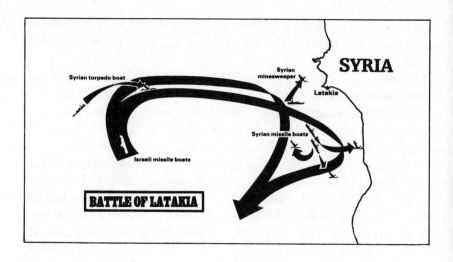

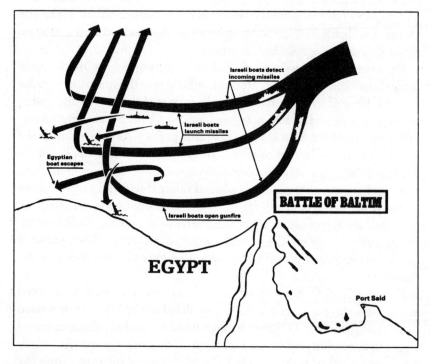

Major sea battles fought in the Yom Kippur War.
(*Based on maps published in* Maarchot *by the
Israel Defence Ministry*)

As soon as the aimer reported the missile in the center of his binoculars, the weapons officer in the CIC below ordered, "Over to beam-ride."

A console operator pushed one of the buttons before him. The missile now flew down the track of the radar beam locked on the target. As it neared the target, the missile signaled that its own radar had picked the target up.

"Missile ready for homing," said the NCO operating the radar.

"Over to homing," said the weapons officer.

A button on one of the consoles lit up, indicating that the missile was now homing in on the target with its own radar, freeing the *Reshef*'s fire-control radar to start a second missile on its way even while the first was still in the air. The first missile, which had been programmed to stay twenty meters for most of its flight to avoid being hit by waves should there be any, had dropped down as it approached the target and was now skimming toward its target just two meters above sea level. As the second missile was being prepared for launch, the image of the first missile on the radar screen merged with the target. The bridge simultaneously reported a flaring of light on the horizon.

The cheer that went up on the *Reshef* was echoed by the cheer in the naval command pit in Tel Aviv, monitoring the task force's radio communications. The first Gabriel fired on a target within range had struck home. Micha pushed the "Permission to Fire" button again, and two minutes later the bridge reported a second hit.

Even as Micha had been preparing to fire his second missile, the *Reshef*'s Israeli-developed search radar picked up three unidentified vessels close to the Syrian shore. The vessels were undiscerned by the Saars' European-purchased radar, on which they were masked by the land mass. The Israelis had presumed that the boats' ESM would give them ample warning of enemy missile boats, but the Saar commanders were totally surprised when fast-moving dots suddenly appeared on the radar screens heading in their direction. On the decks, men could see balls of light arcing up at them over the horizon from the southeast, off their starboard beam. "*Til, til, til.*"

Silence gripped the naval command pit in Tel Aviv the moment Barkai's report of incoming missiles was heard on the radio net. His voice was level, but the men in the command room could detect its tautness. It was the first time missiles were being fired at Israeli vessels since the sinking of the *Eilat* and the *Orit*. The devastating results in both cases were etched in the mind of every man aboard the missile boats and in the pit.

No one in headquarters was tenser than Herut Tsemach, on whose technological intuition the lives of two hundred men were at that instant riding. The success of his EW system, in the absence of any hard intelligence on the Styx, depended entirely on his own educated guesses. The navy's ability to wage war hinged on whether or not he had guessed right. Although Tsemach had tailored most of the chaff to the wavelength he guessed the Styx were using, he had included other lengths as well, as a backup.

The *Reshef* and *Mivtach* were closest to the Syrians and appeared to be the principal target. Both began throwing up chaff clouds as they turned toward the enemy and began maneuvering wildly to confuse the enemy radar further.

The *Reshef*'s deceptor and jammer devised by Tsemach automatically kicked into operation—analyzing the missile radar's characteristics and sending back signals to it on the same wavelength, in the hope of blotting out the Israeli boat's image and creating imaginary images in the distance for the Styx to turn on. It was an attempt at electronic ventriloquism being played out by black boxes, and the men on the boats could for the moment be passive spectators only.

Tsemach had devised the broad mix of EW elements in the hope that at least one of them would prove effective. Some at naval headquarters had objected to his turning the boats into "Christmas trees" with his space-consuming equipment, but Tsemach had convinced them that a multioptional defense was needed to give the boats a reasonable chance of crossing the missile belt safely.

As the Syrian missiles appeared on the horizon, the EW decoys began tugging at the Styx's guidance systems. Unlike the Gabriel, which could be guided directly onto target by an operator in the mother ship if enemy EW tried to confuse it, the Styx was a fire-and-forget missile, whose dispatchers had no control once it was launched.

It took two minutes for the Styx missiles to complete their flight, two minutes in which the radio in the pit remained silent. If the missiles hit, then all the years of intensive effort on the Saar-Gabriel system would have been for naught—the Arab missile boats could simply stay out of Gabriel range and blow the Israeli missile boats out of the water with their longer-range missiles. The wait was excruciating. Finally the flotilla commander's voice was heard again. "They missed."

The normally reserved Tsemach let out an Indian whoop as cheering filled the war room. Cupping the top of his head with one hand, Tsemach spun himself around the room as if he were a top.

On the boats themselves there was little time for celebration beyond a deep sigh of relief. Raising their electronic umbrella, the four attacking craft charged across the missile belt to press home the first head-on missile-boat-to-missile-boat encounter in history.

The Syrian naval command, as reports filtering to the West would later reveal, was astonished at what was happening. The command thought it knew Israel's naval strength, but the number of vessels being picked up by radar was incredible. Three fast-moving boats had been sighted eighteen miles west and slightly north of Latakia, and a group of ten slower vessels was seen moving in pairs southwest of Latakia. At the same time, a cluster of four helicopters and another group of three helicopters were reported approaching coastal artillery positions. Eyewitness sightings were also reported of missiles being fired in the area of the minesweeper, due west of Latakia. To have mustered such strength and such an offensive initiative on the first night of the war meant, as a summary by the Syrian War Command College would subsequently note, that the Israelis had been planning this action for at least two days. Yet it was the Syrians and the Egyptians who had opened the war, with a surprise attack, hardly eight hours before.

The three Syrian missile boats, two Komars and an Osa, fled southward after firing their opening salvo in order to put distance between themselves and the Israeli boats. With their radars showing a vast hostile fleet incredibly erupting around them, the Osa—the only one of the Syrian boats with missiles remaining—turned to face the pursuers. It was a courageous choice, because these Russian-made missile boats did not have EW, relying for protection only on the superior range of their missiles. The Osa chose for its target the fast-moving boats west of Latakia.

Aboard the *Reshef*, in the lead, Micha gave the order to prepare missiles for firing.

"We've got a problem, sir," said the weapons officer. "Looks like a short circuit. We can't launch."

"Execute repairs as quickly as you can," said Micha.

He altered course to the south in order to head the Syrian boats off from the port of Banias, twenty-two miles from Latakia. If the missiles were not operational, he would use his guns.

The *Mivtach*, accompanying the *Reshef*, was not armed with missiles. With the *Hanit* left behind to sink the torpedo boat, this left only the *Gaash* and the *Miznak* among the pursuing Israeli boats capable of launching a missile strike.

The *Gaash*, with Lieutenant Commander Arye Shefler in command, was closest now to the rapidly approaching Osa. Shefler received Barkai's permission to engage. The two boats raced directly at each other. At less than thirty thousand meters, two-thirds of its maximum range, the Osa fired. Spewing chaff, the *Gaash* began vigorous maneuvers. The Styx was still descending when, at its maximum range, twenty thousand meters, the first Gabriel lifted off the *Gaash*'s deck; the two missiles passed close by each other. The Styx exploded in the water harmlessly, but the *Gaash*'s radar picked up a second Styx already coming at them. The first Gabriel was still in the air when Shefler pressed the "Permission to Fire" button, which dispatched another Gabriel at the same target. The Osa's second Styx exploded harmlessly in the water before the first Gabriel had completed its trajectory. The *Miznak*, meanwhile, had fired two Gabriels at a fleeing Komar.

The Israeli bridge officers saw the Gabriels erupt from their containers on the *Gaash* and *Miznak* and head across the dark sea. The missiles were distinguishable for a while by their white exhausts as they rode electronic beams toward invisible targets. Then the exhausts became too small to see, and for a moment all was silent. The horizon abruptly erupted in jagged light, and across the water came the roll of two violent explosions.

A few minutes before, the 560-ton minesweeper had absorbed two Gabriels but remained afloat. However, the effect of the Gabriels, with their 150-kilogram warheads, on the missile boats, only one-third the minesweeper's size and loaded with fuel, was devastating.

Barkai was monitoring the narrowing of the gap between the two forces on the radar screen when he saw the missile trajectories reaching out from his own force toward the enemy. In the CIC in the belly of the *Miznak*, Barkai looked at the radar screen a moment later with puzzlement. The two targets had disappeared.

"Udi," he called to his operations officer.

"Sir?"

"Where are the Syrian missile boats?"

Erell glanced at the screen. "Sunk," he said.

Barkai was stunned. He had sunk enemy vessels innumerable times on exercises in the Haifa simulator, but it simply had not occurred to him that in real life they would instantly be wiped off the radar screen.

The *Gaash*'s second missile exploded in the water, because the target had been destroyed by the first Gabriel a minute before. In this type of warfare, it was quite conceivable for two combatants to blow each other off the surface in their first exchange of missiles, leaving their second volleys, already airborne, to strike their respective oil slicks.

Barkai wasted little time in bemusement: there was another Komar to be accounted for. The radar revealed it heading at full speed straight for the shore.

Its captain had seen the fate suffered by his comrades and made some quick calculations. He had no more missiles to fire even if he wanted to, he could not outrun the Israeli boats, and there was no port he could reach before the Israeli missiles intercepted him. In the circumstances, all he could do was try to save himself and his crew.

When the Israelis drew close, they saw the boat driven up onto the shallow waters off the coast like a landing craft. Barkai was disappointed at not being able to send it to the bottom, but he was determined to finish it off. A missile would be useless because of the land mass, but guns could do the job as well. Coastal artillery had begun to open up on the Israelis as they approached, and Barkai ordered the other three vessels to stay out of range while he went in with the *Miznak*.

The fifth Israeli boat in the attack force, the *Hanit*, which had been left behind to sink the torpedo boat, had been silent for more than an hour, and Barkai had begun to wonder whether it had been hit by Syrian missiles that had overflown the other four boats and continued on in the *Hanit*'s direction. As Barkai was preparing to take the *Miznak* in to shell the stranded Syrian vessel, the *Hanit* captain made radio contact.

"I had a communications failure, but it's all right now," he reported. "The torpedo boat's sunk. It took a long time going under."

Barkai gave the position of the stricken minesweeper and ordered the *Hanit*'s captain to perform the same *coup de grâce* on the larger vessel. It had still been floating when the rest of the squadron had taken off in pursuit of the Syrian missile boats.

The flotilla commander then set about his last chore for the evening.

Moving to within a kilometer of the beached Komar, the *Miznak* opened fire with its three 40mm guns, stitching the target with shells until it burst into flames and began exploding. Ten miles to the northwest, the *Hanit* put another missile into the minesweeper and opened up on it with its 76mm gun. The stricken vessel began exploding, turned on its side, and slowly slipped below the surface.

Admiral Telem had ordered Barkai to return to base. As soon as the *Hanit* rejoined him, the flotilla commander re-formed his force and turned toward home.

It was now shortly after midnight; only an hour and a half had passed since first contact had been made with the Syrian torpedo boat. In this brief period, the nature of naval warfare had been changed. The first missile-to-missile battle in history had been fought, and the results had been spectacular. The Syrian force had been armed with a powerful Soviet missile whose range was more than twice that of its adversary's, but the force was itself defenseless against missiles. The Israeli side had a shorter sword but a sophisticated electronic defense system and well-thought-out battle tactics. The results were more decisive than naval engagements almost ever permit—all five Syrian vessels caught up in the battle destroyed, no Israeli vessel touched.

To Tsemach, the battle of Latakia, small in scale and strategically marginal as it was, would rank in the history of naval warfare with Trafalgar or Midway. A corner had been turned.

As the task force set out on the five-hour journey home, Barkai and Erell sat in the captain's cabin of the *Miznak* with a bottle of whiskey between them. They were exhausted, but euphoria would not let them sleep. Their mouths were dry from tension, and they were hoarse from the constant shouting of orders over the noise of the engines. The implications of what had happened off Latakia seemed greater than they could yet comprehend.

"We just can't grasp it," they kept saying to one another as they tried to subdue their excitement with an occasional swig of whiskey.

For Erell this night had been, apart from everything else, a vindication of his father. Udi had been a student in Nautical High School when his father began to push the missile-boat concept. The young officer recalled his father's visionary gleam as he spoke to him then of this new kind of craft and the special élan that would be needed to command them—a mixture of the dashing "ace" quality of the torpedo-boat man and the discipline and orderliness of the destroyer officer. When the first Saars started to arrive, the young man would often accompany his father, by then commander of the navy, on his dockside visits on Saturdays to observe them like a doting parent. Udi remembered the chewing out his father had once given to a hapless duty officer because the boats were not tied securely enough and could possibly be damaged in a storm.

It was now Udi Erell's duty as flotilla operations officer to wire to headquarters a preliminary battle report of the night's events, but he found it impossible to formulate an emotionless account of movements and times and missiles fired and boats sunk. It would be two hours before he could muster the dry jargon suitable for an official description of the first missile battle in history.

20

Phantom Pursuit

$\mathbf{A}$s Barkai's northern force had been closing on its first target off Latakia, two Saars slid quietly along the Sinai coast three hundred miles to the south and dropped anchor west of El Arish. It was a calm, clear night with excellent visibility. Commander Gideon Raz could hear the surf above the murmur of the idling engines and see the breakers curling toward the beach. A few weeks before, he had arrived at the same point in a rubber boat with Barkai. Measuring the depth with wooden sticks, they had probed for a way between the sandbars, to enable the missile boats to lie in ambush close inshore, where they could not be detected by Egyptian radar. It had been a contingency plan for the indeterminate future, not one that Raz had expected to see implemented in real time. He had received the code word indicating that war had begun but knew nothing of what was happening on the battlefields of Sinai and the Golan. However, the fact that he had been ordered to undertake this dangerous navigation at night was indication enough that serious matters were afoot.

Raz's two boats constituted one arm of an ambush force. Cruising well out to sea was another pair of boats, commanded by Eli Rahav aboard the *Keshet*. The second of the Israeli-produced Reshef-class vessels, the *Keshet* had been launched in Haifa just a month before. Not all the boats had yet been fitted with deceptor-jammers; the *Keshet* force had them, but neither of Raz's boats did. The ambush force was to go into action if the Egyptians attempted a landing behind Israeli lines on the Sinai coast. In the Syrian sector, any engagement would likely be purely a naval affair, but the boats operating in the Egyptian sector had an important supporting role to play on the flanks of the Israeli ground forces in Sinai. The ambush force maintained radar and radio silence so that their emissions would not be picked up by the Egyptians. An Israeli radar station on the coast to the west was to alert Raz if targets were sighted. The radar was located near the northernmost outpost of the Bar-Lev defense line built by Israel along the Suez Canal, the outpost known as Budapest.

Raz's boat was the *Soufa*, which had been Hadar Kimche's command boat on the Cherbourg breakout. Its guest book contained the names of Limon, Corbinais, and others associated with that episode, but its present distinction was as one of the crack boats in the flotilla, both in its technical equipment and in its crew. Raz was relatively new to it. Until five months before, he had been commander of the submarine flotilla, emerging, like Barkai, from beneath the sea in order to seek broader command vistas in the surface fleet. After brief retraining, he had been appointed commander of a missile-boat squadron, and he made the *Soufa* his command ship. With him this night was the *Herev*, commanded by Lieutenant Shmuel Peres.

Tension aboard the boats was high. Action would probably take them into the vicinity of Port Said, and the memory of the *Eilat*'s sinking in those waters six years before was still vivid. If they approached within forty-five kilometers of Port Said they would be in range of missile boats emerging from the harbor.

At 10:00 P.M. the shore radar station reported unidentified vessels approaching from the west. The radar operator saw the boats heading directly toward his part of the coast. Raz was already below decks at his battle station in the CIC when his bridge officer reported flashes to the west. On the radio came the voice of the shore radar officer. "They're firing at us."

"Raise anchor and activate the radar," said Raz evenly. Several targets instantly appeared on the screen as the *Soufa* broke radar silence. The targets were just outside Gabriel range. Raz spoke to Lieutenant Peres on the radio. "Skunks at twenty-five thousand meters," he said, using the term employed by most Western navies to designate enemy vessels. "Raise anchor and close on the targets."

There was no longer any need for radio silence. Raz informed headquarters that he was setting out in pursuit and asked for air-force assistance. His two boats had chaff but no other EW protection; without air cover, they would be too vulnerable.

Out at sea, the other arm of the pincer had earlier been joined by two more boats. The four vessels had been ordered by Telem to pull back to the northeast when they seemed to be circling too close to the Egyptian shore. When Raz's tallyho was heard, Rahav's force found itself more than sixty kilometers from the enemy's reported location. The boats turned and raced at full speed toward the coast.

As the southern force braced for action, Telem informed it that Barkai's force, off Syria, had just been subjected to a salvo of Styx missiles and had come through unscathed. He patched Barkai directly through to Rahav on the communications net so that Barkai could ease the minds of the men in the south. "Their missiles aren't serious," said Barkai, a reassuring message that did not reflect his own concerns about the danger, which no amount of safe passages through combat in the coming days would relieve. However, to the men in the southern force racing toward the Styx-bearing Egyptian vessels, the message perceptibly eased tensions. The captains in Rahav's force, calculating the slow closing of the gap, saw that they could not reach Gabriel firing range before the enemy had gained harbor. It would be up to Raz and Peres.

There were now five targets on the radar screens of the *Soufa* and the *Herev*. The two Egyptian katyusha-firing craft that had fired at the radar station had been picked up by an escort of missile boats as they fled westward. When they drew within missile range, Raz divided the targets between himself and Peres and ordered firing commenced. The boats shuddered with the release of the first missiles. In the CICs all eyes were on the tracking screens, where electronic impulses sent back by the missiles form a line leading toward the target. Instead of intersecting with the targets, however, the missiles fell short, overflew, or went off on a tangent. Subsequent firings did no better. The bridge officers reported some missiles lifting off and falling into the sea after a few seconds. The armaments officers checked the electronic circuits and reported malfunctions in the fire-control radar in both boats. Raz ordered the remaining missiles fired in emergency mode, a fallback procedure that proved to work no better. In all, eleven missiles were fired without even a near miss.

In the midst of this frustrating pursuit, Raz heard his boat's code name on the radio. A single Phantom, the only aircraft the hard-pressed air force could spare the navy this night, was approaching and asking for guidance onto target. Raz could hear the pilot but could not be heard by him, so Peres guided the plane toward the Egyptian vessels. The pilot reported seeing the missile explosions in the vicinity of the fleeing Egyptian craft. Thinking that the missile trajectory could be adjusted, as with conventional artillery fire, he began suggesting adjustments, such as "four hundred meters short and five hundred left," to the momentary amusement of the navy crews.

The boats held fire to avoid hitting the plane as the Phantom dropped a flare to illuminate the area and dived. A bright explosion lit the night as the plane's bombs hit an Egyptian missile boat.

"My fuel's low," said the pilot to Peres. "I've got to head for home. Thank you." The naval officer would long remember the pilot's polite departing-guest salutation.

Not willing to concede the battle to the air force, Raz and Peres continued their pursuit of the remaining boats, slowly closing to gun range. Contact with the enemy vessels was being maintained by the radar, but the bridge officer could sometimes make out through their binoculars a darker shape against the night horizon, which they assumed was the nearest of the blacked-out Egyptian vessels. At four thousand yards, Raz ordered gunfire to commence. To his total disgust, the Soufa's gun jammed after a few rounds. Peres's situation was even worse—his guns would not fire at all. This immobilization of the guns on both boats, following the malfunction of both their missile systems, was more bad luck than Raz could have anticipated from the law of averages in the worst of circumstances.

Maintaining his pursuit, the force commander ordered his chief technician to try to get the gun cleared. With neither gun nor missiles functioning, the Israeli boats would be unable to defend themselves if their quarry turned on them. But the Egyptians either believed the two boats at their rear were part of their own formation or were just intent on escaping them. After twenty minutes, the technician reported to Raz that the fault with the gun was apparently linked to the malfunction of the fire-control system that had aborted the missiles. If at all possible to repair at sea, it would take a long time. They were by now almost due north of Port Said. Raz informed Telem of the situation.

"Disengage," said Telem. "You've done your job. We've already had a success in the north, and I don't want you to proceed westward any more. We're not going to have any more air-force help tonight. Come on home."

Glumly, the two captains turned their boats north. Despite Telem's pat on the back, they did not believe they deserved congratulations. The moment they had trained for so intensively, the supreme moment of their professional careers—a confrontation at sea with an enemy force—had come and gone, leaving them totally frustrated. In the context of Israel's abbreviated wars—the 1956 Sinai Campaign had lasted four days and the 1967 war had lasted six—it seemed unlikely to Raz that they would ever get another chance to command a missile boat in combat.

The captains of the last five Cherbourg boats, the night of their arrival in Haifa, form a semicircle around Navy Commander Avraham Botser, Defense Minister Moshe Dayan, and Chief of Staff Haim Bar-Lev at a welcoming ceremony at the Haifa naval base. Dayan presented each with a Bible for his vessel. Some of the officers had changed into suits for the occasion. Second from the left is Hadar Kimche, the flotilla commander, who led the Cherbourg breakout. *Moshe Tabak*

A Gabriel lifts from the deck of an Israeli missile boat. After arcing upward, it will dive and skim over the surface of the sea to its target. *Israel Aircraft Industries*

Admiral Yohai Bin-Nun. *Israel Government Press Office*

Above: Admiral Shlomo Erell. *Israel Government Press Office*

Top right: Ori Even-Tov, at the head of the table (right), head of the Gabriel missile development team, chats in his office at Israel Aircraft Industries with Deputy Defense Minister Shimon Peres. *Ori Even-Tov*

Right: Ori Even-Tov during an early trial of the Gabriel on the Mediterranean coast, with Defense Minister Moshe Dayan, Navy Commander Shlomo Erell (left), and Israel Defense Forces Chief of Staff Haim Bar-Lev (right). *Ori Even-Tov*

The first test of an armed Gabriel missile on the derelict destroyer *Jaffa*. The pictures show the missile approaching and striking the stationary vessel, and the resultant damage. *Israel Defense Forces*

Above: Captain Michael Barkai, commander of the missile-boat flotilla in the Yom Kippur War. He was subsequently appointed O/C Navy. *Israel Defense Forces*

Top right: Herut Zemach (left), the wizard who developed the electronics umbrella for the Israeli missile boats, awarded the Israeli Security Prize by President Katzir. *Meir Zemach*

Bottom right: Admiral Binyamin Telem. *Israel Government Press Office*

Above: The Israeli missile-boat flotilla on exercises.
Israel Government Press Office

Right: The Cherbourg boats, bereft of armaments and electronic-warfare equipment, docked in Haifa shortly after their arrival. *Israel Government Press Office*

Above: A Gabriel missile in firing position in its open launching box. *Israel Government Press Office*

Top right: A Styx missile fired on Israeli missile boats in the first ever missile-to-missile engagement at sea, off the Syrian port of Latakia, is seen as a ball of fire in this unique photo. The light from the missile's exhaust flames is reflected in the sea as the weapon appears to approach the Israeli boat on whose bridge Israeli naval photographer Oded Yagur was standing. *Oded Yagur*

Bottom right: A missile boat with guns and missile launchers fore and aft and a mast bristling with electronics devices is little bigger than a conventional patrol boat but formidable enough to take on an opponent many times its size. *Israel Government Press Office*

Right: A Dabur patrol boat in the Red Sea, with the mountains of Sinai in the background. *Israel Government Press Office*

Left: The *Reshef*, first of the Israeli-built missile boats, at the dedication ceremony in Haifa harbor in 1973. *Israel Government Press Office*

Israeli naval commandos. *Israel Government Press Office*

21

Zero Range

The two Daburs commanded by Zvika Shachak had entered the Gulf of Suez a day before Yom Kippur. In his briefing before their departure from Sharm, Almog had been guided by naval intelligence's warning of Egyptian war preparations. "I'm going to give you an order I've never given before," said Almog. "Your guns will be manned every day from dawn to dusk against air attack, even when you're docked."

The boats were tied to buoys at Ras Sudar, at the northern end of the gulf, on Yom Kippur afternoon, when the radio began issuing reports of Egyptian attacks along the Suez Canal and at Sharm. At 4:00 P.M. Zvika was ordered to cast off and patrol along the coast toward the Israeli oilfields at Abu Rodeis, to the south. Any Egyptian boats or helicopters they saw attempting to cross the gulf were to be fired on. As darkness fell, the Dabur crews could see the lights of helicopters in the distance crossing from the Egyptian mainland toward Sinai. The horizon to the west was lit by a burning oil-storage tank at Abu Rodeis. To the south, the sky was tinted by the flaring of the Egyptian offshore wells at Morgan. There was no communication with Sharm al-Sheikh, and it was not clear to Zvika whether they were witnessing a large-scale but localized incident or something else. No one had informed them of war.

At 9:00 P.M. Zvika's radar operator spotted a large target just off the

245

Sinai coast. "We've got no vessels in the area," said the officer at Ras Sudar whom Zvika contacted.

"What do I do about it?" asked Zvika.

"Act according to standing instructions."

Standing orders called for Zvika to attack, but instinct counseled caution. With all his vessel's armaments focused on the unidentified target, he closed to firing range and switched on his projector. It illuminated a familiar profile, the Israeli tanker *Cyrenia*, which regularly operated between Abu Rodeis and Eilat. Its captain had decided to flee from the battle zone under cover of darkness. The ship was riding high in the water on tanks empty of fuel but full of combustible fumes that would have easily ignited had the Dabur opened fire. Zvika knew many of the tanker's crew members. With a mixture of horror and relief at the near miss, he notified Ras Sudar of the ship's identity. Within moments, orders were transmitted to the tanker captain to drop anchor. It was far too dangerous to attempt this passage now—more dangerous, in fact, than the Israelis realized. With nightfall, Egyptian naval forces had begun mining the entrance to the Strait of Jubal, which the tanker would shortly have reached.

At 10:00 P.M. Shachak heard his code name on the radio. To his astonishment, he recognized Admiral Binny Telem's voice. The MIG attack on Sharm in the afternoon had knocked out radio communications between Telem and Zeev Almog, so the navy commander was contacting the ensign in charge of the Dabur patrol directly from his Tel Aviv headquarters. Telem ordered the two Daburs to cross the gulf to Ras Zafaranah and attack any boats they found. Shachak set course for the southwest and headed out into the turbulent waters.

At military headquarters in Sharm, Almog sensed something ominous about the way the Egyptian attack had been developing. It had a scope and a rhythm that portended bold steps. The attack on Sharm's communications and airfield in the opening minutes of battle had clearly been a softening up, perhaps for a landing during the night. To guard against the possibility, Almog sent out the two Daburs remaining in Sharm and three LSTs in the late afternoon to patrol the waters between the base and Ras Mohammed, at the southern tip of the peninsula. This was the likely area where Egyptian forces would land if they intended moving on to Sharm. Around the naval base itself, sailors manned defense positions. The army had been able to spare only one armored brigade to defend the vast reaches of southern Sinai, an area larger than Israel proper, and the air force could assign the area only four Phantoms. It would be up to the navy to prevent any seaborne invasion.

At 8:30 P.M., the operator at the air-force radar station at Sharm saw two objects heading rapidly toward the base from the southwest. Almog heard the warning on the radio: "Two helicopters attacking." Before anyone could react, two loud explosions reverberated over the base. In the flames that lit the hill around the radar station, the huge antenna was seen to have disappeared. The commander of the small armored unit posted at Sharm led a platoon of old Sherman tanks up the steep hill to drive back the attackers. Cresting the winding road, the tanks moved toward the radar station with machine guns firing. As they neared the ruined building, a grenade exploded beside the lead tank. In the momentary silence that followed, the tank commander heard a shout in Hebrew: "Don't fire. We're Jews."

Emerging from the ruined building came air-force men carrying four dead comrades. There had been no helicopter attack. The two objects on the screen had been Kelt missiles, which can be fired from airplanes a hundred miles from their target. Homing in on the emissions of the radar station, the missiles carried powerful warheads with 850 kilograms of explosives. A similar missile had been fired at Tel Aviv during the day but was shot down over the sea by an air-force pilot.

If the Egyptians had hit the Sharm radar station, it was because they were preparing something that they did not want seen. But there were other eyes watching the night. At 10:00 P.M. the patrolling Daburs' radar picked up dozens of small targets approaching from the west. At the navy's request, a patrolling air-force plane dropped flares. In their light the commander of the Daburs saw rubber boats filled with Egyptian commandos moving toward the shore. As the Daburs opened fire, the rubber boats turned and escaped through the reefs. The Daburs could not follow, but the attempted landing had been foiled.

At 1:30 A.M. two Komar missile boats were detected by ESM instruments thirty-seven miles out to sea and approaching. Almog called in the air force, and two patrolling Phantoms were over the Komars within minutes. One dropped flares and the other dived to attack. The pilot pulled up sharply as shoulder-held Strella missiles came up at him from the Komars. While circling for another pass, the pilot glanced at his fuel gauge and informed Almog that they would have to break off immediately if they were to make it back to base.

The Komars were now almost twenty-five miles out and approaching Styx range. Raising the LSTs patrolling offshore, Almog issued the code word indicating approaching missile boats. The three landing ships turned and ran toward the shore. At 12.5 miles the Komars fired their four missiles. The Styxes passed just over the three ships and exploded inland.

In twelve hours, the Egyptians had attacked southern Sinai with helicopter-borne commandos, boat-borne commandos, long-range Kelt missiles, and Styx sea-to-sea missiles, and had used a submarine to attack a tanker in the Red Sea. They were plainly working according to a bold, carefully orchestrated plan. Almog had no reason to suppose that it had crescendoed.

Zvika Shachak's two Daburs arrived off the Egyptian coast at 1:00 A.M. The hour's crossing of the gulf had been extremely rough, and most of the men were seasick. In the middle of the crossing, communications had suddenly been re-established with Sharm, which ordered Zvika to break off and return to the Sinai coast. The ensign refused: "I'm operating on direct orders from Telem." In the middle of the conversation, the radio link failed again, to Zvika's relief. He had no intention of being deprived of this chance at combat.

The area of Ras Zafaranah, which they cautiously skirted, was empty of shipping. There was a radar station on the headland, but the Daburs had either not been detected or been taken for Egyptian vessels. Looking at his map, Zvika saw a small anchorage at Marse Telemat, a few miles down the coast. Telem's orders had concerned only Ras Zafaranah, but Zvika decided to extend his mandate. As the boats approached the entrance to the small bay, Zvika's radar looked as if they had come upon a school of fish. Numerous fluorescent blips lit up the screen, indicating dozens of small vessels. Until this point no one had informed the ensign that there was a war on. It was not clear, particularly after his recall order from Sharm, whether Israel was involved in a general conflict with Egypt or in some limited incident in which he did not have the authority to strike at targets not specifically assigned to him. With no radio contact, there was no one to ask. He pondered the question briefly and decided to take his boat in. Ordering the other Dabur, commanded by Ensign Tankovich, to remain in reserve outside, Zvika eased his vessel in slowly through the bay entrance. This time there would be no question about closing to zero range.

There was no moon, and binoculars revealed only vague shapes looming in the darkness. Zvika threw on his projector and flashed it to the right of the entrance. Fishing boats could be seen anchored around the rim of the bay. The Dabur moved in a slow arc as Zvika vainly scanned the vessels for signs of life. If there were Egyptian forces in the bay, they evidently were uncertain who he was. As the Dabur reached the center of the rim, its light picked up a Bertram patrol boat attached to a buoy. Two rubber boats were attached to the Bertram. The boats were filled with Egyptian commandos dressed in black rubber suits.

"Fire," shouted Zvika.

The Dabur's guns opened up as the vessel kept moving counterclockwise around the rim. Two hundred meters from the commando force, the boat shuddered to a stop. They were on a reef. Zvika shut the projector.

The land rim of the bay sprang to life as gun positions dotting the shore opened up on the Israeli vessel. The Egyptians had gathered large forces around the bay, evidently to be transported across the gulf in the fishing boats. Fire from around the harbor was peppering the Dabur, and men were being hit. Zvika ordered his gunners to keep firing on the commando force around the Bertram.

Zvika grabbed the microphone and ordered the other Dabur to enter. Tankovich reported on the radio that he was already inside the bay; he had started in as soon as he heard the shooting. When Tankovich's guns opened on the Egyptian gun flashes, some of the shore fire shifted from Zvika's vessel.

Zvika's chief mechanic went below to start the stalled engine, which could no longer be started from the bridge because of a severed connection. When it ignited, Zvika was to operate the throttle until the boat could work itself free. Because of the racket of the firing, however, he could not hear the sound of the engine starting, and the mechanic would have to run up to the fire-swept deck after every ignition to inform him that the engine was working. After several attempts, the boat floated free. A water pipe cooling the engine had been hit, and the mechanic, taking off his boot, shoved a sock into the hole.

As the patrol boat turned toward the entrance, an officer got down on one knee and fired several signal-flare rounds at the Bertram. One flare arced across the water and hit the Egyptian boat dead center, setting it aflame. In its light the rubber boats could be seen to have sunk.

The other Dabur, meanwhile, had also run onto a reef. One of the boat's gunners was fatally wounded in the chest as he exchanged fire with the Egyptian gunners onshore, and another crewman took his place. After a few moments, Tankovich worked his boat free and headed out into the gulf.

The sky behind them was aglow. There were one dead and eight wounded on the two boats, almost half of their crewmen. But the Egyptian master plan for southern Sinai had been derailed.

22

The Gunfighter

The breakwater at the entrance to Haifa harbor was lined with spectators as the boats of the northern task force returned from the battle off Latakia early in the morning. Word of stunning success off the Syrian coast had quickly spread through the port city. Barkai had decided that there would be no brooms tied to masts in the traditional symbol of naval victory. They had left behind a lot of Syrian sailors lying at the bottom of the Mediterranean. Any flaunting of the victory, he said, "wouldn't be respectful to them or to ourselves." The sailors could see figures crowding the rooftops and windows of buildings overlooking the port.

Admiral Telem had come up from the war room in Tel Aviv to lead the debriefing. With him was Herut Tsemach, eager for the first reports from the EW officers. The central figure in the room was the unshaven, bleary-eyed flotilla commander. Hoarse from the night's exhortations, Barkai spelled out in his salty tongue impressions of the new era they had sailed into. The theories they had developed thus far about missile warfare were fine, he said, but in combat, opportunity mattered more than theory. "When you're outside his [the enemy's] harbors you never know when he's going to sortie out. It's like fighting in a built-up area, like shooting around corners."

Whipping both hands up to imaginary holsters like a gunfighter in a shootout, the wiry officer added, "What you need is quick reaction—not to go by the book, but to shoot to hit."

251

Borrowing from the air force's system of quick turnarounds, the navy set about getting the boats ready for another sortie in a few hours. For Telem this meant not only refueling and rearming but also drawing tactical and procedural lessons from the previous night's combat to be implemented for the second night's mission. The short wars Israel was accustomed to precluded any leisurely battle analysis if the lessons were to be effective.

In the Yom Kippur War the Israeli army would undertake few night actions, once a highly favored mode of operation. The navy, however, would undertake almost all its operations at night. The darkness made the enemy reliant on his radar and thus gave the Israeli boats' EW advantage full play. The darkness also offered better protection against air attack in enemy waters.

Technicians quickly located the problem with the missile systems on the *Soufa* and the *Herev*—cables to the radar had simply been misconnected. Tsemach introduced some new calculations into the EW system as a result of the first debriefing but found that on the whole it had worked beautifully.

Looking out at the exultant men on the boats, Admiral Telem turned to Tsemach and said, "If not for you, Herut, many of them would be dead by now."

While service personnel swarmed over the boats to ready them for their next mission—augmented by top civilian experts mobilized into the reserves—the crews descended to their bunks for a few hours' sleep. The officers lay down on foam-rubber mattresses on floors or desktops in headquarters. A succession of well-wishers appeared in Barkai's office, and it was late morning before he could lie down. It seemed to him that he had only closed his eyes when he was roused to lead his boats out on their second mission. He had already informed his operations officer that this night they would go south with the squadron commanded by Nitzan: "It's time to let the Egyptians feel us."

Nitzan's task force lay all night west of Port Said, but the Egyptian navy declined to come out. The only untoward incident occurred when the *Hanit* ran onto a sandbar off Bardiwill on the Sinai coast on the outbound voyage and could not pry itself loose. Before dawn, Telem summoned the force back to Haifa. Nitzan sent his three other boats back and set course for Bardiwill on the *Miznak* in order to get the *Hanit* free.

The weight of their accumulated weariness descended upon the officers and men as tensions receded with the conclusion of their combat sweep. Nitzan could no longer keep his eyes open. Before going up to his cabin to nap, he drew an arc on the plotting-table map extending forty-five kilometers outside Port Said, the range of a Styx fired from the harbor. Tapping the arc, he told his duty officer, "Keep your distance from Port Said."

With the night's mission over, Barkai, who had chosen the *Miznak* as his flagship, had also gone to rest in his cabin. Udi Erell remained for a while sitting on a chair in the CIC, savoring the release of tension that follows a combat patrol. In the dim light, the sailors around him seemed to be half nodding from sleep even as they sat at their screens and consoles. When he looked more closely, he saw that some were sound asleep, and he rose to shake them.

Glancing at the plotting-table map in the oddly silent room as he sat down again, Erell sensed through the curtain of sleep that seemed about to close on him that something was amiss. The plotting showed the boat sailing in a straight line parallel to the Egyptian coast. Suddenly the flotilla operations officer realized what was wrong: they should not be sailing in a straight line but swinging out to avoid Port Said. Egyptian radar must certainly be tracking them, and they were almost abreast of the port. As a lone boat they would make a tempting target for the missile boats in Port Said.

Erell was electrified into wakefulness as he rose again and began to focus on the consoles. The instruments were issuing unmistakable indications that Egyptian boats were coming out. It was like the familiar nightmare in which a monster is about to grab you while all the people around you are uncomprehending. Missiles were about to be fired at them, the EW had not been activated, and everybody seemed to be at least half asleep.

At this instant, a voice crackling urgently over the loudspeaker roused the drowsy men in the CIC. It was Captain Moshe Tabak, Telem's operations officer at navy headquarters, warning that the Egyptians at Port Said might fire missiles at an Israeli vessel. There was no time to encode the message, and Tabak spoke in the clear, even though the Egyptians themselves would certainly pick him up. Erell sounded the alarm.

Nitzan and Barkai, sleep gone from their eyes, rushed down the steps into the CIC. As the bridge officer swung the boat away from the coast and opened full throttle, the officers and the CIC scanned the map and made instant calculations. The instruments indicated two boats moving out of Port Said.

"Let's turn and charge them," urged Erell.

Barkai was measuring the distance from their own vessel to the Egyptian boats and the distance between the latter and Port Said.

"No," said the flotilla commander. "We need only a few miles to be out of their range. If we attempt to charge them, they can fire and get back to port before we can hit them."

Erell tried to argue that one of the Egyptian boats might break down in the pressure of the pursuit, but Barkai stuck to his command decision. In the absence of a full EW deployment, the risk was too great for such a slim chance at the enemy.

The Egyptians were taking time getting into firing position, and every minute was bringing the Israeli vessel closer to the edge of Styx range. From the bridge, Nitzan saw a powerful reddish-yellow flash briefly illuminate the predawn sky far to the south. Three more flashes followed in quick succession as two Komars fired their salvos. The missiles themselves soon flew over the horizon into view. Nitzan saw the first ball of fire plunge into the sea far astern and sighed with relief. The second missile also exploded astern, but the third missile kept coming. It passed over the boat and continued for another three miles before exploding in the sea. The fourth missile appeared to be descending straight toward the *Miznak*. It plunged into its wake only one hundred meters astern, and the men in the CIC could feel the explosion. As the Komars on the radar screen turned back toward Port Said, the Israeli boat turned after them, but they made it back to port easily.

"Well, that woke us up," said someone in the CIC.

The *Hanit* was a pitiful sight on its sandbar when Nitzan's force reached it. A boat from the *Hanit*'s squadron that had been guarding the stranded vessel all night was relieved by the *Miznak*, and Nitzan began rescue operations. After lowering a rubber boat into the surf, he placed towlines aboard the stranded vessel and began pulling. But the task proved prodigious. The *Hanit* had been traveling at high speed when it ran aground, and its keel was deep in the sand.

At Nitzan's request, a Dabur patrol boat joined him to help provide leverage in the towing operation. The smaller vessel's lines kept the

Hanit from going broadside to the waves and thereby being pushed farther onto the sand.

The operation continued all day, and by late afternoon the *Hanit* had edged well forward. Nitzan was feeling confident that he would soon see it slide free when his radio operator handed him a message from headquarters. A tug was on its way from Ashdod. As soon as it arrived, he was to pass it the towlines and make for the Port Said area, where the other boats would be rendezvousing with him. The Egyptian naval force in Port Said was expected to come out during the night; the missile-boat flotilla would be waiting.

23

The Battle of Baltim

The order for the flotilla to sail immediately for Port Said reached Haifa before all the missile boats had completed refueling. The orderly scene exploded into frenzy as supply personnel leaped ashore, fuel lines were disconnected, and engines roared to life. A gantry was maneuvering a missile toward the deck of the *Herev* when the skipper shouted to his men to halt the loading operation and prepare to cast off. Within twenty minutes, eight missile boats had pulled away from the naval docks and were heading southwest from Haifa at thirty knots.

Barkai was lying off Port Said with two boats when the others arrived five hours later. A powerful force was now at his disposal, but the reason for their presence had dissipated even before they arrived. The Israeli army had launched a counterattack this day—the third day of the war—hoping to push the Egyptian forces back across the Suez Canal. The naval command had expected that ground pressure on Port Said just opposite the Israeli lines would compel the Egyptian boats in the harbor to flee to their main base at Alexandria, 110 miles to the west, for fear of being captured or shelled. But the ground attack had failed, and the Egyptian boats were not coming out.

Barkai and Telem decided to attempt to provoke them out by shelling coastal targets in the area of the Nile delta. The Israeli boats had just begun this task when they picked up targets to the west on their

256

electronic sensors, shortly after 9:00 P.M. Forming a broad skirmish line, the boats charged. They made a gallant sight, ten warships plunging abreast through the sea at forty knots like a cavalry squadron at full gallop. After half an hour, however, it became apparent that they had been chasing electronic shadows—reflections of clouds or some floating objects.

As they halted to regroup, Barkai asked each skipper to report on his fuel supply and armaments. The boat he was on, the *Miznak*, was low on fuel, he knew. When the reports came in, he saw that three other boats also had barely enough fuel to get back to Haifa. Barkai informed Telem that he was debating whether to return with his force, in view of the fuel problem.

"Why don't you send home the boats low on fuel and stay on with the rest?" suggested Telem.

It was a simple solution but Barkai, his mind full of weighty calculations, hadn't thought of it and was grateful that Telem had. Bidding Commander Nitzan on the *Miznak* farewell, Barkai descended into a rubber boat with his staff, clutching his vertical plotting board like Moses descending Mount Sinai with the tablets. He had just cast off when the task force picked up indications that four Osas were coming out of Alexandria harbor and heading eastward. When Operations Officer Udi Erell heard the report shouted at them, he had a momentary vision of the six missile boats speeding off, leaving the command staff adrift in the rubber boat. The boats, however, remained in place until Barkai reached the *Herev*. As soon as he clambered aboard, he ordered the force to begin moving toward Alexandria.

It was now 11:00 P.M. Barkai formed his boats into three pairs moving in parallel lines across a broad front. The northern pair was made up of the two large Israeli-made boats, the *Reshef* and the *Keshet*. The central pair consisted of the *Eilat*—named for the sunken destroyer—and the missileless *Misgav*. Barkai positioned the *Herev* with the *Soufa* on a southern wing. It was still not clear that the Egyptians were sailing to meet them: they had not been picked up by radar or by long-range electronic sensors.

Close to midnight, Barkai took his pair of boats close in to the shore to shell targets at Damietta on the Nile delta. As the gunnery officer of the *Herev* was preparing to open fire, the boat's ESM picked up readings off Baltim, to the west. Uncertain whether this was another electronic fluke, Barkai ordered Commander Eli Rahav on the northern wing to disperse long-distance chaff to his north to see if it would draw fire. In a few moments, missiles began arcing toward the chaff cloud from the west. The squadron switched on its electronic defenses and opened full throttle. Once again Barkai did not call on the air force for help.

The battle line this time was banana-shaped, the two Reshef-class boats on the north having moved farther forward than the others before contact was made. Two pairs of Osas were moving directly toward them but were still beyond Styx range. This time it was indeed like a cavalry encounter, with two hostile forces galloping directly for each other. Such head-down charges had become as rare in sea battles as on land. In 1798 Nelson had destroyed Napoleon's fleet off Egypt at Abukir, just a few miles from Baltim, in a battle full of maneuver and deployment of strength against weakness. The midnight charge of the missile boats at Baltim was more reminiscent of that long-ago encounter between English and French troops, in which the respective commanders, after marching their men up to within musket range, gallantly saluted each other with sweeps of their hats and each offered the other side the first shot.

It was clear who would be getting the first shot at Baltim. Unlike the first night's tumult off Latakia, where the Syrians had been able to snap off their first salvo before the Israelis were expecting it but at less than maximum range, the battle of Baltim was classic in its neatness. The Osas would plainly fire when they reached the Styx's forty-five kilometer range. The Israeli boats, if they survived this salvo, would attempt to close to within the Gabriel's twenty-kilometer range. The major maneuvering would not be of boats but of electronic beams.

Tension gripped the men aboard the Israeli vessels as the gap closed. In the CIC on the command vessel, sailors at the consoles and screens began shouting when the Egyptians came into view.

"Here they come."

"Four—four boats."

"Coming right at us."

Barkai and Erell began shouting at the men to quiet them down: "Shut up. Everybody shut up."

As the Osas approached to within Styx firing range, the excitement aboard the Israeli vessels gave way to fear. Despite his cool demeanor,

Barkai felt it no less than on the first night. "They can tell you what the missile can or can't do," he would say to his colleagues, "but you can't be sure that the missile knows it, too." The EW defenses lowered the odds of being hit by offering the Styx a wider choice of targets, but the missile boat itself remained one of those targets.

At fifteen minutes past midnight, the Israeli sensors indicated an Egyptian missile launch at forty-eight thousand meters.

"They're firing," said a console operator.

Lieutenant Peres bounded up the steps leading to the bridge.

"Where are you going?" shouted Barkai. "You're the boat's commander."

"You've seen the missiles already," said Peres. "I haven't." In fact, Barkai had not seen a missile in the air, because he remained at his below-decks CIC post in every encounter.

From the bridge Peres could clearly see flashes on the horizon to the west. Pillars of flame curved in the sky and began rushing toward them. In two minutes the balls of fire began descending on the Israeli boats. Tracers lifted from the decks toward the approaching missiles, and guns barked. The missiles exploded as they landed on the sea, their half-ton charges sending up lofty geysers. Meanwhile, the Egyptian squadron kept coming, firing three more salvos in the next ten minutes.

Fire seemed to be concentrated against Rahav's boats on the northern wing. The absence of any secondary explosion was reassurance to the bridge officers elsewhere on the Israeli line that none of the missiles had hit their targets. With the last Egyptian barrage, fired at a distance of thirty kilometers, the two pairs of Osas executed a classic figure-eight maneuver as they turned from a confrontation course and began racing back for Alexandria. The pursuit was on.

Barkai addressed his commanders. "We're going to close to seventeen kilometers before firing. Anybody who fires longer I will dismiss on the spot." He did not want any repetition of the long shot that had marked the first Israeli missile response at the battle off Latakia. Quick calculations he made on the map showed that they would catch up with the slower Osas before they could make it back to port. He divided the targets on the radar screen among his commanders. All that had to be done now was to maintain the pursuit at maximum speed.

In the naval command pit in Tel Aviv, Admiral Telem stared intently at the three-story-high Plexiglas screen in the dimly lit chamber; the chase was magically taking shape before his eyes in the form of six "friendly" boat markers slowly closing on four "unfriendlies" making for Alexandria on the giant map depicted on the screen. Unseen behind the screen, young women sailors moved the boat markers as position reports were fed to them over earphones.

In the CICs of Barkai's force, the men settled down for the long chase. They worked in overhead light kept purposefully dim so as not to interfere with the light on the screens and plotting table. The captains had ample time to brief their men and to ensure that all systems were operating properly. At the plotting tables, seamen continually adjusted the relative positions of the Egyptian and Israeli boats. Reports from other parts of the boat and from other boats—sometimes even from Telem—issued constantly from the overhead loudspeakers, some restrained and precise, some almost chatty. Sometimes an officer took one of the overhead headsets to talk to the bridge, gun positions, or engine room. Armaments officers checked the electrical circuits of the missiles to prepare them for firing. Each captain at his plotting table measured the distance between his boat and his assigned target.

The crews fell silent as the gap narrowed. On the *Keshet,* an officer brought water to the men sitting at the consoles and wiped sweat from their brows as they kept their eyes fixed on the instruments. Barkai's calm and confident voice issuing from the loudspeakers cautioned the captains again to wait until the range was certain. Although the Gabriel's range was twenty kilometers, the target was moving away, which meant that any missile fired at maximum range would find the target already gone by the time its two-minute flight was completed.

After a chase of twenty-five minutes, the *Keshet,* on the northern wing, reported itself within seventeen-kilometer range. Ensuring that the fire-control radar was locked on the nearest Osa, Commander Rahav pressed the "Permission to Fire" button on the console. A Gabriel leaped from its pod, and the missile aimer on the bridge, picking up its white exhaust in his binoculars, guided it into the radar beam with his joy stick. There was a flash on the horizon and the bridge officer shouted, "We hit." At this point Rahav was notified that the *Keshet*'s engine room was taking on water from a burst pipe. He brought his vessel to a halt two kilometers from the burning Egyptian missile boat he had hit while the missileless *Misgav* dashed in from the center of the line to finish off the stricken boat with gunfire.

As the *Keshet* slowed down, the *Reshef,* sailing behind it, fired at the second Osa and hit it. Together with the *Eilat,* from the center, which had also fired a missile at the target, the *Reshef* closed on the burning Egyptian vessel and hurried it to the bottom with gunfire.

The southern pair of Osas had split, one heading toward the coast and one racing west toward Alexandria. The former was hit by a missile and came to a standstill close to shore but refused to sink. Even when the *Herev* and the *Soufa* poured dozens of shells into it, the boat remained afloat. Not until the captains checked their charts did it become apparent that the Osa was aground.

Glancing at his radar screen on the *Reshef,* Commander Micha saw that the fourth Osa had meanwhile fled out of range. Either the Saar assigned to hit it had fired at a different target or its Gabriels had missed. The *Reshef* was closest to the fleeing boat, and Micha ordered pursuit. As his weapons officer prepared another missile for firing, the console operator checking its system reported a short, such as one suffered the first night, off Latakia. Micha maintained pursuit as the technicians labored to repair the missile system. If they failed, he hoped to reach gun range.

On the command vessel, Barkai watched the *Reshef* drawing rapidly away from the main force with growing concern. If the boat got much closer to the Egyptian coast, it would be vulnerable to air attack without backing from the rest of the task force. Barkai took the radio handset and addressed Micha.

"Come on back. You're getting too far out."

"Just give me five minutes," implored Micha. "We'll have the bug fixed by then."

It would take several more moments of argument before Micha broke off and rejoined the main force, leaving the last Osa to disappear over the horizon in the direction of Alexandria.

Years later Micha would meet an Egyptian naval officer who had commanded one of the Osas in the battle of Baltim. Both were enrolled in the same course at the U.S. Naval War College and quickly established friendly relations.

"Where were you in the line?" asked the Egyptian when he learned that the Israeli had commanded a missile boat at Baltim.

"Second from the north," said Micha.

"Then you were the one who sank me." The Egyptian officer said he and two or three members of the crew had survived the explosion and managed to swim to shore.

Barkai would later tell headquarters that he had experienced a sense of *déjà-vu* during the battle, as if he had already fought it before. He had in fact done so on several occasions in almost identical fashion, in the tactical simulator at the Haifa naval base.

Retired Admiral Shlomo Erell, who had arrived from Europe earlier in the day, had joined Telem in the war room during the battle. The first voice he heard on the radio net was that of his son, reporting from off the Nile delta near Damietta. In his own youth, Shlomo Erell had been a seaman on small freighters sailing between Damietta and Latakia, one of the few Jewish sailors in Palestine. His son was now operations officer of an Israeli missile-boat flotilla making naval history in those same waters.

Telem ordered Barkai to break off his chase. The force was now too close to the main Egyptian naval base, at Alexandria. The shore was lined not only with gun batteries but also with shore-to-sea missiles, a weapon the Syrians did not have, and the Egyptian air force was a threat. At 1:30 A.M. the six Israeli missile boats turned northeast, toward Haifa.

24

Skirmish

Thewaratseahadtakenonarhythm of its own, detached from the main battlefields, where the Israeli army and air force had been staggered by the Arab attack. The navy had succeeded, in its actions off Latakia on the first night of the war and Baltim on the third night, in establishing its clear superiority—tactical and psychological—over both Arab fleets. Telem was determined to keep the Arabs' heads down by constant pressure.

On the fifth night, Barkai was dispatched north again with seven boats, more than he had commanded in either of the previous encounters. With luck, the Syrian missile boats still in harbor could be provoked into coming out to fight. Squadron Leader Yaacov Nitzan led five of the boats on a wide sweep out toward Cyprus and up toward Turkey before turning back south and pausing off the northern Syrian shore to organize. It became apparent to them as they prepared the attack that the Syrians had become aware of their flanking movement and knew where they were. Barkai and his staff were with Nitzan aboard the *Hetz*, the last of the boats to be built in Cherbourg. The two Reshef-class boats had not joined the flanking move. They were to come at the southern port of Banias straight out of the sea from the west. At ten minutes to one, the two larger boats were ordered to begin their attack. As they moved up to gun range of Banias in the darkness and reported themselves going in, Nitzan and his five boats opened full throttle and swept down the Syrian coast at forty knots, unleashing their electronic decoys.

The Syrian radar screens between Latakia and Tartus suddenly began flickering. Five groups of targets, showing seventeen different ships from twelve to twenty miles out to sea, appeared on the screens simultaneously. Helicopters were reported over several different coastal points, and loud explosions were heard at sea. The Syrian naval command ordered two missile boats in Latakia harbor to fire at the oncoming vessels. Two other Osas—in Tartus, to the south—were ordered to fire at the targets off Banias, just up the coast to their north.

Once Nitzan's five boats had rounded the cape, two of them swung out of line almost immediately and turned in toward Mina al-Baida. The pair opened up with their 76mm guns on the naval harbor as heavy shells from coastal artillery began to explode around them. The other three boats, including the flagship, continued eight miles down the coast toward Latakia. They were greeted with a barrage of missiles.

To their astonishment, the Israelis saw that neutral foreign merchant ships had been anchored outside the harbor and were being used by the Syrian missile boats as floating sandbags behind which they could take cover after firing. When Barkai informed Telem of this, the admiral ordered him to fire if he saw a target, despite the risk of hitting the merchantmen.

Extremely accurate coastal artillery fire straddled the Israeli boats and forced them to keep zigzagging at top speed as they tried to get a bearing on the enemy warships. Barkai ordered shelling of the port area and oil-tank farm in Latakia. The sharp turnings made it a nightmare for the bridge officers, who had to keep the boats from ramming one another in the darkness while avoiding incoming salvos. The battle turned into a melee as the Israeli vessels sought targets of opportunity yet tried to avoid becoming targets themselves. The *Hetz* was the first to fire a missile, when it got a bearing on a Syrian missile boat dodging between merchantmen. *Herev* and *Haifa* soon joined in. The Israelis saw indications that an Osa and a Komar were hit, but there was no clear confirmation. Two freighters—Japanese and Greek—were set afire by the Gabriels and sank.

Some of the boat commanders left the CIC for the bridge in an effort to understand more clearly what was happening in the close-range skirmishing. At one point Nitzan was on the bridge of the *Hetz*, and the other two boats in his force were in line behind him, when he saw a Styx coming straight toward them. The missile passed just over his boat, and then over the other two boats astern, before exploding in the sea behind the last one.

The boat's cook, of Yemenite origin, was at a machine-gun position when he saw a missile heading for them. Pronouncing the prayer *"Shma Yisrael"* ("Hear, O Israel"), he opened fire. The missile kept coming and he shouted again: "There is a God." His tracers caught the missile, which exploded in mid-air.

In the coming days, at least two other instances would be reported of missiles downed by machine-gun or cannon fire, but many of the officers were inclined to believe that the missiles would have been diverted from the boats anyway by the EW. Although the boats failed to ignite the Latakia oil tanks, a glow in the sky to the south verified the southern force's report that it had set the tanks at Banias ablaze, despite heavy missile and artillery fire.

For the Syrians, the unimagined intensity of the Israeli attacks and the tactics employed obliged a total reappraisal of the naval situation. "The pace of their sorties," Syrian Defense Minister Mustafa Tlass would subsequently write, "indicates either the existence of reserve crews or an error in Syrian intelligence's estimate of the size of the Israeli fleet." A Syrian naval assessment would declare it self-evident that Israel could not keep putting the same boats and crews to sea on consecutive days. The assessment acknowledged that the prolonged stay at sea of the Israeli boats, even on individual sorties, reflected a high technical standard. Most boats and crews would in fact be going out almost every night for three weeks.

After the first night, the Syrian naval command had come to realize that the Israelis were using electronic measures to confuse their radar. They nevertheless continued to perceive the Israeli forces as far larger than they actually were. In addition, they were convinced that helicopters were being used to spot targets for the Israeli boats and to strafe shore targets. They came to believe, too, that submarines were being used for spotting, and that Israeli commandos were being landed by rubber boats, probably from the submarines, for the same purpose. After the first night's engagement off Latakia, the Syrians would avoid battle on the open sea, limiting their missile boats to short forays from harbor mouths and relying principally on coastal artillery for defense.

The Syrians saw themselves as successfully defending their harbors from numerically superior and technologically advanced Israeli forces. The military leadership would acknowledge that the Israelis, by their aggressive tactics, were keeping the Syrians on the defensive.

For Barkai, the second battle off Latakia, which had lasted close to two hours, was a nerve-racking, frustrating exercise with no clear results. But the strategic aim had been achieved. The Syrians were no longer thinking about implementing their prewar plans for attacks on the Israeli coast and Israeli-bound shipping. What concerned them now was protecting their own harbors against the fierce and astonishing attacks the Israelis were mounting.

25
Commando Operations

Fighting their own war far to the south, the four patrol boats of the Red Sea fleet had managed thus far to thwart the Egyptian attempt to reinforce by sea the initial helicopter-borne commando landings. Captain Almog knew that his force was too weak to fight a successful defensive battle much longer. The Egyptians had close to 150 fishing vessels and other small boats in their harbors on the gulf, which could be used for a seaborne landing on the long Sinai coast. They seemed plainly determined to reinforce the twelve hundred commandos who had been helicoptered across in the first wave, and they had four missile boats to protect such a landing. Even one was enough to neutralize Almog's entire force.

The Egyptian intention was not merely to stage diversionary raids but to cross the gulf in strength and seize southern Sinai. Their plan called for elements of the Third Army, which had crossed the Suez Canal to the north, to push down along the eastern shore of the gulf, whose defenses would be undermined by the strong Egyptian commando units landed by helicopter and boat. Faced only by a single Israeli armored brigade, the Egyptians would be in position to capture half of the Sinai Peninsula speedily—the half with the oil. The bulk of the Israeli army was pinned down in desperate battles along the canal and could send little help southward.

At this point Almog was unaware of the Egyptians' plan, but it was clear from the scope of their attacks that they intended to gain a solid foothold in southern Sinai. Given his weakness, his only hope of foiling them was to take the offensive. If the Israelis could apply heavy enough pressure on the enemy's bases, the Egyptians would have to invest their energies in defense rather than attack. Almog did not have the boats for offensive operations, and the air force could not spare the planes for the major operation that would be needed to break through the SAM anti-aircraft defenses in the gulf in order to get at the Egyptian anchorages. There was, however, one unit that Almog believed could do the job economically, and whose services were at the moment unemployed—the unit that he himself had commanded for many years.

The transport plane carrying the small commando force he had requested from navy headquarters landed at Sharm al-Sheikh on the third day of the war. Almog received with less enthusiasm reinforcements in the form of two former naval commanders, Admirals (ret.) Yohai Bin-Nun and Avraham Botser, who had come to offer their services. Almog made it clear that he would be happy to benefit from their experience as long as they did not interfere in the chain of command.

Top priority was given by Almog to neutralizing the Egyptian missile boats in the early stages of the battle. No Israeli invasion force could safely cross the gulf unless the Komars were removed from the area. An invasion exercise had been carried out in the presence of the General Staff only a few weeks before in which a brigade of Russian-made tanks was landed on the coast by the LSTs near Sharm. The tanks had been captured in the Six Day War and refitted. Although far less comfortable for their crews than the American and British tanks in use by the Israeli army, they were effective fighting machines and could pose a formidable threat if loosed into the Egyptian hinterland. The tanks were stored at Sharm, near the LSTs that were to transport them across the gulf.

The missile-boat threat to this strategic option came mainly from the Red Sea anchorage of Ardaka, one hundred kilometers southwest of Sharm. Two Komars were based there. Two others were located at a port farther south in the Red Sea, where they did not pose an immediate danger. Ardaka was protected from Israeli air attack by batteries of SAM anti-aircraft missiles like those that had already taken a heavy toll of Israeli planes along the Suez Canal. Komars venturing out under this long-range umbrella could safely reach the Egyptian-garrisoned island of Shadwan, halfway to the coast of Sinai. From the protected waters around Shadwan, at a range of about forty kilometers, Styx missiles could sink any Israeli vessel trying to swing around the southern tip of Sinai in order to enter the Gulf of Suez. The Israelis would not even know that the missile boats were there if the Komars shut off their radar and were kept informed of the Israeli movements by the large radar station on Shadwan itself.

In the absence of air or surface forces to deal with the threat, Almog proposed getting at the Egyptian boats with bare hands. The commandos had been trained for precisely this kind of mission—penetrating defended harbors and affixing limpet mines to target vessels. In previous months Almog had proposed a contingency plan for a commando attack on Ardaka in the event of war, but it had been dismissed as impossible of execution both by the naval command and by his own successor as leader of the naval commandos. To reach Ardaka meant crossing a hundred kilometers of very rough waters in rubber boats, aided only by simple navigation devices in finding the target on the dark desert coast. Once there, the commandos would have to penetrate a three-kilometer-long channel, barely eight hundred meters wide, before reaching the anchorage. If they succeeded in penetrating the anchorage and hitting their target, they would have to return the same way, this time with the hornets swarming out of their nest. Because of the SAM missiles, there would be no air cover if anything went wrong, and no chance of rescue by helicopter.

Granting the soundness of these arguments, Almog believed the operation could nevertheless succeed. In the predicament his command was left in by the massive Arab attack, he saw it as the sanest option open to him. However, when he spelled it out again in his war room to his successor as commando leader and the two former navy commanders, the opposition to it was unanimous.

"You've gone off the rails," said one of them.

"You haven't yet plugged yourself in to what's happening here," said Almog angrily.

Almog decided on one more try. Seeking out a commando officer who had participated with him in numerous operations, Lieutenant Commander Gadi, Almog put to him the choice of undertaking the mission.

"It's important that you understand the background," said Almog. "We've heard what's been happening on the canal and on the Golan. I believe the Egyptians intend to capture southern Sinai."

Briefly spelling out his Ardaka proposal and the opposition to it, Almog said, "I'm convinced that this is possible, but if you say it's impossible I apparently have no choice but to raise my hands. In that case, however, our fate is sealed."

The young commando officer, a kibbutznik from the upper Galilee, did not hesitate. "I'll do it," he said.

Gadi set out the next afternoon with two rubber boats the commandos had brought with them. Each boat contained a pair of divers and two backup men who were to remain aboard after the divers went into the water.

The six-hour journey was like a passage across Sambatyon—the roiling river of Jewish legend—as waves from the north mercilessly tossed the small boats. Gadi's navigation was pinpoint, and the command force arrived off Ardaka shortly after dark. The channel they had to traverse to reach the anchorage lay between a small island and the mainland. As the commando boats silently eased their way forward, the men saw the silhouette of an Egyptian patrol craft blocking the channel. The Israelis had evidently not been seen, and Gadi steered his boats toward the cover of the mainland shore, where they laid up waiting for the patrol boat to move.

They had not been there long when they heard a faint purr of motors. Out of the darkness appeared a line of Egyptian commando boats that seemed to be returning from a mission against the Sinai coast. The Israeli boats lying close to the rocky shore offered no silhouette, and the Egyptian boats moved past them into the channel. The patrol boat did not move from its position, and after several hours Gadi decided to return: waiting longer would necessitate crossing Egyptian-controlled waters in daylight. On the return run, the boats' fuel ran out before they reached Sinai, and Almog dispatched two Daburs to refuel them, despite the patrol vessels' vulnerability to Styxes fired from Shadwan's waters.

The mission's abortion did not discourage Almog: Gadi had shown that it was possible for rubber boats to carry out the task. In the debriefing, Almog determined from the commando officer's description that the boats had actually penetrated the channel for some distance. If his calculation was right, they had been close enough for the divers to go into the water and swim to the anchorage. He told Gadi that after a night's sleep he would repeat the mission, this time with a third boat carrying extra fuel.

When Gadi's force returned to Ardaka the next night, there was no patrol boat barring the way. The two boats carrying divers moved cautiously up the channel. At the predestined point, the two pairs of divers went into the water, and swam separately toward the anchorage. Strapped to their chests was combat breathing apparatus, which emitted no telltale bubbles. On their backs they carried limpet mines. The Egyptians shifted their missile boats to other anchorages periodically, and there was no certainty that there were any in Ardaka this night. If they could not find missile boats, the commandos were to sink any other vessels they encountered.

The sound of explosions could be heard underwater as the commandos neared the anchorage, and the divers could feel shock waves. Egyptian guards were periodically tossing explosives into the water to protect against frogmen. Easing his way slowly upward, Gadi quietly broke the surface and looked about him. The explosions were occurring over a wide area, but there was one point where they seemed to be especially frequent. Apparently there was something there that needed special protection.

Having gestured to his partner to follow him in that direction, Gadi slipped back beneath the surface and swam toward the ever louder explosions. When he surfaced to get his bearings, he could make out the silhouette of a Komar imposing itself on the darkness dead ahead of him. The frogmen treaded water as they studied the frequency and location of the explosions. Once they had determined an opening in the pattern, the two commandos swam under the boat and attached their mines and timing devices.

Meanwhile, the other pair of divers had poor hunting. Buffeted by strong currents, they had been unable to find any targets. Both pairs made their way back to the rendezvous point at the fixed hour. As the last man clambered aboard the boats, which had been tied up to rocks onshore, the backup men cast off. However, the engine on one of the boats failed to start. Repeated efforts to start it were heard by sentries at the nearby Egyptian navy base, and tracer bullets were soon searching out the Israeli force. The four men in the stalled boat hastily tumbled into the one alongside, which headed toward the channel exit, the Egyptian bullets speeding them on their way. As the boat reached open waters, a loud explosion erupted in the anchorage behind them. Almog would have one less Komar to worry about.

The Egyptian commandos who had landed by helicopter on the first day were rapidly being hunted down or giving themselves up. One group even surrendered to a navy logistics convoy on the road from Sharm to Ras Sudar. As prisoners were questioned, it became clear how important Zvika Shachak's action had been at Marse Telemat. The commandos were to have gone into action after receiving reinforcements and supplies from the landing force, whose sailing had been disrupted by the Daburs' bold incursion into the Egyptian anchorage. Marooned and without supplies in the vast reaches of Sinai the commandos had lost their will to fight.

Meanwhile, the Israeli high command called on its own naval commando force in Sinai to undertake a desperate mission to which even its planners gave little chance of success. All sixteen Israeli fortresses along the Bar-Lev line had fallen except the northernmost, flanked by the Mediterranean, and the southernmost. The latter, called the Mezach or pier position, was not on the Suez Canal like the others but on the Gulf of Suez. In it were thirty-seven men, several of them wounded, commanded by a twenty-one-year-old lieutenant. With them were the bodies of five men killed in warding off the Egyptian assault. They had been cut off since the first day of the war by the Egyptian Third Army. It was impossible to break through to them, and with Egyptian troops surrounding the position, the men inside could not infiltrate out. Army headquarters believed there was a chance, admittedly slim, that a commando force could take them out by sea.

A small commando force was hastily assembled on the sixth day of the war at Ras Sudar, the northernmost naval base on the gulf, and briefed on maps laid out on the hood of a jeep. As they studied the disposition of forces, it became apparent that the operation was close to suicidal. The Egyptians were maintaining a tight ring around the isolated outpost, and their guns covered the sea approach. To penetrate it unseen and bring out a sizable garrison, including wounded and dead, would require more luck than anyone was entitled to expect.

The mood was grim as the commandos set out in half a dozen rubber boats, escorted by three Daburs to protect against Egyptian patrol boats. Each of the rubber boats held only three men, leaving enough room for the soldiers in the garrison if they could be extracted. The rubber boats were to proceed to a point offshore from which several frogmen would swim to the pier. They would report on the Egyptian force besieging the fortress and attempt to find a route by which the men inside could make their way to the water unobserved. Headquarters would then contact the men in the Mezach position by radio and persuade them to venture out of their defended perimeter to the pier, carrying their wounded and, if possible, their dead.

The message would have to be transmitted in such a way that the Egyptians, who were undoubtedly listening, would not understand its import. It would also have to be transmitted by radio operators or officers whose voices were familiar to the men in the garrison, who might otherwise suspect an Egyptian ruse to draw them out. If the garrison commander indicated that he was coming out, the message would be transmitted to the commandos waiting offshore in the rubber boats. They would then head for the pier while maintaining maximum silence. For its entire length the operation was treading a razor-sharp edge, and the chances of pulling it off seemed smaller the closer it came to execution. Lacking any other hope of saving the garrison, and unwilling to abandon the besieged men as long as there was even a theoretical chance to save them, the high command ordered the operation to be attempted despite the risk.

The sea was tranquil as the force proceeded northward but the moon was nearly full, which boded ill for a commando operation. Halfway to their target, the Daburs picked up radar sightings to the west and swung off in pursuit. It soon became apparent that they were chasing false radar echoes, and the patrol boats turned northward again. The rubber boats had meanwhile been proceeding on their own.

The commandos could already see the outline of the Mezach pier jutting out into the moonlit water when the skyline to the west flickered. A few moments later the silence gave way to the shriek of heavy artillery shells. The water fountained as shells exploded all around them. The Egyptian coastal artillery, directed by radar, also reached out toward the Daburs. Army headquarters in Sinai, closely following the progress of the mission, ordered the force to break off the operation and return to base. There would be no point in attempting the operation again. Two days later the men of the Mezach went into captivity.

Along the Suez Canal, an Israeli counterattack that had been confidently expected to smash through the Egyptian lines to the canal had failed, with heavy losses. The Israeli ground forces were now braced for a massive Egyptian armored push toward the passes leading to central Sinai. The Egyptians in the Gulf of Suez were again assembling boats for a landing on the Israeli shore. Almog pushed all his Daburs into the gulf. To avoid ambush by the Egyptian missile boats at the main entrance to the gulf, the Strait of Jubal, Almog had before the war designated an alternate passageway, a thousand-meter-wide channel between the shore and a line of reefs. The Daburs had practiced passage in the darkness at high speed through the channel, called the Milan Straits. With the outbreak of the war, a fifth Dabur, which had been laid up at Eilat without a crew, had joined Almog's force. The clear supremacy won by the Israeli missile boats in the Mediterranean obviated the need for the large Dabur force deployed there. The navy command decided to truck most of the patrol boats overland to Eilat, but they would take several days to arrive.

Meanwhile, the commander of the Dabur squadron, Lieutenant Commander Ami, took two of his boats across the gulf one night to hunt an Egyptian de Castro patrol boat that had been sighted near the offshore oilfields at Ras Sadat. Four years before, while serving as a section leader with the naval commandos, Ami had won Israel's highest medal for bravery for his exploits in the capture of Green Island in the Gulf of Suez. Now Ami sailed north hugging the Egyptian shore, in the hope of finding the Egyptian patrol boat at sea and silhouetted against the moon. At Ras Sadat, tankers were anchored peacefully offshore. Except for the air attack on the Israeli oil tank at Abu Rodeis on the opening day of the war, both sides were honoring the unspoken agreement not to attack each other's oil facilities. The Israeli command believed that this mutual restraint extended also to mining, but the Egyptians had in fact mined the Israeli side of the Strait of Jubal on the opening night of the war. Fortunately for Israel, its boats were avoiding the strait for fear of missiles.

As Ami moved cautiously among the tankers, he spotted his prey just where he had hoped—sailing through the wake of the moon. The two Daburs closed range rapidly but held fire until five hundred meters. Their first bursts exploded on the superstructure of the de Castro. The Israeli boats circled as close as fifty meters from their target, pouring fire into it until it burst into flame and its ammunition started to explode. As the boat began to sink, Egyptian artillery zeroed in on the Israeli vessels. With shrapnel cutting into their hull from near misses, the Daburs zigzagged out of range.

A week after Zvika Shachak's attack on the Egyptian commando force on the opening night of the war, a new fishing-boat armada was at Ras Arib, midway up the gulf. Ami was ordered to attack with all five boats in his command. The squadron commander was at Sharm with three boats, to take on fuel and ammunition. The two other boats were at A-Tor, in the gulf. On the afternoon of October 14, Ami set out from Sharm for the Milan Straits. The other force set out several hours later by a route that would bring it to Ras Arib at the same time but from a different direction.

Ever since Shachak's inconclusive skirmish with the Egyptian patrol boat a month before the war, Almog had been pressing for installation on the Dabur of a weapon with enough power to sink a patrol boat, not merely prick it. It had been decided to experiment with a light antitank weapon, but the war had broken out before it could be tried. On the third day of the war, a shipment of the weapons had arrived at Sharm, and one was rigged on the stern railing of a Dabur for testing. A sailor balancing the back part of the weapon on his shoulder fired at targets in the water and was able to achieve reasonable accuracy. The five Daburs closing on Ras Arib had all been armed with the antitank devices, and in the past few days crewmen had been trained to use them.

Ami led his three boats toward the southern of two anchorages at Ras Arib. As he approached in the darkness, his radar showed the anchorage crowded with small craft. He divided the sectors among the boats, and ordered them to hold fire until they were close to their targets. The Egyptians did not pay attention to the three boats slipping into the anchorage until their guns opened up.

After a stunned pause, fire was returned from the shore and from the anchored boats. Ami led his vessels out of the anchorage after their first sweep, reassigned target areas, saw to the reloading of weapons, and went in again. Ten times the three boats made sweeps of the anchorage, firing everything they had into the massed Egyptian transport fleet. The Israelis also threw grenades and satchel charges as they brushed past the anchored vessels. Secondary explosions indicated that the Egyptian boats were carrying ammunition.

When all the ammunition of his own force was gone, Ami called on the other two Daburs to take over. This pair had found the northern anchorage empty. They now moved into the southern anchorage and in the light of the burning boats emptied their guns into the targets still afloat. Accurate fire was now coming from the shore, but the pair of boats made it safely out after completing their work. Remaining behind in the flames garishly lighting the harbor were nineteen sunken or sinking fishing boats, several of them large vessels. Only a handful of boats were still afloat.

Three nights later, Almog himself led a repeat attack on Marse Telemat, the anchorage attacked by Zvika on the war's opening night. The Egyptians had begun assembling boats there again. The anchorage was too well defended now to permit another incursion by Daburs. A suggestion had been made to send in the commandos, but Almog had said it was too risky in those confined waters. He decided instead on a totally novel approach—using an LST as a gunboat. The idea had come to him at 2:00 A.M. a few nights before. If a mortar mounted on a halftrack could be accurately fired from the open hangar of a landing craft, the Egyptian anchorages could be bombarded from offshore, thus compensating for the lack of Israeli vessels with firepower.

The army commander at Sharm agreed to lend Almog a halftrack and a reservist mortar crew after engineers had determined that the powerful mortar recoil would not punch a hole in the LST's bottom. The LST was duly dispatched in darkness through the Milan Straits into the gulf. At A-Tor, on the Israeli side, it halted during the day to permit practice firing at a sunken ship. The hits were satisfactory. With nightfall the LST and two Dabur escorts crossed the gulf in an area not covered by Egyptian radar. They sailed along the Egyptian shore to a position three kilometers south of Marse Telemat.

Numerous targets could be seen on the radar. Almog estimated sixty to seventy boats in the anchorage. The mortar crew adjusted range and at the fire command began dropping shells down their tube. Moments later the explosions could be heard from the anchorage. The startled Egyptians recovered quickly. Shore guns opened up and shells began exploding around the LST. When the mortar commander shouted that he had used up his ammunition, the LST captain began pulling the vessel back out of range.

Almog, who had been counting the outgoing shells, had tallied only 120. "We took on 150 shells," he told the captain. "Better check to see if there are any left." When the captain reported finding the thirty shells, Almog ordered him to take the vessel back to firing position: "We're not going home with unused ammunition." The mortar crew hastily fired off the thirty rounds, and the LST backed once again out of range of the Egyptian guns. Flames from the anchorage lit the horizon behind them as they crossed the gulf to the Israeli side.

Only eleven days had passed since the Egyptians' bold opening moves in the Gulf of Suez. They were now being assaulted in their home ports by frogmen, patrol boats, and even LSTs. The Egyptian naval command, which had begun the war with a clear view of the inferior Israeli naval disposition in the Gulf of Suez, was confused now by the fierce opposition it was facing. It would become even more confused in the days ahead.

26
Sixth Fleet

Udi Erell winced at the sight of the buckled plates and the missing propeller of the *Hanit* on the ways in the Haifa navy yard. With a bit of luck, however, it might yet provide his first wartime command. Barkai had relieved the *Hanit* captain following the mishap and given command to Erell. Working round-the-clock, yard personnel would have the boat back in the water in three days.

Since the *Hanit*'s crewmen were all unknown to Erell, it perforce became a very "official" boat, in which Erell addressed his men by their rank or job title rather than their first names. He could sense their resentment at his having displaced their popular commander. The *Hanit* was the boat that had finished off the Syrian torpedo boat and minesweeper off Latakia the first night of the war, and its crew was well knit. Erell discussed the problem with a navy psychologist, who explained that the men faulted themselves for their captain's reassignment.

On his first night at sea with the *Hanit*, Erell joined the squadron attempting to relieve pressure on the northern position of the Bar-Lev line, the only position that had not fallen. The boats harassed Port Said and shelled Egyptian commandos who had landed on the coast behind the Israeli lines.

As they sailed near the coast, Erell was startled to hear the shout of "*Til, til*" from the bridge. A moment later a machine gun began firing sustained bursts.

"Cease fire," shouted Erell as he scanned the instruments in the CIC. "There is no missile."

On most of the boats the officers had run up on deck to verify the missile firing, but Barkai and his staff—Erell among them—had never left the CIC. The new skipper's calm certainty that there was no missile without even going up topside to look impressed the crew. When Erell did go up it was to berate the machine-gunner for having fired without permission.

"I'm going to take you off the boat when we get back," said Erell.

The machine-gunner went by the nickname Starter because of a stutter that sounded like a car engine trying to come to life. A giant of a man who worked as a merchant seaman in civilian life, he was one of the few reservists to have won a place on the boats in the war.

He implored Erell not to beach him. "I'll even bring a case of whiskey for the crew," he said.

Satisfied that his message of fire discipline had sunk in, Erell relented. "All right, you can stay aboard. And if you bring that case of whiskey you can even stay at the machine gun." When they headed back toward Haifa, Erell felt that the atmosphere aboard the *Hanit* had grown a bit less frigid.

The Syrian and Egyptian missile boats would not challenge the Israeli fleet in open combat again after their initial encounters. For the remainder of the war, the Osas and Komars of the Arab Mediterranean fleets would make no more than brief sorties from their harbor mouths to fire missile salvos at the Israeli boats before dashing back to shelter. For the Israelis, this missile sniping would be no less nerve-racking than fleet actions. As the days passed and the missiles kept missing, it was not a sense of immunity that the Israelis developed but a sense of shortened odds. The officers often talked about it as they sat on the jetty in the late afternoon, waiting for the signal to cast off for the night's action. They and their men were becoming more fearful of the Styx with every mission.

There were sometimes two or more missiles in the air simultaneously. In the CIC, faces would pale and sweat break out as the instrumentation indicated a missile heading directly toward them. Sometimes the men sitting at the consoles could not control their bowels in their fear, but kept doing their job without faltering. Any deviation from the proper orchestration of the electronics and chaff would leave a hole in the defense umbrella that the Styx could penetrate. Even properly deployed, the umbrella was not penetration-proof. The constant drilling the crews had undergone proved critical in keeping them functioning flawlessly even when a missile with half a ton of explosives had locked its eye on them.

Off the Syrian coast one night, the *Hanit*'s radar operator, tracking an incoming missile, reported it heading straight for them. In a level voice he reported, "Missile off the screen," which in this context meant that it was too close to be seen.

Udi Erell instinctively looked up from the plotting table at the bulkhead opposite, half expecting to see the missile bursting through the thin steel. A detached inner voice said to him, "Look, you've escaped lots of missiles so far. One has to catch up with you." But the bulkhead did not disintegrate, and a faint vibration indicated an explosion in the water nearby.

The nearest misses were not from missiles but from the radar-controlled shore batteries supplied by the Soviet Union. For Bridge Officer Gadi Ben-Zeev it was like swiveling through a slalom run as he conned his boat through geysers thrown up on either side by straddles off the Egyptian and Syrian coasts. Ben-Zeev, who had arrived in Cherbourg a few days before the final breakout to captain Boat Number Eleven, had resigned his commission a year later to take over the family hotel in Eilat. When the need for experienced bridge officers on the missile boats became evident after the war's first night, he had been detached from his normal reserve duty as captain of a landing craft in the south to rejoin the missile-boat fleet. On the bridge of a Saar off Port Said one night, his boat was lifted out of the water by explosions alongside. When they returned to Haifa, he found a hole in the bow where a shell had passed through one side and out the other without exploding.

The sailors were so engrossed in their own efforts that it was several days before they realized that, despite their own spectacular successes, the rest of the war was not going well. The army and the air force had been surprised not only by the timing of the Arabs' attack, but also by their will to fight and by the new weaponry they were employing. Masses of Syrian tanks had broken through on the Golan Heights, swept past hastily abandoned Israeli settlements, and reached within six miles of Israel's pre–Six Day War border before Israeli reserves thrown piecemeal into the battle halted the drive. On the Egyptian front, almost all of the Bar-Lev line had fallen in the first hours of the war, and hundreds of Israeli tanks had been destroyed, many by rocket-carrying Egyptian infantry. The air force had lost scores of planes to SAM missile batteries drawn up in dense array behind the Arab lines.

The battlefield turnaround would come, but at an agonizing cost. In the north, Israeli armored units assisted by tactical air strikes pushed the Syrians off the Golan Heights and reached within artillery range of Damascus's suburbs. Shortly after midnight on the tenth night of the war, Israeli paratroopers, penetrating a gap in the Egyptian lines, crossed the Suez Canal in rubber boats and established a tenuous bridgehead on its west bank. Armored units would pour through the opening in the coming days to raise havoc in the Egyptian rear.

A massive airlift by American air-force Galaxies had begun delivering military supplies to Ben-Gurion Airport as Israel's strategic stockpiles rapidly dwindled. In the entire military effort, it was only the navy—the hitherto marginal service—that was performing the way the army and the air force had performed in the Six Day War. The sailors' pride in their own achievements was offset by concern over the general progress of the war and the Israeli death toll, which would pass twenty-five hundred, the most intensive killing in any Israeli conflict since the yearlong War of Independence, which had claimed six thousand lives.

Admiral Telem knew from the General Staff meetings he attended each day just how serious the situation was. It was for this reason that he had proposed the rescue attempt by the naval commandos at the Mezach position as a way of helping the ground forces even though the chance of success was minimal. In harassing the enemy coasts, the navy was also drawing off some Arab forces from the main battlefronts—the Syrians had reportedly deployed at least two armored brigades along their coast. The navy's most direct contribution to the efforts of the ground troops was in the Gulf of Suez region, where it had broken up the Egyptian landing attempts on the first night of the war. Telem admired the chief of staff, General Elazar, for the steadiness he had shown even in the first, desperate days, when others around him were seeing apocalyptic visions. Elazar scheduled fifteen minutes every day for a briefing by Telem on the naval situation.

The success of the navy astonished the chief of staff. "I underestimated the navy," he admitted to aides. "All I expected from them was to defend the coast." On the first night of the war, Elazar had told Telem to recall Barkai's force as it was making its way north toward Syrian waters. With the Israeli lines collapsing on the Suez Canal and on the Golan Heights, the general did not want the navy getting involved in an adventure that might require the air force to bail it out; every plane would be needed this night to stave off catastrophe on the ground. Telem, in one of his major decisions of the war, chose to ignore the order. When he next spoke to Elazar, several hours later, it was to inform him of the stunning victory off Latakia. Buoyed by that one positive report in a night of unremitting grimness, Elazar made no mention of his earlier order.

If he had realized what the navy was capable of, the chief of staff would later say, he would have assigned it a far greater role. The navy, however, had assigned itself its own roles beyond anything ever considered by the General Staff. Elazar heartily approved Telem's proposal to attack Syrian coastal oil installations, noting that the navy was saving him warplanes he would otherwise have needed for the task.

Naval task forces prowled every night off the Syrian or the Egyptian coast, or both, to keep up the pressure. Telem directed these efforts from his underground command center in Tel Aviv, choosing missions and designating forces. From his glass-enclosed room on the "command bridge," he could watch the precise deployment of friendly and hostile forces in the Mediterranean battle zone and in the Gulf of Suez on the giant Plexiglas screen in the situation room outside his glass walls. The screen also showed relevant factors like the state of the sea, wind direction, and position of the moon. There was something godlike in his real-time surveillance of distant battlefields and his ability to direct the movement of his forces instantly by radio.

Telem communicated with his commanders at sea in the clear for the most part, rather than in coded messages, despite the risk of interception by Arab listening posts. He believed it essential to maintain voice contact so that he and his captains understood one another clearly. It was sometimes as important to hear how something was said as what was said. In his navy career he had been witness too often to written messages interpreted differently from the intentions of the sender, sometimes directly contrary to those intentions. Telem addressed his captains by their nicknames, and his reassuring voice offering practical advice was a welcome presence in the boats' CICs.

In flanking rooms on the pit's command bridge, separated from him only by movable glass partitions, were his intelligence chief, Captain Lunz, and other senior staff officers. When the fleet entered battle, Telem's communication link would be hooked into the loudspeaker so that all could follow its progress. An odd tradition had developed among the staff officers since the first night's battle. On that occasion, Telem's deputy began biting into an apple to relieve the tension when Barkai announced "incoming missiles." The officer chewed his way through the excruciating silence and was just down to the core when Barkai reported the boats' safe passage. Every night thereafter, the deputy laid in a supply of apples for the entire staff, and the sound of crunching apples filled the otherwise silent command post as the enemy Styxes flew toward the Israeli boats.

One night Herut Tsemach asked Telem's permission to bring a visitor to the command post. "Everyone's forgotten about Ori Even-Tov," said Tsemach. "He deserves to be here." Even-Tov had left the IAI amid controversy in 1970, shortly after the Gabriel had become operational. He found himself labeled as problematic and for many months could find no employment. When he finally did, it was in a routine industrial job that made little use of his talents. Ushered into the pit by Tsemach, he listened emotionally as distant voices announced the launch of Gabriel missiles at enemy targets.

Every morning Telem emerged into the Tel Aviv dawn to drive north to debrief the returning officers in the Haifa base. Lessons were being learned each night, from the effectiveness of battle tactics to the way the engines stood up to different stresses.

As the navy's success became apparent, Telem pressed the General Staff to expand the fleet's mission by authorizing sustained attacks on strategic infrastructure along the enemy's coasts, particularly oil-tank farms and ports, missions that had not been conceived of for the navy before the war. The oil was owned by international interests, and attacking them might bring on political complications. As for the shelling of ports, this could provide the Russians with an excuse for active intervention if a Soviet vessel was hit. However, after Frog ground-to-ground missiles fired by Syria in the opening days of the war against an airbase in northern Israel hit surrounding civilian settlements, Elazar gave Telem a go-ahead.

On the night of October 12 a Russian freighter was indeed sunk by

Gabriel missiles during an attack on a Syrian harbor. Telem was informed in an ominous tone the next morning by a senior member of the General Staff that Dayan wanted to see him.

"You can take your badge of rank off already," said the general tartly as he led Telem down the hall.

Dayan was anything but irate when Telem was ushered into his office. He greeted the admiral warmly and asked him to relate what had happened. There was no rebuke and no exhortation by the defense minister to avoid such incidents in the future. Soviet men-of-war would escort Russian freighters carrying military equipment to within a few hours' sailing of Latakia all during the war. The Israeli navy did not attempt to interfere with these convoys, but the presence of Soviet freighters would not inhibit in any way the Israeli attack on the Syrian harbors. Although the eastern Mediterranean had been filled with Soviet warships since the war began, it was presumed by Israel that the equally augmented presence of the U.S. Sixth Fleet would stay any direct Soviet action against the Israeli warships.

While the Israeli and Arab fleets battled off their coasts, the most powerful naval forces ever deployed in the Mediterranean cast Olympian shadows on the western skyline.

With the beginning of the war, the U.S. Sixth Fleet and the Soviet Mediterranean squadron had begun maneuvering toward a massive confrontation. The Sixth Fleet commander, Vice Admiral Daniel Murphy, learned of the war's outbreak after sailing from Istanbul into the Aegean aboard his flagship, USS *Little Rock,* en route to his home port of Gaeta, Italy. The day before, U.S. intelligence sources had monitored Soviet ships evacuating Soviet civilians from Latakia and from Alexandria, but that had not been interpreted as signaling imminent war.

Murphy's forces were spread along the length of the Mediterranean, mostly in Greek and Spanish ports. Closest to the battle area was the task force centered on the carrier *Independence,* making a port call in Athens. Murphy ordered its commander to recall all men from liberty and prepare to sail on four hours' notice.

A second carrier, the *Franklin D. Roosevelt,* was operating with its escorts in the western Mediterranean. Murphy wanted to shift the task force toward the eastern Mediterranean, but Washington forbade it.

The orders from the Joint Chiefs of Staff were strict—to maintain a low-key, even-handed attitude and to continue routine activity. Above all he was to avoid any overt move that could be construed by the Russians or the Arabs as a prelude to direct involvement in the conflict.

Close to midnight Washington time on the first night of the war, the high command modified its policy. Murphy was ordered to dispatch a task force into holding position southeast of Crete. The force could reach the battle zone quickly from that station, but it was far enough removed to avoid provocation or unwelcome encounters such as the attack on the *Liberty* six years before. It was dawn in the Mediterranean when the message was received. At 0520 hours Murphy ordered the *Independence* to weigh anchor with its escorts and join him off Crete. By 0900 hours the task force was under way.

As it took up its new position, the naval force's commanders reviewed standing plans for the evacuation of American citizens from the region. There were an estimated sixty thousand Americans in the area, forty-five thousand of them in Israel. The planning concentrated on the evacuation of those in the Arab countries, but within a few days it would become clear that it was not the Arab countries that were in trouble.

The carrier *John F. Kennedy,* which had been in the North Sea, was ordered south to the eastern Atlantic with its three destroyer escorts. It was not to transit the Straits of Gibraltar into the Mediterranean until further orders, so as not to provoke the Russians or the Arabs. For the same reason, the *Roosevelt* would stay in the western Mediterranean while transport ships carrying close to two thousand marines would remain on the northern side of Crete at Suda Bay rather than with the *Independence* group on the side of the island closer to the battle zone.

The Soviets, meanwhile, were deploying a vast fleet. Lookouts in the hills above the Dardanelles reported ships from the Soviet Baltic fleet streaming southward at an alarming rate, both missile-armed surface ships and missile-armed submarines. The Soviet Mediterranean squadron had had fifty-seven vessels at the war's outbreak and would rise to the unprecedented number of ninety-seven during the next three weeks. The American ships would increase only from fifty to sixty.

Never before had there been such a massive U.S.-Soviet naval face-off. Virtually bereft of a deep-water navy in World War II, the Soviets had steadily increased their ability to project a strategic presence across the world's oceans. They had not been ready during the Cuban missile crisis in 1962 to stand up to the American navy, but they were ready now.

The Soviets had initiated their naval presence in the Mediterranean in 1958 on an intermittent basis. By 1964 the presence was permanent and growing, a response to the positioning there the previous year of U.S. Polaris submarines bearing missiles targeted on the Soviet Union. The Mediterranean squadron served under the command of the Black Sea fleet. Its primary mission was to neutralize the nuclear threat to the southern part of the Soviet Union posed by the missile-carrying submarines and aircraft carriers of the Sixth Fleet. The squadron also had a traditional gunboat role to play in the volatile political developments on the rim of the Mediterranean, particularly those involving its allies in the Arab world.

The Sixth Fleet had replaced the British navy as the dominant force in the Mediterranean after World War II. Since 1952 the fleet had included two carrier task forces.

Although the Soviet fleet in the Mediterranean was larger than the Sixth Fleet on the eve of the Yom Kippur War, the presence of 180 fighter-attack aircraft on the Sixth Fleet carriers righted the strategic balance. The Russians were devoid of any air cover in the region. The Soviet naval air arm that had been based in Egypt had been ordered out of that country the previous year.

Both fleets had abandoned the gun as their principal weapon. The Americans, with the vast experience gained in the Pacific in World War II, relied on their naval air arm. The Russians, with no hope of matching the Americans in aircraft carriers, had developed sea-to-sea missiles with ranges of up to 250 miles. The two fleets could thus stand well away from each other and deliver lethal strikes.

The American fleet would rely for its defenses mainly on its own aircraft. Murphy kept a constant cover of planes over the Soviet missile warships with the intention of attacking at the first clear indication that the Soviets were about to launch. In the event that the Soviets nevertheless succeeded in launching, a screen of F-4s was maintained over the carriers in order to shoot down any incoming missiles.

Murphy's rules of engagement were, in broad terms, to defend his fleet. It was for him to determine at what point to attack—whether at the first indication of intent, such as movement of the Soviet launchers into firing position, or only after missiles were actually launched. In any case, there would be no time to consult with Washington. As the sea steadily filled with Soviet and American vessels, Murphy reckoned it a 40 percent chance that the Soviets would attempt a first strike. Confident that naval intelligence would provide him with clear warning of Soviet intentions, in part through electronic monitoring, he hoped to emerge from the opening exchange unscathed. It was his intention, if hostilities commenced, to hunt down every Soviet vessel in the Mediterranean and sink it. Years later, with the revelations of the Walker spy ring that had penetrated U.S. naval intelligence, Murphy realized with a chill that his every move and plan might have been known to the Russians.

The Sixth Fleet also had EW defenses, but Murphy hoped he would not have to fall back on them. The fleet's electronic monitors could pick up Soviet missile vessels constantly targeting the American ships. Murphy kept his two carriers seventy-five to one hundred miles apart—close enough to render mutual assistance but far enough away from each other to be able to determine which was being targeted by the Soviet missile batteries.

Work on chaff and jammers, begun in the early 1960s, had been accelerated considerably following the sinking of the *Eilat*. Their combat effectiveness was as much an unknown as the Israeli EW system had been until the first missile encounter off Latakia a few nights before. The American and Israeli EW systems had been developed independently, and there was no way of knowing how successful the Americans' would prove in the ultimate test, particularly if the Soviets launched many missiles simultaneously. As for sea-to-sea missiles of their own, the Americans' cupboard was bare. The Harpoon would not become operational until near the end of the decade.

Soviet vessels tailing every American task force in the Mediterranean were a constant reminder of the possibility of a missile strike. Dubbed "tattletales," these Soviet shadows had as their main task to keep constant track of the position of the American carriers, so that missiles fired at the American task force from surface ships or submarines well beyond the horizon would be targeted on the carriers rather than on escort ships. These tattletales in normal times generally consisted of a single destroyer.

Two days after the *Independence* task force took up its position off

Crete, it was joined by a Soviet cruiser and submarine tender. A week later the Soviet tails were reinforced by another cruiser and a missile destroyer. Although ranking Soviet commanders almost never participated in such encounters, the Americans became aware of the presence of two admirals aboard the shadowing craft. "The object of this presence may simply be to let us know that they are aware of our activities and to make us aware of theirs," cabled Murphy to Washington.

The American naval commanders had long lived with the possibility of "D-Day shootout" in which the Russians launched their missiles without warning at the beginning of hostilities, the tattletales presumably having gotten out of the way first. The Russians had even begun arming their destroyer tattletales with aft-facing Styx missile launchers so that they could unleash their own volley as they scuttled away over the horizon. Zumwalt had told colleagues that if the Russians in this tactical situation got in the first shots, the Sixth Fleet would be defeated. Meanwhile, there was nothing to do but keep a close watch on the watchers.

Radio monitoring and satellite reconnaissance gave the Russians a constant reading of ship movements in the Mediterranean surpassing in precision even that of the Americans. The Israelis discovered that the Soviet presence beyond the immediate battle zone was ubiquitous. Israeli scout vessels on clandestine long-distance missions inevitably found themselves picked up and followed by Soviet escorts two or three hours before reaching their designated objective.

The main Russian anchorage was south of the Greek island of Kithaira, just outside territorial waters. Soviet destroyers escorted Soviet merchantmen coming through the Dardanelles with war matériel for Syria. The warships did not go farther east than Cyprus, for fear of provoking either the Americans or a *Liberty*-like attack from the Israelis. The Soviet merchantmen made the last leg of the run to Latakia on their own, and the sinking of the Soviet merchantman in the Syrian harbor did not provoke any threat of Soviet retaliation.

The American fleet offered protection to merchant ships west of Crete, but not between Crete and Israel. With the initiation of a massive American airlift of war supplies to Israel after the first week of the war, Murphy deployed U.S. picket destroyers the length of the Mediterranean to render navigation or rescue assistance if necessary. In this context, a single destroyer took up position off Cyprus, the closest any American vessel came to the war zone.

The American fleet had a more direct role in the transit of warplanes being rushed to the Israeli air force to replace its heavy losses. With European countries refusing the use of their airfields for fear of Arab retaliation, the planes crossed the Atlantic to the Azores and hopped to Israel via the deck of the *Independence*.

Vaguely aware of these superpower maneuverings beyond the horizon, the Israeli naval command was too busy with its own affairs to pay much notice.

27

The Grand Piano

The trepidation felt by the military photographer as he boarded the missile boat in the late afternoon at the Haifa naval base for his first combat mission was somewhat assuaged by the smile and easy manner of the young boatswain who welcomed him. But the sailor's words quickly restored the knot in the visitor's stomach.

"It's going to be lively tonight. You'll have plenty to photograph."

The reservist photographer was astonished at the youth of the crew members who had assembled on deck to be briefed by the captain before departure. Almost all seemed to be under twenty—but they were clearly no longer teenagers. He saw in their eyes a sheen of confidence and something like toughness that almost certainly had not been there two weeks before.

On the bridge the photographer conversed with an eighteen-year-old sailor cleaning a machine gun. "What's a battle against a missile boat like?" he asked, certain that the tremor in his voice betrayed him.

"We wait for them to come out," said the sailor as he rubbed oil into the weapon with a piece of flannel, "they shoot at us a bit, and then we pound them."

"And what becomes of us if we get hit by a missile?"

The young sailor glanced up to study his questioner.

"We become an oil stain."

The large moon that night silhouetted the mountains near Latakia, which seemed to come down almost to the water's edge. The sea itself was a languid, rippling pool. Aboard the *Herev,* Lieutenant Peres was struck by the beauty of the scene. In a few minutes, he knew, it would all erupt, but he clung to the picture for as long as he could before descending to the CIC. Soon missiles were lifting off the *Herev* deck toward the harbor, and the Syrian defenses were bursting into life.

When the Styxes started descending toward the boat bearing the photographer, he had to use his thumb to push the camera shutter—his other fingers seemed to have petrified.

"The bastards aren't coming out," an officer on the bridge said as he stared toward the harbor from whose mouth the Syrian boats had fired.

The coast was aflame from hits on oil tanks, and the ship's gun thundered. To the north, points of light flew through the sky where Styxes were seeking out the other wing of the attack force. Through the noise of the guns and missiles, the voice of the skipper on the loudspeaker could barely be heard. "We're going in to see if we can make contact with the enemy missile boats."

The boat dashed toward the inferno on shore as if rushing for the gates of hell. Hell seemed to be coming out to greet them as geysers from shore batteries sprang up all about them, but the boat seemed to weave its way through these almost playfully. The Syrians refused to be tempted out, and the captain finally gave the order to break contact and rejoin the rest of the force.

More than two weeks after the Banias oil tanks had first been hit, a four-boat force was dispatched to set fire to the tanks still intact. As they headed north, Udi Erell asked Barkai for permission to take the *Hanit* in first. The boat's gun had been jamming, and Barkai said he would agree if it could test-fire eight rounds without clogging. The gun fired eight rounds into the sea, but when Erell ordered a ninth round fired for good measure it jammed. He raised Barkai aboard the *Soufa* to report.

"You've got eight," said Barkai. "I was counting."

"I've got to tell you it clogged on the ninth," said Erell.

"Well, I promised," replied Barkai. "You're going in first."

The sea was a dead calm when the *Hanit* moved close inshore. The other three boats lay back out of range of shore batteries and braced for possible missile-boat forays from nearby Syrian ports. The shore batteries were not firing, and Erell was almost tempted to shut off his own engines in order to provide a more stable firing platform. The boat's 76mm gun opened fire, and tank after tank erupted in flame, like targets in a shooting gallery. Although the gun clogged periodically, the crew swiftly cleared it. After pumping in eighty shells, the *Hanit* pulled out to let the *Haifa* take over the job of "lighting torches," as the navy men had come to call this kind of mission.

On their instruments the missile-boat commanders saw a Syrian missile boat emerging from Latakia, up the coast. Breaking off contact with Banais, they raced north. The Syrian vessel launched its Styxes at maximum range and dashed back to harbor. Almost simultaneously, missile boats emerging behind the Israeli boats from Tartus to the south fired their Styxes in a neatly laid ambush. By utilizing their superior range, the Syrian missile boats were able to unleash their volleys and scamper back to the safety of harbor before the Israeli boats could draw within Gabriel range. The Styxes were coming on so steadily through the Israeli deception screens that officers in the CICs thought that this time it might be Russian crews firing.

An Israeli war correspondent who had joined the *Hanit* for the mission grew animated as the balls of fire began descending straight toward them. Standing on the deck next to "Starter," he urged him to begin firing his machine gun.

"My captain says not to fire until ordered," said Starter. "Even if that missile goes through my belly and comes out my backside, I'm not firing until he says so."

When the reporter grew insistent, Starter held him in his giant's grip at arm's length, keeping his other hand on the machine gun. A moment later the hapless reporter was stunned as a cluster of chaff rockets just above his helmet detonated.

On the Egyptian front the reins on the Israeli boats were loosened as the war progressed, to permit the boats to prowl farther and farther westward, past the Nile delta toward Alexandria, shelling military targets along the coast and raising the threat of a seaborne landing. On the night of October 21, a patrol led by Barkai was dispatched toward Abukir Bay, on the approaches to Alexandria. Near Rosetta, a large fishing boat close to shore signaled by light toward the *Herev* and the *Hanit*. The sighting was reported to Tel Aviv headquarters.

"Sink it," ordered Admiral Telem.

Peres and Erell were taken aback by the order, but the *Herev*'s gun opened fire at close range, shattering the wooden vessel. Three Egyptian sailors were pulled from the water. They identified themselves as naval personnel and confirmed that the fishing boat had been on picket duty to warn of Israeli raids. Half an hour later, the *Hanit* sank a fishing boat farther west. Two more Egyptian naval personnel were rescued. The four Israeli boats sailed into Abukir Bay prepared for action.

When the Egyptian command declined to send out its boats to meet them, the Israeli task force began shelling shore targets, in the hope of drawing them out of Alexandria, twenty-five kilometers to the west. Barkai asked permission to fire a Gabriel at a large coastal radar: a special technique had been developed in the past few days for using the missile against shore targets, but it had not yet been tried.

"We've got to do it, if only to honor the name of this place," said Barkai to Telem, a reference to Abukir's place in naval history as the site of Nelson's destruction of Napoleon's fleet.

Telem gave Barkai his go-ahead, and the Saar (Boat Number Seven, which Tabak had sailed from Cherbourg in the first breakout) paid homage to Nelson by firing a missile over the shallow waters in which Nelson had broken the French line. It struck the coastal radar dead center.

In the Red Sea command, Zeev Almog had decided to have another go at Ardaka. At least one other missile boat was believed to be anchored there. Even if the commando attack failed to sink it, the very fact that the anchorage was again penetrated would keep the Egyptians busy looking to their own defenses, he believed, rather than planning another crossing. Telem visited Sharm on October 18, and Almog obtained his permission for the strike.

On the Suez Canal the tide of battle was to turn as Israeli armor poured into the bridgehead on the Egyptian side of the waterway. Pressure on the Egyptians in the Red Sea, Almog believed, would help the effort. This time the attack on Ardaka would be made on the surface, using a device similar to the one Yohai Bin-Nun and his men had used so successfully in the War of Independence—a small boat loaded with explosives that would be sped into the target as the operator leaped clear. The seaborne bomb was an American pleasure speedboat that had been modified for the task by the commando unit. Testing of the system had been completed just before the war, and it had not yet been declared operational, but Almog had two of the boats flown down to Sharm.

The attack force set out on October 19, eight days after the previous penetration. The Israelis hoped that the Egyptians would not believe them so foolhardy as to try entering the same harbor twice. (This would actually be their third visit, but the Egyptians were unaware of the first foray, which had not been pushed home.) In addition to the two attack boats, each loaded with 270 kilograms of explosives, the force included two retrieval boats, which were to pick up the operators of the attack boats after they went into the water.

The crossing of the gulf was extremely rough. As the commandos reached the mouth of the Ardaka channel in the darkness, they found no sign of Egyptian alertness. With the boats' exhausts below water level, the attack force made scant noise as it proceeded cautiously toward the anchorage. The commandos scanned the shore on either side of them for signs of ambush, but all was still. At last the jetty came into view. The outline of a missile boat could be made out alongside it. Nearby the hulk of the missile boat holed in the previous attack lay half sunk in the shallow waters.

The commander of the operation ordered the first boat to make its run. The silence exploded as the operator opened his throttle and headed in toward the jetty, aligning his bow with the dim outline of the missile boat. As the attack vessel gathered speed, the operator ejected, and the retrieval boat that had been following him swooped in to pick him up.

Fire was coming at them now from the shore. As the operator of the attack boat was being hauled aboard, he and the retrieval team heard the sound of a motor racing toward them. To their horror, they saw that the unmanned attack boat had turned full circle and was coming toward them. It missed by a few feet. The boat's jammed steering mechanism kept it going in circles until a self-destruct device set off the explosives with a tremendous roar.

The commander ordered the second attack boat to make its run. The craft missed the anchored missile boat but exploded against the jetty. Its operator was picked up, and the two retrieval boats sped up the channel as the Egyptians fired into the darkness behind them.

The men returned to Sharm disappointed, but Almog was elated.

The penetration of Ardaka was itself the accomplishment. The commandos' report that the Egyptians were firing wildly in every direction was exactly what he had hoped to hear. It was safe to assume that the Egyptians would be busy fighting ghosts for a while.

The small commando force had been operational now almost every day for two weeks in extremely difficult conditions involving rough waters, long periods at sea, and enemy fire at close quarters. In addition to their attacks on Ardaka and the attempted rescue of the garrison on the Bar-Lev line, they had also harassed the Egyptian garrison on Shadwan Island. With the Israeli bridgehead across the Suez Canal now secured and the end of the war in sight, Almog decided to let the exhausted commandos return to the north. They were already at the airfield at Sharm on the morning of October 21, the day after the return of the Ardaka attack force, when Almog was ordered by Telem to recall the men immediately.

"I want you to hit Ardaka again tonight."

Almog was stunned. Ardaka was a difficult target in the best of circumstances. To hit it for a third time—just two nights after the previous attack—was pushing luck past acceptable limits. He remained silent for several seconds. "I think the chances of success are small," he said finally. "I'd like your permission to command the operation myself."

Almog's request was intended to signal to Telem the grave dangers he saw for the mission—dangers so grave he could not ask his men to go on it while remaining behind himself. Understanding the gesture, Telem gave Almog his assent. The high command was preparing finally to stage the cross-gulf landing in order to gain territory for bargaining before the looming cease-fire. It was imperative to eliminate the remaining Egyptian missile boat at Ardaka and any other that might have joined it, to ensure safe crossing for the loaded Israeli LSTs.

At Telem's suggestion, the attack was to employ an antitank weapon fired from the shoulder. The Egyptians could be expected to have reinforced their close-in defenses against underwater attack and boat bombs, but the commandos would stand off and hit their target from a distance.

Yohai Bin-Nun asked to join the mission. Almog tried to convince him of the psychological blow it would be if an admiral, even a forty-nine-year-old retired admiral, were to be killed or to fall into enemy hands, but Bin-Nun insisted on going along.

"Well, if Binny agrees, I'll agree, too," said Almog, convinced that Admiral Telem would turn down Bin-Nun's request.

To his astonishment, Telem gave his assent.

Almog assigned Bin-Nun command of the backup boat that would follow the two attack craft. Donning his rubber combat suit for the first time since leaving the commandos almost two years before, Almog joined the lead boat with the major commanding the unit.

Ardaka would be hit this time, Almog decided, in the last hour before dawn. After a long night's uneventful watch, there was a chance that the Egyptians might conclude that the Israelis would not attack so close to sunrise so far from their own base. The boats set out from Sharm several hours after darkness following a brief training exercise in which one man from each of the two attack boats fired several anti-tank rounds. The results from a rocky boat had not been very encouraging. Halfway to target, the motor of Almog's boat began to act up, and he and his crew swapped boats with Bin-Nun, to the latter's consternation.

From a great distance, a halo of light could be perceived from the direction of Ardaka. As they drew closer, the commandos could see that the Egyptians had installed giant floodlights on the approaches to the naval base, but it was not clear whether the lights were covering the northern entrance to the anchorage, from where the previous penetrations had been made, or the southern approach. As they drew near, it became apparent that the light was at the southern end. The Egyptians seemed convinced that the Israelis would not attack from the same direction three times.

An eerie silence lay about them as the attack boats moved noiselessly down the narrow channel toward the anchorage. It seemed inconceivable that the Egyptians had left the approach unguarded. Perhaps the timing of the attack had indeed deceived them. Or perhaps they had prepared an ambush. At eight hundred meters the commandos could make out the outline of a Komar missile boat.

"Maybe it's the one we already hit," said the officer next to Almog. "Maybe they set it out to draw us in."

At four hundred meters it was clear to Almog that the missile boat was riding high in the water and was undamaged. Oddly, it was not tied up at the jetty but anchored offshore. At 150 meters fire was opened at them, from the shore and from the Komar as well.

"Move up to firing range," shouted Almog.

In each boat the designated gunner rose and braced himself with the weapon on his shoulder. Each had only five rounds. As the roll of their boats brought the target into the sights, they fired. The first rounds missed. So did the next three. Almog ordered the boats to halve the range to forty meters before the gunners fired their last rounds. If they hit at this distance and the missiles aboard the target exploded, they would go up with it. If they missed, Almog was determined to close on the missile boat and destroy it with satchel charges.

The last two rounds exploded on target, setting the Komar ablaze. In the light of the flames, Egyptian crewmen could be seen jumping into the water. Almog's boat began to turn away, but shuddered to a stop as it ran onto a reef.

The commander of the boat fired the craft's machine guns to keep the swimming Egyptian sailors away. As Almog looked about him, he saw why the Komar had been anchored where it was. The reef surrounded it almost completely. The anchorage had plainly been chosen to foil any repeat of a boat-bomb attack. Almog ordered his men into the water. As the lightened boat floated free of the reef, they clambered back aboard. The boat zigzagged uncontrollably as it began to move off, the propeller having been damaged. The second boat took Almog's in tow, and they headed back up the channel. As they reached its mouth and turned eastward into the gulf, dawn began to brighten the sky ahead of them.

Although the Arab missile boats in the Mediterranean had been effectively neutralized, six Egyptian submarines still constituted a serious danger to Israel-bound shipping. Egypt had broadcast a warning at the beginning of the war to all maritime interests that the eastern Mediterranean was a war zone and that any ships entering it would be proceeding at their own risk. Merchant shipping to Israel was halted with the outbreak of war but resumed after a few days, when it became evident that the Arab surface vessels were bottled up. Some foreign vessels refused to make the final leg of the run and offloaded in Italy or Greece, where Israeli freighters picked up the cargo.

As the war stretched into its third week, the seaborne cargo, including tanks, artillery shells, and other armaments, became increasingly vital to Israel's staying power. The freighters coordinated the timing and route of the final leg with the Israeli navy. During the three weeks of the war, more than a hundred merchant ships entered and left Haifa harbor.

In the third week, Telem dispatched one of the Reshef-class boats and a Saar-class boat to the Strait of Messina, a thousand miles to the west. An Egyptian destroyer operating out of Bengazi in Libya was reported to be stopping merchant vessels and searching for Israel-bound cargoes. The Egyptians had shifted their destroyers to distant ports before the war, in the knowledge that they could not stand against the Israeli missile boats or air attacks. The central Mediterranean was a relatively safe area for the destroyers, since they were out of operational range of Israeli aircraft and of the Cherbourg boats. However, the two Reshef-class vessels had been designed for precisely this range, and they began to undertake four- and five-day sweeps.

Apart from protecting Israel-bound shipping by this long-range mission, the navy was hoping to catch up with the Egyptian destroyer in order to even the score for the destroyer *Eilat*. But when the Egyptians learned of the Israeli naval presence in the central Mediterranean, the destroyer would no longer venture from Bengazi.

However, revenge for the *Eilat* would be wreaked on the southern front. The Komar sunk in the last attack on Ardaka had been the missile boat that had crippled the *Eilat*, the Israelis would learn. The Komar's demise had come one day after the sixth anniversary of the *Eilat* sinking. The next day the Egyptians packed up and abandoned Ardaka. A naval base so powerfully defended with SAM missiles that Israel's air force had been reluctant to attack, and so difficult a surface target that the naval command had at first shunned the idea of trying an attack, had been closed down by fewer than a dozen naval commandos displaying superb skill, daring, and imagination.

Shlomo Erell joined the flotilla during one of the final forays against the Syrian coast. Udi Erell had not agreed to have his father sail with him. Still adjusting to his new command, he did not want the extra pressure of his father the admiral looking over his shoulder.

The battle that night was another of the seemingly chaotic skirmishes in which the Israelis raked the Syrian ports and fruitlessly attempted to draw the Syrian missile boats. But to Shlomo Erell, aboard one of the Reshefs, it was a fabulous sight. He was captivated by the way Barkai and his captains coordinated their operations despite the wild weavings and intense confusion of a night battle at forty knots.

Coming up from the CIC as the boat approached Banias, Eli Rahav found Erell standing on the bridge bareheaded. "How am I going to explain it if you're injured?" said the squadron commander, handing Erell a helmet. The boat was to shell the oil tanks at Banias. Erell and the officers on the bridge debated what kind of fuel the tanks likely held, and whether they would burn if hit. The debate ended when the first shells set the tanks aflame.

From the direction of Tartus, four Styxes suddenly appeared in the sky. The missiles, heading straight for them, looked like a formation of planes. Erell was petrified but if the others on the bridge were too, they masked it well. This was the vision Tsemach had seen a decade before when Erell had called him in to discuss the Styx and ask "Do we have a problem?"

"They're beginning to turn," said the bridge officer.

To Erell the lights still seemed to be heading straight between his eyes but the bridge officer, with two weeks of missile watching behind him, could already perceive the missiles succumbing to the tug of the electronic decoys. Soon Erell could make it out as well.

It was plain to Erell that the complex offensive and defensive systems crammed into the small boats functioned in the ultimate test of battle better than anyone could have hoped for when they were being conceived. Recalling his first conversation about the boats in the German Defense Ministry ten years before, the retired admiral smiled to himself and thought, "They've even put in the grand piano."

Since the second week of the war, Daburs had been arriving overland at Eilat from the north and speeding off toward Sharm as soon as they were fueled. Almog pushed them on through the Milan Staits into the Gulf of Suez. Now, in the final days of the war, he had thirteen Daburs under his command—more than three times as many as at the war's outbreak. They had an important role to play in maintaining the encirclement of the Egyptian Third Army, trapped on the Sinai side of the canal by the Israeli armored crossing of the canal, which had severed its supply lines. The Daburs broke up attempts by the Egyptians to ferry supplies across the gulf at night in small boats.

On October 23 Almog was informed that an Israeli armored brigade that had crossed the canal was moving south to capture the port of

Adabiya, on the west side of the Gulf of Suez. Almog decided to try to take the port first. He flew by helicopter from Sharm to Ras Sudar, where he boarded a waiting Dabur. All Daburs in the area were ordered to proceed at top speed to Adabiya.

A column of smoke rising from the harbor told Almog as he approached that he had lost the race. Israeli tanks could be seen along the waterfront, and others were clanking down the road from the north. An Egyptian patrol boat, hit by a tank shell, was burning in the anchorage. Two Arab freighters, one from Saudi Arabia, were tied up at a jetty.

On leaping ashore, Almog shook hands with the Israeli brigade commander, Colonel Dan Shomron. "We got here twenty minutes ago," said the dust-covered colonel.

Desultory fire burst around them from pockets of resistance as they talked. Shomron said the Egyptian naval commander for the Red Sea—Almog's opposite number—had been captured in his command bunker. "I think it would be more appropriate if you took his formal surrender," said Shomron.

The Egyptian officer saluted when Almog was presented.

"I'm sorry we have to meet under such circumstances," said Almog in English.

"So am I," said the Egyptian.

In the command bunker Almog noted a large wall map on which the Egyptian plan for the capture of southern Sinai was depicted with arrows and timetables. Almog invited the Egyptian commander for lunch aboard his vessel.

Over lunch, the two commanders discussed the war they had been fighting for the past three weeks. The Egyptian, acknowledging the Israeli naval successes, said, "But you had missiles." Almog did not reply, so as not to reveal what he had or did not have, but it occurred to him that the Egyptians may have believed that the antitank shells had been guided missiles of some sort. The planned Israeli transgulf invasion had in the end been canceled, but a use was found for the LSTs when Shomron asked Almog if the navy could transfer fifteen hundred prisoners to the Sinai shore. Instead of transporting Israeli troops westward across the gulf into combat, the landing craft were called in to transport Egyptian soldiers eastward into captivity.

Gadi Ben-Zeev was on the bridge of a Saar escorting an ammunition-laden freighter on the last leg of its run through the eastern Mediterranean when he saw an almost forgotten glow limning the sky as they neared Haifa. The lights of the city, blacked out since Yom Kippur, were glittering again, from the port at the foot of Mount Carmel to Stella Maris on the crest. The war was over, at least officially.

Although a cease-fire had been reluctantly accepted by Israel on October 22 under strong pressure from the United States and the Soviet Union, the situation was now approaching a highly dangerous point. Fighting on the Egyptian front was continuing on the ground—both sides blaming the other for initiating it. The capture of Adabiya completed the sealing off of the Egyptian Third Army and confronted the leadership in Cairo with the prospect of forfeiting all that had been gained in the war if the Third Army was forced to surrender. In a message to President Nixon on October 24, the Soviet leadership made it clear that it would not let its client—and itself—be humiliated.

The Israelis had violated the cease-fire and were "embarked on the path to their own destruction," warned the Russians. If the United States did not join with the Soviet Union in sending troops to ensure the cease-fire, as Cairo had requested, then Moscow would find it necessary to take unilateral action. The Soviet Union had earlier warned Israel of "grave consequences" if the fighting did not stop.

In Western intelligence circles, alarm bells began ringing as signs mounted that the Soviets were preparing for direct involvement in the fighting, including possibly the use of tactical nuclear weapons. A ship apparently carrying nuclear devices was monitored as it passed through the Dardanelles. On October 25 it docked in Alexandria. An unusually large number of Soviet transport planes had been landing at Egyptian airports. The flights halted completely on October 24, as if the planes that had returned to the Soviet Union were being readied to carry other cargo—perhaps troops. Two Russian brigades armed with ground-to-ground missiles were shown by American satellites to be deployed between Cairo and the Israeli forces. Some forty thousand Soviet airborne troops had been reported transferred to staging areas in the southern part of the Soviet Union in the previous week to await airlift to Egypt, and Soviet air units were also moving south. Soviet combat pilots were back in Egypt, flying the modern Foxbat aircraft. The Soviet fleet buildup in the Mediterranean was continuing and included sixteen submarines on the flanks of the Sixth Fleet, as well as cruisers and landing craft with several thousand troops and tanks.

At a White House meeting running into the early hours of October 25, the National Security Council reacted to the Soviet moves by ordering a worldwide alert—Defensive Condition 3—of American forces, including the Strategic Air Command. An airborne division was put on standby for imminent departure to the Middle East, and more than fifty B-52 strategic bombers were recalled from Guam to the United States.

Admiral Murphy did not learn of the heightened state of alert until 7:30 A.M.. He was taking a shower when an aide rapped on his cabin door to inform him that they had gone to Defcon 3. Murphy had been pressing for four carriers to cope with the Soviet vessels swarming over and under the Mediterranean. The Pentagon now informed him that he was going to get a third, the *John F. Kennedy*. The *Roosevelt* was ordered to sail east to join the *Independence* off Crete. The amphibious ships at Suda Bay were to join the *Independence* task force as well, placing the marines in position for quick commitment should the Russians land their amphibious forces.

The deployment of the Soviet squadron changed ominously as October 25 dawned. The State Department had informed the Soviet ambassador in Washington of the new alert status and the admiral commanding the Soviet Mediterranean squadron knew about it at almost the same time that Murphy did. The tattletales shadowing the American naval units were joined by first-line missile-carrying warships. Admiral Murphy calculated that the Soviet fleet confronting him this day had a first-strike capability of forty sea-to-sea missiles and 250 torpedoes. Within a few days, this capacity would rise to eighty-eight missiles and 348 torpedoes. With the two fleets thus locked in high-alert confrontation in the confined waters of the eastern Mediterranean, the highly unlikely scenario of an old-fashioned naval shootout at close quarters no longer seemed a fantasy.

Slowly, however, the tension eased. Succumbing to American pressure, the Israelis agreed to let Egypt send supplies eastward across the Suez Canal to its surrounded Third Army. On October 29 trucks from Cairo bearing food, water, and medical supplies were driven by UN personnel through the Israeli lines to the edge of the canal, where they were ferried across by Third Army personnel. As the cease-fire on the ground between Israel and her Arab foes continued to hold, and both sides announced readiness for peace talks, the American and Soviet fleets slowly disengaged and slipped over the horizon to the west on their separate ways.

There was no victor in the shadow sea encounter between the two superpowers—neither had blinked—but for the first time since World War II the American navy had found its deterrent power effectively checked by the Soviet fleet, which had been armed with a new equalizer, the sea-to-sea missile.

Ironically, the tiny Israeli navy might have fared better than the Sixth Fleet against the Soviet naval force. The Israeli missile boats carried sixty-three missiles, a larger missile capacity than the Russians had in the Mediterranean before the cease-fire. Although the Russian missiles had far longer ranges than the Gabriel, the Israeli boats had a proven EW system that had performed perfectly against fifty-four Soviet missiles in a hard-fought war. It is questionable how effective the Soviet EW defenses would have been in thwarting the sea-skimming Gabriel. The Americans had no sea skimmers for the Soviets to develop defenses against. The vessels supplied by the Russians to their Arab clients had no EW systems at all.

The Russians would doubtless have attempted to defend against the Gabriel with gunfire or anti-aircraft missiles, but it would not have been easy to knock down a missile coming in two meters above the waves. Any attempt by the Soviets to support their naval forces against the Israeli missile boats with planes based in Egypt or Syria would doubtless have been met by the formidable Israeli air force. If the Israeli boats had passed through the initial Soviet missile barrage and closed on the Russian fleet, the results could have been astonishing. Admiral Binny Telem had no desire for any encounter with the Soviets—he operated on the assumption that they would be neutralized by the Americans—but if Russian warships had acted belligerently he fully intended to meet them head-on.

Israel had come through the Yom Kippur War bloodied and sobered. It had glimpsed its own mortality and been shaken out of the sense of invincibility engendered by the Six Day War. The navy had been the one military arm not burdened by glory in that earlier conflict, a fact that would account in good part for its performance in 1973. Driven by the need to prove itself, and free of any cause for arrogance, it had invested original thought and years of intense labor to enter a new era of its own creation.

As a traumatized post–Yom Kippur War Israel tried to grasp what had stalled its vaunted military machine, the navy's performance was little noted, its astonishing success seemingly as marginal to the overall picture as its failure had been in 1967. But the navies of the world had taken note. The United States navy sent to Israel a large team, including top EW experts, shortly after the war, to learn how a small navy had managed on its own to so overwhelmingly defeat a Soviet weapon system that the U.S. navy itself had been deeply concerned about since the sinking of the *Eilat*. The U.S. had invested astronomical sums in shipboard antimissile systems in an attempt to cope with the threat of Soviet missiles, whereas the Israelis had performed superbly with a system so seemingly simple that the Americans were amazed it had worked at all.

The American naval team subjected the results of the Israelis' experience to intense scrutiny over the course of weeks, including computer analyses of the missile clashes. One of the team leaders, an admiral who subsequently undertook a worldwide study of the impact of modern weapons on the battlefield, would say more than a decade later that the way the Israeli navy had analyzed the nature of the threat facing it and then taken the necessary steps to solve the problem "stands out as the one clear example [in the development of modern weapon systems] where everything was done right." The Israeli experience would have a powerful impact on the development of missile boats, missiles, and EW systems throughout the world.

In the Yom Kippur War, the Israeli missile boats—outnumbered and outranged by the Arab missile boats—had completely cleared the eastern Mediterranean of the Syrian and Egyptian navies, prevented attacks upon Israel's vulnerable coastline, kept the Mediterranean sea lanes open, sunk at least eight Arab warships and perhaps two others, caused severe damage to Syria's oil reserves, shelled targets the length of Egypt's coast, and pinned down Syrian troops far from the main battlefield. All of this was accomplished without a single casualty in the flotilla or any damage to the missile boats. The navy had lost two frogmen who penetrated Port Said harbor; two more men were lost in clashes in the Suez Gulf. But the missile boats themselves had successfully eluded fifty-four homing missiles and thousands of shells fired by coastal batteries. Rarely has there been such a sweeping naval victory so unmarred by loss.

The missile-boat program, including the Gabriel, had spurred Israel into the era of high tech on which much of its future economy would rest. It was the first major weapon system Israel developed, and its success would encourage others, from the Merkava tank to the aborted Lavi warplane. The technological standards it demanded would spill over into the civilian sector, and brilliant engineers who had honed their talents on the project, such as Tsemach and Lapid, would assume top research positions in civilian firms.

Apart from their military and technological impact, the Cherbourg boats were a reaffirmation of a beleaguered nation's most important asset—national will. In daring to conceive and undertake something so unorthodox and risky, in the dedication invested in the Shalechet development program, and in the tough-mindedness with which the boats were snatched from Cherbourg and deployed in the Yom Kippur War, the small band of men associated with the missile boats proved that, a generation after independence, despite the apparent passing of the heroic age, Israel's life force had not ebbed.

In the weeks after the war, cases of whiskey, champagne, and gourmet foods filled the corners of Yomi Barkai's office in the Haifa naval base. Although most of the nation was unaware of the dramatic missile battles that had been fought at sea and the magnitude of the navy's victories, the maritime community did know, and naval suppliers, shipping companies, and importers were sending an endless stream of presents to the naval base in appreciation. As the cases began to edge toward the center of the office, Barkai said to Udi Erell one day, "We've got to get rid of this stuff. Let's have a party."

The party was set for the Hanukkah holiday, two months after the war. The flotilla commander organized it the way he would a military operation, assigning tasks to his officers, setting timetables, and establishing a chain of command. Erell's job was to get an appropriate song written about the missile boats for performance at the celebration.

The party was held in a large customs shed. Barkai had issued an order that all the liquor must be consumed this night, and the men did their best to comply. As the festivities swirled around them, Barkai and

Erell, each sitting on the shoulders of two men, engaged in a chicken fight in which each tried to knock the other off his perch.

The party would last until dawn. Midway, Barkai mounted the makeshift stage and took the microphone. As the noise died down, he thought about the first time he had addressed the flotilla, just half a year before. Looking about him now at the officers and men in the shed sitting with their wives and girlfriends, he began with the same salutation he had used then: "Fighters of the Missile Flotilla."

This time, no one laughed.

Abbreviations and Technical Terms

Bertam   Class of patrol boat
CIC   Combat Information Center
Dabur ("Hornet")   class of Israeli patrol boat
ECM   Electronic Countermeasures
ESM   Electronic Support Measures
EW   Electronic Warfare
Frog   Soviet ground-to-ground missile in Syrian arsenal
Gabriel   Israeli sea-to-sea missile
IAI   Israel Aircraft Industries
Kelt   Soviet air-to-ground missile used by Egypt
Komar ("Mosquito")   class of Soviet missile boat used by Egyptian navy
LST   Landing craft
Osa ("Wasp")   class of Soviet-made missile boat, larger than the Komar
Rafael   Israeli Authority for Weapons Development
Reshef ("Flash")   class of Israeli missile boat, larger than Saar
Saar ("Storm")   class of Israeli missile boat
Skory   class of Soviet destroyer used by Eygptian navy
Styx   Soviet sea-to-sea missile used by Egyptian and Syrian navies

Bibliography

ENGLISH

Abu Zikra, Lt. Gen. Fouad, Commander of the Egyptian Naval Forces. "The Role of the Naval Forces in the War of October, 1973." Paper delivered at International Symposium on 1973 War, Cairo, October 1975.

Almog, Rear Admiral Zeev. "Israel's Naval Theatre." *Israel Defence Forces Journal* (Spring 1986): pp. 20–26.

Baker, David. *The Rocket.* New York: Crown, 1978.

Brecher, Michael. *Decisions in Crisis: Israel, 1967 and 1973.* Berkeley: University of California Press, 1980.

Coleman, Herbert J. "Gabriel Outmatches Soviet Styx." *Aviation Week* (December 10, 1973): p. 20.

Colvin, R. D. "Aftermath of the *Eilat.*" *U.S. Naval Institute Proceedings* 95 (October 1969): pp. 60–67.

Davenport, Elaine, *et al. The Plumbatt Affair.* London: André Deutsch, 1978.

Deutschkron, Inge. *Bonn and Jerusalem*. Philadelphia: Chilton, 1970.

Erell, Rear Admiral Shlomo. "Israeli Saar FPBs Pass Combat Test in Yom Kippur War." *U.S. Naval Institute Proceedings* (September 1974): pp. 115–18.

Engel, Shimon. "The Way Ahead—C³I in Naval Warfare." *Israel Defence Forces Journal* (Fall 1986): pp. 24–28.

Eytan, Walter. "The Cherbourg Boats, Memoir." *Midstream* (December 1981): pp. 34–38.

Fairhall, David. *Russian Sea Power*. Boston: Gambit, 1971.

Friedman, Norman. *U.S. Naval Weapons*. Annapolis: Naval Institute Press, 1982.

George, James L., ed. *Problems of Sea Power*. Washington, D.C.: American Enterprise Institute for Public Policy Research, 1977.

Jacchia, Enrico. "Origins of the Plumbatt Affair." *International Herald Tribune* (26 May 1977): editorial page.

Jane's Missile Handbook. London: Jane's Publishing, 1978.

Jane's Weapon Systems. London: Jane's Publishing, 1981.

Kehoe, Capt. (retired) J. W., and Brower, Kenneth S. "The Israeli Reshef Class Missile Boat." *Naval Engineers Journal* (November 1984): pp. 63–67.

Kissinger, Henry A. *Years of Upheaval*. Boston: Little, Brown and Company, 1982.

Lapid, Capt. (retired) Peleg. "Electronics in the Israeli Navy." *Israel Defence Forces Journal* (December 1984): pp. 13–18.

"Mideast War Spurs Missile R & D Effort." *Aviation Week* (December 31, 1973): pp. 17–25.

Moore, John E. *The Soviet Navy Today*. New York: Stein and Day, 1976.

Moorer, Admiral Thomas H., Chairman, Joint Chiefs of Staff. "Report on United States Military Posture for FY 1975." Extract of testimony before House Armed Services Committee, released by Joint Chiefs of Staff, pp. 81–91.

Nitze, Paul H., *et al. Securing the Seas.* Boulder, Col.: Westview Press, 1979.

Polmar, Norman. *Guide to the Soviet Navy.* Annapolis: Naval Institute Press, 1983.

Price, Alfred. *Instruments of Darkness.* New York: Scribner's, 1967.

Rahav, Rear Admiral (retired) Eli. "Missile Boat Warfare." *Israel Defence Forces Journal* (Fall 1986): pp. 37–43.

Streetly, Martin. "Israeli Naval EW." *Jane's Defence Weekly* (6 December 1986): pp. 1348–51.

Telem, Rear Admiral Binyamin. "Strategic and Naval Policy." Speech on Israeli navy at International Symposium on Military Aspects of the Israel-Arab Conflict. Reported in *Jerusalem Post* (19 October 1987): p. 2.

U.S. Naval Historical Division, Washington, D.C. Declassified reports on Sixth Fleet operations during 1973 Arab-Israel War.

Vogel, Ralph, ed. *The German Path to Israel.* London: Oswald Wolff, 1969.

Wilson, Andrew. "West Seeks Answer to the Styx Missile That Sank the *Eilat.*" London Observer Foreign News Service printed in *Jerusalem Post* (3 September 1968): p. 3.

Zumwalt, Elmo. *On Watch.* New York: Quadrangle, 1976.

HEBREW

Days on the Water. Tel Aviv: Israel Defence Forces, Navy, 1974.

Dreznin, Zvi. *Israel's Military Industries.* Tel Aviv: Israel Defence Ministry, 1980.

First Missile Battle in the World. Tel Aviv: Information Branch, Israel Defence Forces, Navy, 1978.

Goodman, Hirsh, and Mann, Shlomo. *Israel Defence Forces Encyclopedia: The Navy.* Tel Aviv: Revivim, 1982.

Israel Defence Forces Radio Station. Transcription of interview with participants in Cherbourg boat escape, broadcast 31 December 1979.

Levi, Moshe. *The Forty-Eighth Soul.* Tel Aviv: Maarchot, 1981.

Mardor, Munya. *Rafael.* Tel Aviv: Israeli Ministry of Defence, 1981.

Rehav, Rear Admiral (retired) Eli. "The Gabriel Boats." *Maarchot* (December 1984): pp. 31–40.

————."A Toast to the Small Boats." *Maarchot* (July–August 1985): pp. 19–25.

"Syrian Naval Performance in the 1973 War." Translated from the Arabic. *Al Fakr al Askri* (September 1974).

Tlass, Mustafa, Syrian Defense Minister. "The Syrian Navy in the 1973 War." Translated from the Arabic. *Al Fakr al Askri* (September 1974).

FRENCH

"Affaire des vedettes." *L'Express* (11 January 1970): pp. 14–19.

Fenwick, Jean-René. *Les Vedettes de Cherbourg.* Paris: Elsevier Sequoia, 1976.

Index